AF579308

KEN BARRINGTON

A TRIBUTE

KEN BARRINGTON

A TRIBUTE

by Brian Scovell

First published in Great Britain 1982
by HARRAP LIMITED
19–23 Ludgate Hill, London EC4M 7PD

ISBN 0 245–53867–4

Designed by Michael R. Carter

Composition by Ronset Ltd, Darwen
Printed and bound in Great Britain
by Book Plan Ltd, Worcester

Contents

Illustrations

Preface

If Sir Neville Cardus was to be believed, all the great characters of English cricket played in the Nineteen Twenties. Cardus enriched cricket's literature with his stories, some apocryphal, of the Tyldesleys, Wilfred 'we'll get 'em in singles' Rhodes, Walter Brearley, Archie MacLaren, Emmott Robinson and the other giants of Yorkshire and Lancashire of that time.

In later years the myth grew that there were no characters left in English cricket – well, not the characters there used to be – which of course was nonsense. Every generation of sportsmen provides its legendary figures, and no generation has offered us a more loved 'funny man' than Ken Barrington, 'The Colonel' to cricketers and cricket-followers all over the world.

The story of how this son of a soldier fought his way from poverty to become one of the most successful Test batsmen in the history of the game has been well documented. But behind it lies a host of amusing stories, all true, about this most humorous of men.

As a tribute to Ken Barrington's memory I have collated many of them in this volume, and I am indebted to the people who spared time to help me. The Lord's Taverners are perpetuating Ken's respected name in cricket with their Ken Barrington Under 13 competition, and part of the profits of this volume will be devoted to that worthy cause.

BRIAN SCOVELL

Bromley, October 1981

PART ONE
'THE COLONEL'

CHAPTER ONE

The Boy from the Barracks

The most quoted epitaph when Ken Barrington died in the early hours of Sunday, 15 March 1981, was the remark made by his friend, the former Australian wicket-keeper Wally Grout, on the occasion of Ken's retirement in 1968.

'Whenever I saw Ken coming to the wicket I thought a Union Jack was trailing behind him,' said Wally. It summed up Ken Barrington's attitude to cricket. When he played for England he was playing for his country, and that meant striving to achieve the ultimate. Ken Barrington wasn't an instinctive cricketer, as Peter May – who was born eleven months earlier in the same place, Reading – Colin Cowdrey or Ted Dexter were instinctive cricketers.

'He was a fighter, and he had to fight to get where he did,' said Bernie Constable, a Surrey team-mate. This determination and dedication made him one of England's greatest batsmen, a man whose records will stand as long as the game of cricket is played.

But he was more than a run-accumulator who set records: he was a character, a genial, engaging man whose personality endeared him to cricketers and cricket-lovers all over the world. The stories about him are legion, and we have recounted some of them in this book, which is a tribute to his memory. He was cricket's Mr Malaprop, a man who said the right thing but often in the wrong way.

After he retired from playing cricket he became a selector, and then manager of successive England touring teams. He was the man the players turned to first when they had a problem. Near the end of the disastrous England 1981 tour of the West Indies, after his body had been flown home to England, Ian Botham (the England captain at the time) said, 'We still think he'll be coming round the corner.'

English cricket has never replaced him, nor will it be able to. Those who were privileged to know him well agreed that there had never been a more popular cricketer. He was a man who never spoke ill of anyone, or who had anyone speak ill of him.

Ken Barrington had his first heart attack in Melbourne while playing in a double-wicket contest on 12 October 1968. A doctor was called, and Ken was taken to hospital and treated for a mild coronary. He was advised to quit playing cricket and he did so, but his life of pressure continued as he carried on running his garage in Bookham, near Leatherhead, producing ghost-written columns in newspapers and being an England Test selector.

He was a man who worried a lot, and it was stress, not the game of cricket which he loved, which probably gave him his second (and this time fatal) heart-attack in the Holiday Inn, Barbados in March 1981.

Twenty-eight days after Ken's first coronary in Melbourne, Wally Grout, a fit man of forty-one, himself died of a heart-attack. The two men were firm friends. 'He and Bobby Simpson helped Ken with his benefit when they toured England in 1964,' recalled Ann Barrington.

'Ken was recovering from his heart-attack, convalescing in Rye, when someone marched in and told him that Wally had died. The person came right out with it. The news could have given Ken another attack!'

Ken Barrington was fifty, and still fit enough to bowl for two hours in the nets, when he died, his last ambition unfulfilled. He sought to become England's first permanent manager, a man who could make England paramount again in world cricket. He called it 'a jigsaw I am determined to finish so that we can have a team to beat the world'.

Kenneth Frank Barrington was born on 24 November 1930, the eldest son of a serving soldier in the Royal Berkshire regiment. Percy, his father, an orphan, was a POW in the First World War, and his mother, with four children to bring up, used to take in the officers' washing.

Life for the Barrington children in Brock Barracks, Reading, consisted of a mixture of school and playing cricket, football and 'soldiers'. His military upbringing left Ken with a deep love of brass bands, and he used to say, 'When I go to a football match my friends reckon I enjoy the band as much as the match!'

Percy was a medium-pace bowler in regimental cricket matches, and taught his son the rudiments of picking up a bat and bringing his arm over properly to bowl from the age of four. The family couldn't afford to buy cricket-bats, so Percy shaped primitive bats for his children from hunks of wood. Ken retrieved the ball for the soldiers in the nets, and soon they were letting him have a bat.

There was no radio or television in the house, no newspaper to follow the scores, so he had no hero except his father. And as most of his boyhood, between the ages of nine and fifteen, came at a time when there was no county cricket because of the Second World War, he never saw a professional game until he joined the Surrey staff at the age of seventeen.

At Katesgrove School, Reading, he was a fast bowler in the school side, although he was only 5 feet 4, and a good enough footballer to be picked along with Roy McCrohan, the former Reading, Norwich and Colchester player, and Johnny Brooks, ex-Reading, Spurs, Chelsea, Brentford and England, in the Reading Schools side. For a time he captained Reading Schools from midfield, and harboured thoughts of becoming a professional. The thought of being a 'pro' cricketer never occurred to him.

He left school at fourteen, and worked as an apprentice mechanic in a garage for a weekly wage of 87½p. Tinkering with cars and engines, along with listening to brass bands, were to be the other non-sporting interests of his life, and it was appropriate that he should invest his benefit money from cricket in a garage of his own at Fetcham, Surrey, which is now run by Ann.

He stayed at the garage in Reading a year, until one day while working on a large American car he drenched himself in oil and went home saying to himself it was about time he found an easier job. That night a schoolmaster, Jim Brown, knocked at the door and invited him to apply for the job of ground-staff boy at Reading Cricket Club. 'When you're not working you can play for the club,' said Mr Brown, a genial man who knew he was a promising cricketer.

The next week he started work as assistant to the groundsman, Charlie Brockway, a Minor Counties player with Dorset and Berkshire. Besides helping with the preparation of pitches, he was able to spend a great deal of time in the nets bowling to members, and it was in the nets at Reading's Church Road ground that he began to learn the art of bowling leg-spin.

One of the Reading members recommended him to Surrey, and on 24 May 1947 he made his debut for Surrey Colts at Hook and Southborough Cricket Club. It was the first time he had travelled so far from home. He took 5–43 and scored 4 not out and played the rest of the season for expenses only, taking 30 wickets at 13·46 apiece and averaging 5·33 with the bat. He was a bowler in those days.

His life changed one day in August that year when Andy Kempton, who captained the Colts side until within a few months of his death in his seventies, arranged to meet him at the Oval and drive him to a game at Dorking. England were playing South Africa in the Fifth Test, and the ground was almost full when he arrived clutching a handgrip with a bat protruding. 'Here he is,' shouted a wag, 'England's last hope.'

The atmosphere so affected him that he resolved to become a Test player. The following year, 1948, he joined the Surrey ground-staff and made his debut for the 2nd XI against Norfolk at Norwich that summer along with Peter May.

His figures in his early seasons were so poor that he was surprised he wasn't sacked. It was this more than anything else which turned him into a percentage player when he finally made the grade, for as he related in his first book *Running into Hundreds*,

> A player is judged mainly on his figures. Not all county committees are prepared to wait for a player to come good and that's the reason why professional cricketers have a dull, defensive streak. No matter what is said about encouraging brighter cricket, players are judged on results. To a professional cricketer, figures are the same recommendation as they are to a salesman.

In his first season his highest score was 6, and being away on National Service the following two years probably saved him from being dismissed. There was a staff of fifty at the Oval at the time, and the competition was tough.

On matting wickets playing for the Wiltshire Regiment in West Germany his confidence returned, as he took a crop of wickets and was selected for the Army. From 5 feet 4½ he grew to 5 feet 8½ inches. He used to recall with amusement the time he was chosen to play for the Army and found himself the only squaddie in the side when the team arrived at Ostend by boat. Four staff cars took the officers to the game, whereas he had to travel alone in a lorry in the rear!

Back at the Oval he assisted groundsman Bert Lock for a weekly wage of £2 10*s*., and out of season worked as a lorry-driver, a mechanic, a solicitor's office boy and a British Rail painter. While his bowling deteriorated between 1950 and 1952, his batting started to mature, and after scoring 1,000 runs for the second team in 1952 he began to open the innings.

His first-team debut came on 6 May 1953 against the MCC at Lord's, and the same bowler, Alan Oakman – now the Warwickshire coach – dismissed him in both innings, for 8 and 17. This was not an auspicious start, but better than most players could boast. On the final day Stuart Surridge, the Surrey captain, told him that he was to keep his place in the next game against the Australians at the Oval.

That night he took his fiancée whom he had met at a dance at the Olympia Dance Hall, Reading – a publican's daughter named Ann Cozens – to the pictures, and halfway through the feature film, told her he was playing against the Australians. Miss Cozens – who was to become Mrs Barrington the following year – was a keen tennis-player, and not too knowledgable about cricket, but she knew enough about the game to realize it was a big moment in the career of her new boy-friend.

Barrington was sixth in the order, but with Surrey 22–4, found himself going in to bat twenty minutes after the start of play. Ray Lindwall bowled, he tried to leg-glance and the ball went past Neil Harvey at cover for a single. When Alan Davidson bowled short he hooked the ball for 4, and a voice in the slips said, 'Cripes, he hits those bouncers like Bradman!'

At this stage in his career Barrington was a dashing batsman who liked playing shots. It was only later, after he had been discarded by England, that he changed his style and aimed more for occupation of the crease than spectacular shots that might have caused his downfall. The threat of not making the grade was still in his mind. Even when he became an internationally acclaimed batsman, he still couldn't sleep well when he was in the middle of an innings. He was an incessant worrier, constantly making cups of tea and smoking cigarettes.

Richie Benaud caught him at slip off Ron Archer that day at the Oval, and Surrey were all out for 58. In the second innings he again fell to Archer, this time for 4. Australia won by an innings and 76. In those days the Australians were good enough to beat England's best county by such a margin. Today, with some of the world's leading players appearing for the counties, it is rare for a touring side to win so convincingly.

Barrington found himself left out of the side, but returned in July to play seven matches with indifferent results: 237 runs, average 18. The following year, 1954, was the season he made himself a regular in the side, scoring 845 runs and finishing second in the averages. His six-year apprenticeship in company with some of the finest craftsmen in the business – including Alec Bedser, Jim Laker, Tony Lock, Stuart Surridge and Andy Sandham, the Surrey coach – was over, and he was ready to go out and earn a living on his own merits.

He started the 1955 season – the year he played his first Test innings – by scoring 3 and 27 for the MCC against the South Africans at Lord's. Each time Trevor Goddard, who bowled accurate left-arm over-the-wicket seamers, was the bowler. Left-arm medium-pacers had a habit of getting him out, which was the reason why he later changed his stance to a two-eyed one. Alan Davidson, the great Australian bowler, dismissed him probably more times than any other opponent, and it was Davidson more than anyone who inspired the new stance. One night Barrington invited Jim Laker to his Mitcham home to show him what he intended to do, using a broom-handle as a bat and two kitchen chairs as the wickets. By moving his body more towards the on-side, he said he would eliminate a blind spot against left-armers who brought the ball back into him.

Laker, eight years older, acted as a kind of mentor, advising him with typical Yorkshire caution to 'get his head down'. Laker had been his partner in 1954 when he scored his maiden first-class century against Gloucester at the Oval, an unbeaten 108 in a stand of 198 for the eighth wicket.

When Barrington was 30 not out he came up the pitch and said, 'I'll have a belt now.' Replied Laker, 'No, you don't. You stay there. I'll race you to a hundred. We'll have a bet on it.'

Laker reached the 100 mark first, and won his bet. In 1955, against Lancashire, Barrington played what he always said was one of his finest innings, 135 not out against Brian Statham, a bowler for whom he had enormous respect whatever the conditions.

During an innings of 126 in the next match at Trent Bridge the twelfth man came out to hand him a piece of paper on which was written 'Well played. Delighted to award you your county cap, W.S.S.' The cap, the ceremonial indication that a cricketer has graduated with honours, meant a substantial increase in wages, and also security. But for Ken Barrington no job, particularly cricket, could mean security. That was something he had to strive for every day of his playing career.

A week later, while playing in a benefit match at Luton, he received a message from the England selectors. Len Hutton was out with lumbago, and he was needed for the First Test against the Springboks at Trent Bridge.

On 9 June 1955 Ken Barrington joined the long list of famous batsmen who made a duck on their debut in Test cricket. The England team had players of the quality of May, Compton, Graveney, Bailey, Evans, Tyson, Statham, Wardle and Appleyard, with Hutton and Cowdrey unavailable, and it was a strong side. But so was the South African side, whose bowling attack of Neil Adcock, Peter Heine, Trevor Goddard and Hugh Tayfield was one of the most difficult to play against of that era.

Aged twenty-four and comparatively inexperienced, Barrington thought his chance had come too soon, despite what the newspapers had been writing about him. Peter May – making his debut as England captain because Hutton was absent – decided to bat first, and Barrington was number 5 in the order. At 228–2, with May and Compton still there, it seemed to the fidgety Barrington that he might not have to go in. Several lower-order batsmen had their pads on in case May wanted a nightwatchman.

But with twenty-one minutes remaining Adcock appealed for lbw, and Compton was out. Tyson was the first-choice nightwatchman, and with no signal from May for Tyson to go in, Barrington reluctantly left his seat by the window and started the short walk down the stairs and out through the white-painted pavilion doors.

He was, as he confessed later, 'In a right state'. His first-class career had been confined to a mere forty-four innings, and he wasn't prepared for the ordeal of Test cricket. Eddie Fuller, the least lethal of the Springbok bowlers, was to bowl.

The first ball Barrington pushed nervously into the off-side, and called for a run. May sent him back. Second ball he played defensively. Third ball the same. But the anxiety was building up. He wanted to get off the mark. The fourth ball was short outside the off-stump. He tried to force it square on the off-side off the back foot, and nicked a catch to wicket-keeper Johnny Waite, who was standing up.

Throughout his career Barrington had a reputation for walking. This time he stood there, too shocked to move as umpire Jack

Bartley raised the finger. The other players murmured their sympathies in the dressing-room, but all he wanted to do was slip out the back door.

In the hotel that night he felt the odd man out as the players drank with the reporters who were covering the game for their Fleet Street papers. When he became an established player he would always seek out new players and help ease their way into the set-up. It was a lesson he never forgot. Inadvertently some of May's team may have made it harder for him at Nottingham, and he was determined not to let any other succeeding young England player be affected the same way.

There was no chance to redeem himself in the second innings because England won by an innings and 5 runs. He went back home feeling he had been rushed into Test cricket before he was ready for it. This, and the fact that he had to wait four more seasons before he was next to play in a Test series, influenced his beliefs as a selector. He believed that batsmen didn't reach their peak until they were in their late twenties. To put them in too soon, before they were temperamentally suited to it, could put them back years. This probably explained why so few young batsmen were chosen between 1975 and 1981, when Bedser and Barrington were the key men on the selection committee. Barrington accepted that it was possible for a genius like Gary Sobers to play at seventeen, but an ordinary player needed to serve a long apprenticeship.

The selectors retained him for the Second Test in 1955, and he went to Lord's hoping that the match would be played on a flat, easy-paced pitch. Instead it was green and liberally covered with grass, ideal for the South African bowlers! The first ball from Adcock flew off a length and went over the head of Don Kenyon, the England opening batsman. In the right-hand dressing-room of the pavilion Barrington was even more nervous than he had been at Trent Bridge.

To help calm him, Sandy Tait, the Surrey masseur, had given him some pills. This time England were 30–3 when he went in to bat, conscious of the need to be patient about scoring his first run. He took his time, got off the mark with a 4 and finished up with a top-score 34 in England's 133. With the honesty that was one of his hallmarks, he said afterwards that he had been lucky. 'I could have been caught several times,' he admitted.

In the second innings he was more assured, but made only 18 before falling to Tayfield. Statham bowled magnificently in the South African second innings, taking 7–39, and England won by 71 runs. Denis Compton wasn't the only one in the side who thought that Barrington had done enough to keep his place. But when the team was announced for the Third Test Barrington's name was missing.

He was twenty-eight before he was picked again, and in the

intervening four years he sought doggedly to prove that a mistake had been made. At the end of the 1955 season, when he was voted Young Cricketer of the Year by the Cricket Writers' Club, he was chosen for the MCC 'A' team tour of Pakistan. Newly elected to the then Imperial Cricket Conference, Pakistan had drawn a series 1–1 in England the year before, and were keen to have a full England side back as soon as possible.

The tour was known as the 'Water Treatment' tour after an incident in which Idris Begh, the Pakistan umpire, was 'kidnapped' from his hotel by some England players and taken back to the hotel where the England party were staying, and doused with water. Weary of having to listen to interminably boring speeches at official functions, the England players used the 'trick' on numerous occasions. Barrington himself was a victim.

These rituals are often a part of England tours, but to some people in Pakistan they appeared less than funny. Begh was put in a chair and asked if he wanted some refreshment. He said, 'Give me some water', whereupon two members of the team emptied two bucketfuls of water on him from an alcove above.

Begh, a natural showman, laughed along with the players, but when some Pakistan players arrived later and mocked his plight he stormed off to his hotel.

Next day there were demonstrations by students who chanted, 'MCC go home.' The MCC party needed a police escort, and the incident rapidly developed into an international incident with Lord Alexander of Tunis, President of MCC, offering to withdraw the team from Pakistan. An apology was made by the Governor-General on behalf of MCC, and the Pakistan Board of Control accepted it, but not before Donald Carr, the MCC captain, and Geoffrey Howard, the manager, found themselves having to defend their players against charges of insulting Pakistan's leading umpire. Unfortunately, the umpiring had been poor in several of the unofficial Tests, which the MCC lost, and the Begh incident was looked on as an act of revenge.

It was an unhappy tour, relieved only by the sense of humour of several of the players, notably Ken Barrington. During a big-game hunt he nearly shot Peter Richardson and Alan Moss by mistake!

The next three domestic seasons were the worst of his career, and for a time he worried about whether he might have to seek another, less precarious, form of employment. After being tried unsuccessfully as an opener in 1956 he was dropped from the Surrey side, returning as a Number 5. In 1957 he scored 1,642 runs, including 103 not out against a West Indian attack that included Roy Gilchrist, Frank Worrell, Gary Sobers, Sonny Ramadhin and Alf Valentine.

But his worries were far from over. In 1958 Peter May (who had succeeded Surridge as Surrey captain) told him he was being left out for the home game against Lancashire. Aged twenty-seven, Barrington faced the prospect of an in-and-out career and the collapse of his ambitions to play for England again. He was so upset that he went downstairs to the basement in the pavilion, sat down and cried unashamedly.

When he returned to the side he was run out for a duck against Yorkshire. He spent the remaining weeks of the season practising to correct his mistakes. He decided that he was getting out too often to the in-swing and off-break bowlers, usually caught round the corner. Once a batsman shows on the county circuit that he has a weakness the bowlers and captains in the opposing sides probe it relentlessly.

Though he consulted the other Surrey players, he worked his salvation out himself. As a golfer, he was used to examining his technique at regular intervals. He applied this method to his cricket, and would have a private post-mortem after every dismissal to find out where he had gone wrong.

The fault which had appeared now, he reasoned, was having the bat too far ahead of his pad when playing forward. If the ball nipped back, or turned, it would either go through the gate or find an inside edge, and provide a catch to the short legs or leg slip. He decided to copy Colin Cowdrey's method – which had been perfected against Ramadhin in the 1957 Test series – and play forward with the bat an inch or two behind the pad. If the ball came back the nick would bounce harmlessly into the pad. He spent hours every day developing his new style in a way which only Geoff Boycott of today's players finds time to copy.

He knew that he wasn't a cricketing genius like Sobers, so he had to work at his game. He also made another vital decision that summer: to take fewer chances, and become a grafter. If he could assure everyone that he would be getting a certain quota of runs they wouldn't be able to drop him again. He was to become an 'averages' man, a less exciting player to watch but a dependable anchor man in whatever side he played. The transformation was soon to win him back his England place.

CHAPTER TWO

Making It

Ken Barrington nearly scored 1,000 runs during the month of May 1959. It was one of the few records that eluded him. An innings of 186 against Warwickshire at Edgbaston was followed by 118 not out in the second innings and an unbeaten 113 at Trent Bridge. At the age of twenty-eight he was ready to return to the Test arena, and he clinched his place after scoring 85 and 59 not out against the Indians at the Oval.

The Indians had no fast bowlers in their team. Surendranath and Desai, the opening bowlers, were both medium-pacers, 'Fergie' Gupte was past his best and had no appetite for the task, and the only bowler who looked like a Test bowler was Nadkarni, the slow left-hander whose stock delivery was the arm ball, the ball that moves in to a right-handed batsman from the off. The patient Nadkarni dismissed Barrington seven times that summer.

Captained by D. K. Gaekwad and managed by His Highness the Maharajah of Baroda, the Indians were a social success off the field but a disaster on it, losing all five Tests. Brian Statham, with 17 wickets at 13·11 and Fred Trueman, with 24 at 16·70, rolled them over almost every time. It was an ideal time for an earnest young batsman, out to regain his Test place, to return to the side.

Ken Barrington came fourth in the England averages, scoring 357 runs for an average of 59·50. He failed to make a century, which was a matter of great regret to him, but was unlucky not to do so for Surrey in the match against the tourists at the Oval. He was 85 when he drove a ball from Nadkarni to extra cover and called for a run. The fielder threw to the bowler's end, and Barrington was certain he would make his ground until he suddenly saw Nadkarni in his path.

He tried to dart past him, but the ball struck the stumps direct, and umpire Paul Gibb raised the finger. 'I've been obstructed,' said Barrington, never a man to surrender his wicket without a fight. 'I'm afraid you're out,' said Gibb.

Shortly afterwards Peter May confided that he was in the England team for the First Test at Trent Bridge. As in 1955, there was acute pressure on him when he went in to bat at 60–3 with Arthur Milton, Ken Taylor and Colin Cowdrey out cheaply. This time he was prepared to wait for the first run. It took him twenty minutes to get off the mark. May reassured him in almost *Boy's Own* terms. 'Don't worry too much about scoring,' he said. 'Play yourself in, then we'll fight 'em. We've got runs plenty of times for Surrey. Let's do it here.'

By lunch May and Barrington lifted the score to 93, and in the afternoon May opened up, eventually scoring 106. Together they put on 125 for the fourth wicket, with Barrington bowled by Nadkarni for 56. He reached his 50 with two 6s after surviving a difficult caught and bowled to Nadkarni at 33.

That was the first time he reached a batting milestone with a 6, and it was to be followed by many other such occasions. It was an anomaly in his career: the batsman who could be so restricted and sometimes irritating to crowds could break out at the moment of crisis and reach the target with a flourish. It was as if he wanted to say, 'There you are, I can do it when I want to.'

England's easy win at Trent Bridge was followed by a sterner contest at Lord's which they won by 8 wickets. Again England's first three failed, and the total was 35–3 when Barrington marched in. He held firm while wickets fell at the other end, and at 100–7 England were in danger of failing to reach India's first-innings total of 168. Brian Statham proved to be the stalwart of a long tail by adding 84 with Barrington for the eighth wicket, complaining all the time about his partner's habit of running quick singles.

Barrington made 80 out of England's 226, and he followed it with scores of 80, 87, 46 and 8 in the rest of the series. In one of the later Tests an Indian fielder said to him as he walked to the crease, 'Haven't you scored enough runs against us?' Norman Preston, Editor of *Wisden*, recognized his consistency by naming him as one of his Five Cricketers of the Year.

The series against the Indians was scarcely the preparation England's players needed for the winter tour of the West Indies. Instead of medium-pacers the England batsmen were now confronted with a pair of fast bowlers in Wes Hall and Chester Watson, who bowled three and four bouncers an over. Several players on both sides were injured, although ironically the West Indians who started the bumper controversy suffered worst when Easton McMorris and Conrad Hunte were hurt. England's injuries were mainly confined to bruising, with Ken Barrington the chief sufferer. As Leslie Smith wrote in *Wisden*, 'Nobody relished the short pitched bowling but Barrington showed his dislike more than most and as a result became a special target.'

It was a strong England party, one of England's best sides to go abroad, with a batting line-up of Geoff Pullar (whose consistency belied his supposed lack of class), Colin Cowdrey, who was played as an opener, Ken Barrington, Peter May, Mike Smith, Ted Dexter at Number 6 and Ray Illingworth at 7.

Fred Trueman and Brian Statham spearheaded the bowling, supported by David Allen, Illingworth and Barrington, who bowled 106.5 overs in the five Tests. England won the Second Test at Port of Spain and went on to win the rubber 1–0, the first time they had won in the West Indies. Luck played a part, with Peter May, then Cowdrey (who replaced him as captain in the final two Tests when May returned home ill) winning all five tosses.

Barrington finished the series England's third most successful batsman, with 420 runs and an average of 46·66. He made his maiden Test hundred in the First Test at Bridgetown on a flat, easy-paced pitch on which there was no chance of a result because neither side bowled more than fourteen overs an hour. He started his innings just before lunch at 50–1, survived the opening overs from Hall and Chester Watson, and went in for a snack lunch and a beer confident that he could start hooking the short-pitched deliveries when he resumed.

The first time he tried the hook shot, against Hall, he was so late that he missed, and the ball brushed his cap. Sprinting in off a 33-yard run, Hall was far quicker than he had been in England two years before. He was genuinely quick, quicker even than Statham and Trueman, and supported by a noisy, intimidating crowd, he was a daunting bowler to face, even though the pitch was so docile that only eighteen wickets fell in five days.

Watson was slower through the air, but his bent-arm action – which Barrington thought was unfair – made his shorter deliveries hard to pick up. When Barrington reached his hundred after 285 minutes Watson hit him in the kidneys with an intended bouncer and left him writhing in agony. He was still able to retain his sense of humour through the paralysing pain. 'Thanks very much,' he told Watson. 'That's done me the world of good!'

Remembering Jim Laker's advice about going on for the 200, Barrington was on 128 when he shaped to turn an off-break from Sonny Ramadhin to leg, changed his mind and withdrew his bat only for Gerry Alexander, the West Indies wicket-keeper, to appeal for a catch as the ball brushed his pad.

Cortez Jordan, the number 1 West Indies umpire of the day, put his finger up. Barrington was so amazed that he stood his ground. 'How am I out, then?' he asked. 'Lbw?'

'No,' replied Jordan. 'Caught!' Barrington left the wicket head down, barely acknowledging the applause of the crowd. When he reached the dressing-room Walter Robins, the England manager (who was a man of high principles, and a strict disciplinarian) said pointedly, 'That's not good behaviour on your part. I want you to apologize to the umpire and captain.'

During tea Barrington went to the West Indies dressing-room and the umpires' room to express his regret to Alexander and Jordan, and they accepted his apology. Robins also reprimanded Barrington during the Second Test in Trinidad, which England won by 256 runs after a riot on the third day.

After England lost Pullar, Cowdrey and May cheaply, Barrington, with an innings of 121, and Ted Dexter, 77, put on 142 for the fourth wicket in the face of a hostile exhibition of short-pitched bowling by Hall and Watson which saw both bowlers eventually warned by umpires Lee Kow and E. L. Lloyd for excessive use of bouncers.

Barrington was struck a dozen times, once on the head by Hall, and several times on the hip, arm and chest. He was 93 not out at the end of a torrid day's play after May had again won the toss, and came in complaining bitterly about the tactics of the West Indian bowlers. 'This is a fine bloody way to play cricket,' he said. 'If they don't watch out, they're going to kill someone.'

No one had thought of wearing protective headgear in those days. Batsmen were expected to take their punishment uncomplainingly and bowlers were warned less frequently by umpires than they are today. Robins felt Barrington was making himself a target by doffing his cap when a bouncer sailed by, or pretending to fire his bat like a gun at the bowlers. These acts amused the crowd but only incensed the bowlers.

Before the next day's play began Robins spoke sharply to him. 'It's no use talking like you did last night,' he said. 'I don't like that sort of thing on my tour, and I certainly don't expect it of you because you're not that sort of chap. You should set a better example.

'You're not the first batsmen to be hit and you won't be the last. It's foolish to doff your cap and use your bat like a gun. You'll get all the more bouncers acting like that.' As he left the room Robins, who was really a kindly, paternal man, said, 'Now will you bear that in mind? And jolly well played!'

Hall had him caught behind by Alexander for 121, and with Mike Smith making 108 England totalled 382. On the third day there were 30,000 people packed into the ground – far too many for the facilities to cope with – and many of them had been drinking and betting on individual batsmen. In the event, Trueman captured five wickets for 35 and Statham 3–42, and the West Indies were bowled out for 112.

With the total 98–8, local player Charran Singh was given run out, and the crowd started throwing bottles and cans. Soon hundreds of people invaded the field. The England team gathered together in the centre of the pitch before Alexander came out to lead them away. Police tried vainly to clear the pitch, and when a fire-engine was summoned to squirt water at the rioters the firemen were drenched when the hosepipe punctured!

Play had to be abandoned, and there was discussion about calling off the tour. The following day was a rest-day, and to compensate for the seventy-five minutes lost an extra half-hour was added on to the remaining two days. May declined to ask the West Indies to follow on, and set them 501 to win in ten hours, a task which was well beyond them.

In the drawn Test at Kingston Barrington was struck painfully on the forearm by Watson, and when another short ball struck his gloves on the way through to the wicket-keeper he walked before being given out. McMorris, the West Indies opener, was rushed off to hospital with a contused lung after being hit by Statham, and the players of both sides began to realize that the bouncer conflict had become too hazardous. Thereafter the bouncer was used more sparingly.

Barrington, however, was again injured in the Fourth Test at Georgetown, Wes Hall hitting him just below the left elbow. His arm was so swollen that he was unable to straighten it, and he had to go off the next morning. He was also hurt on the hand in the Fifth Test in Trinidad by Hall while making 69 in the first innings. After his lecture from Robins he decided to duck under bouncers, but the bounce of the ball was often so low that sometimes he had to fling himself to the ground. The other players told him, 'Your backside is hitting the ground so frequently you ought to take a cushion out there to protect it!'

The travelling Press corps criticized his antics, and he defended himself by saying, 'If I stand up straight the ball is likely to hit me. If I duck I'm still in trouble with you lot. I don't know whether to stick or twist!'

The bouncer is a traditional part of West Indies cricket because the pitches are so true that the bowler is at a severe disadvantage, but there is no doubt now, looking back, that the umpires allowed too many bouncers to be bowled in that series. Cowdrey pioneered the use of a chest-pad, but the arm protector favoured by Geoff Boycott and Graham Gooch had still not arrived. Barrington's prophecy that someone would be killed nearly came true a year later when the Indian batsman Nari Contractor ducked into a bouncer from Charlie Griffith which didn't get up, and was dangerously ill for several days.

The English season of 1960 was notable for a fast-bowling controversy of another kind – chucking. Geoff Griffin, the 23-year-old South African, was a pleasant, uncomplicated young man who had the most blatant throwing action of any bowler who had toured England. Ken Barrington was just one of a host of English batsmen who couldn't see him finishing the season. The end of Griffin's Test career came at Lord's in the Second Test when he was no-balled eleven times by Frank Lee and four times by Sid Buller in an exhibition match.

Barrington started the year in form, but a pair at Hove against

Sussex was the start of a bad patch which saw him being left out of the First Test at Edgbaston on the first morning. He would probably have missed the Second Test at Lord's – where he scored 24 – had Geoff Pullar not broken a wrist.

His anxieties were relieved when he scored 80 in the first innings in the Third Test at Trent Bridge (also won by England), while his 76 and 35 in the Fourth Test at Old Trafford ensured him a place at the Oval for the Final Test. Out of six dismissals in the series, four had been at the hands of Trevor Goddard, a defensive bowler who was used to restrict the opposition scoring. Nearly half his 202 overs were maidens.

That winter Barrington evolved a new batting style which he reasoned would be needed to counter Alan Davidson, the Australian pace bowler who toured England with Richie Benaud's side in 1961. He opened up his stance, bringing his left shoulder round more, so that he was facing the bowler two-eyed and full-chested. It may have prevented him playing some of his off-side shots, but he felt it was necessary to stand that way to combat the ball which was bowled across his body. Jim Swanton, the noted critic, lamented, 'It is, to be frank, far from beautiful.'

Davidson, a popular performer who spent a good deal of his time on the treatment table that summer, was Australia's leading bowler with 23 wickets, and he dismissed Barrington twice in the Lord's Test. During the First Test at Edgbaston Barrington kept wicket for a while when John Murray had to go off for treatment.

England managed to hold on to draw the Birmingham Test, with Barrington batting 3 hours 10 minutes for his 48 not out in a partnership of 161 with Ted Dexter, whose mercurial 180 stamped him as one of England's outstanding post-War players. That night came the first indication that the Establishment – which for many years in English cricket has been personified by Gubby Allen, former England captain and treasurer of the MCC – were disapproving of Barrington's ability to occupy the crease in his new style, without trying to force the pace.

Barrington was having dinner in Dexter's flat with their respective wives when the phone rang. Dexter answered it, and was greeted by Allen, who was then chairman of the selectors. Allen congratulated him on his innings, and asked what Barrington had been doing all that time scoring only 48. Dexter defended his colleague, but Barrington, who was in the same room and heard the conversation, was disturbed that the chairman of selectors could have been so critical of him when there had been no chance of any result other than an Australian victory.

Born in 1902 at Sydney, Australia, Allen was a bachelor who lived near Lord's, a man who dedicated much of his life to cricket administration. He seemed to represent the old, amateur approach to the game, which he now saw typified by his latest prodigy, Dexter.

Barrington's professionalism clearly wasn't to his liking. 'I felt he wasn't a great fan of my batting,' said Barrington.

The Lord's Test was famous for the controversy it aroused about the ridge. The Australians, who included four seamers in Davidson, Graham McKenzie, Frank Misson and Ken Mackay to England's three, Trueman, Statham and Dexter, bowled England out for 206 in the first innings and 202 in the second, after scoring 340 themselves.

Barrington's second-innings 66 took 3 hours 20 minutes, but even Gubby Allen couldn't complain this time because it enabled England to set their opponents a modest 69 for victory, which they achieved for the loss of 5 wickets. After the match a team of surveyors went out to measure the undulations in the pitch. They confirmed that there was a slight rise at the Nursery End, and the MCC said that part of the square would be relaid and flattened. The work was carried out, but nineteen years later the Australians were still complaining about a ridge.

In the Third Test at Headingley Ken Barrington was one of many batsmen who failed on a dry, powdery pitch which started breaking up on the first day. Though basically slow, the pitch never enabled batsmen to feel confident: the ball came through at different heights, and Fred Trueman's 11 for 88 in conditions more suited to spin bowling gave England an 8-wicket win with two days to spare.

An exciting series was decided at Old Trafford in the Fourth Test more by the elementary mistakes of England's batsmen than by the inspired bowling of Benaud, who switched to round the wicket in England's second innings and took 6–70 in England's 201 when a comparatively easy target of 256 in 230 minutes was offered them. England started to let the game slip in the morning, as Davidson's last-wicket stand with McKenzie reached 98.

From 150–1, England lost nine wickets for 51 runs. Barrington played across the line and was lbw to Mackay for 5, but the major criticism was heaped on skipper May, who was bowled round his legs by Benaud, and on Brian Close, caught by Norman O'Neill lashing out wildly against Benaud.

In the quietened England dressing-room afterwards Barrington sat muttering, 'Isn't it ruddy marvellous?' The Ashes had been thrown away, and he felt it more than anyone.

He played in the Fifth Test at the Oval with a hairline fracture of the wrist, and no one knew about it at the time except Peter May and the physiotherapist. He injured the wrist batting at Lord's in a county match a few days earlier, but was so determined to play that he kept his injury quiet. In a drawn match he scored 53 in the first innings and 83 in the second, and finished second in the England batting averages next to Surrey colleague Raman Subba Row, who retired after the Oval Test at the age of twenty-nine to go into public relations. It was a heroic performance in keeping with his character.

CHAPTER THREE

Dropped for Slow Scoring

Ken Barrington's natural sense of fun was seen at its most impish during the MCC tour of India, Pakistan and Ceylon in 1961–2. He quickly became the team's leading character, and the huge crowds chanted his name and laughed at his antics.

Perhaps India and Pakistan was where he was more at home than anywhere else in the world. The spectators there love record-breaking batsmen who occupy the crease for days on end, and consider them heroes to be garlanded and fêted.

Realizing that the fans were appreciative of a little showmanship, he kept them amused with various routines and imitations. When a policeman came on the pitch to chase off an invader he pretended that the policeman was chasing him. If a bowler stopped a shot, and threatened to shy at his stumps, he would dart behind the wicket-keeper and seek refuge.

He used his 'Slasher' Mackay run-up in a match at Poona when skipper Ted Dexter, leading England abroad for the first time, asked him to bowl. His fan-mail was enormous, with many letters coming from young girls who wanted a date, or in a few cases to marry him!

In a match at Jaipur he hit the spin bowler Durani for three successive sixes, and took 25 off the over. Durani was to finish India's chief wicket-taker in the Test series, which India won 2–0. In the Pakistan section of the tour, when England won the rubber 1–0 with a victory in the First Test at Lahore, he started with an innings of 139 in 7 hours 15 minutes.

With Mike Smith, he put on 192 for the third wicket, before Smith was run out for 99. A few seconds before Smith was out he said to him, 'Right, don't let's do anything stupid getting that final run.' Smith struck the ball towards mid-on, called for a quick single and was sent back. 'I wasn't convinced I would make it,' said Barrington afterwards. Smith accepted his apology. It was a source of amusement later when Barrington's own innings ended in a run-out.

The five-month tour was one of the most gruelling ever arranged by the MCC, because after playing six matches in Pakistan the party went on to India only to return to Pakistan again, finishing up in the humidity of Sri Lanka (or Ceylon, as it was known then). Few Englishmen spend such a long time in those countries without succumbing to illness, and Barrington, despite his sturdy constitution, was no exception.

Before the First Test against India in Bombay he woke at three in the morning with acute pains in his left side. A doctor was called, and he was given an injection to put him to sleep. Luckily for him, it wasn't appendicitis! Next day a specialist examined him and said he had some grit in the kidneys which needed flushing out. He lost half a stone, and was feeling weak and ill when the Test started in a temperature of 100 degrees.

Again he batted seven hours, compiling a laborious 151 not out in England's 500–8 declared. Many times in that painstaking but courageous innings he felt like giving it away and retiring to the dressing-room to lie down, but his professionalism and desire to succeed kept him going.

The crowds were less well disposed in the drawn Second Test at Kanpur. There were numerous stoppages as mirrors and biscuit-tin lids were shone in the eyes of the batsmen. Missiles were thrown at fielders, and fights broke out among bored spectators and police had to charge in among them with batons raised. In the second innings Barrington made 172 in just under seven hours, which up to then was his highest Test score. He proved he could bat longer than any of the Indian Test players, Contractor, Manjrekar, Umrigar and Borde among them.

An unbeaten 113 followed in the Third Test at New Delhi, which was an even more boring match, and he failed in the Fourth Test at Calcutta, where India won by 187 runs, only the second time in their history they had beaten England. The final Test at Madras was also lost, and local students carried a 'corpse' draped in MCC colours around the ground to celebrate.

For Ken Barrington it was a prolific tour. He scored 139, 6, 151 not out, 52 not out, 21, 172, 113 not out, 14, 3, 20, 48 and 84 in the Tests, and topped the tour averages in both countries. He had a Bradmanesque average of 99 in the Indian series. On docile pitches he was the most difficult of England's batsmen to remove. In twelve Test innings, he reckoned he had been got out only four times. He was not out three times, run out twice, caught twice having a slog and once dragged a wide ball on to his stumps.

Back in London he went down with septic tonsils, and started the 1962 season disastrously. In a warm-up game against London University he was bowled for 0, and the students roared with laughter. Afterwards the captain explained, 'We weren't laughing at you but at the look of amazement on the bowler's face!'

His failures were ignored by the selectors, who kept him in the side for the series against a second-rate Pakistan side led by an unfit Hanif Mohammed. In his first three innings against the tourists he made just 10 runs, including a first-ball duck at Lord's when he was caught by wicket-keeper Imtiaz off the fast bowler Farooq.

Grossly over-bowled, Farooq finally broke down in the Third Test at Headingley and limped off the field for treatment just before lunch. Brigadier Hyder, the Pakistan manager, ran the tour like a military operation, and when he saw Farooq back in the dressing-room, he shouted, 'Get back on the field, you coward!' The crowd were surprised to see Farooq limping back into action so soon! Earlier he had dismissed Barrington again, this time for 1.

Barrington was dropped for the Fourth Test at Nottingham, and it was a surprise that he had lasted so long in the side. His form began to return in county games, and he was recalled for the Fifth Test on his home ground, where he scored an undefeated 50. With a batting average of 20 in the Tests, it had been his worst season internationally, and it made him more determined than ever to eliminate errors in future and play safe. He was worried he might be left out of the touring party for the winter tour of Australia, but while out on a drive with Ann on the Sunday of the Fourth Test he heard his name included in the party.

'I'm sorry, darling,' he said. 'It means another winter away.' 'Don't worry,' replied Ann, 'it's your career. Let me be the first to wish you good luck.'

That long tour of Ceylon, Australia and New Zealand which began at Colombo on 3 October 1962 and ended in Christchurch on 19 March 1963 was to be one of the most successful undertaken by Ken Barrington. Leslie Smith, the Press Association reporter who accompanied the team everywhere without a single day off, wrote in *Wisden*: 'Barrington once more showed his remarkable consistency abroad, scoring 1,763 runs, only 18 short of Denis Compton's 1,781 in South Africa in 1948–9, the highest ever recorded up to then by an MCC player in first-class matches on tour.

'He hit six centuries, three of them in Tests, and whether at number five, where he started, or number three, where he finished, he played in the same solid way, rarely producing anything of an exciting nature but showing an excellent temperament and the ability to take runs off any attack. Without his steadiness, the team might well have been in trouble on a number of occasions.'

Ken Barrington was thirty-one, and at the height of his powers. He was sound in the field, but some of the other players lacked his agility, and the failure of Ted Dexter's ageing side – average age twenty-eight – to regain the Ashes was blamed on their inferior fielding, both close to the wicket and in the deep field, where Bobby Simpson's Australians were faster and threw better.

He took seventeen catches, more than anyone else in the party except first-choice wicket-keeper Alan Smith. He topped the batting averages in the Tests in Australia with an average of 72·75 from 582 runs, and came second to Colin Cowdrey in New Zealand with 73·50 from 294 runs.

The West Indian side which toured England in 1963 under Sir Frank Worrell's undemonstrative leadership was a far better side than Simpson's, particularly in bowling, and Barrington failed to score a century in the five Tests, three of which were won by Worrell's magnificent side. His highest score, 80, came in England's first innings in the Second Test at Lord's, the match which was called by the popular newspapers 'The Greatest Test Ever'.

He was overshadowed by Dexter, whose 70 off 73 balls against the fiery pace of Wes Hall and Charlie Griffith was positively brilliant. But when England needed 234 to win Barrington showed the qualities which had made him England's most dependable player, withstanding many bruising blows from Hall and Griffith on a lively pitch to compile 60.

Earlier that summer he had his first clash with the moody Griffith, who was touring England for the first time. During his unbeaten 110 against the tourists at the Oval for Surrey, Barrington drove a half-volley from Griffith straight past the bowler, and when he arrived at the bowler's end Griffith scowled and said, 'Wait till I get you on a fast wicket.'

'What's the matter?' replied Barrington. 'Aren't I supposed to hit the ball? Should we stand away from the wicket to give you a free go?'

Right from his first meeting with Griffith, Barrington felt there was an element of unfairness about his action. He was a student of bowlers' actions, and was quick to spot any irregularities. Griffith, he believed, threw his faster delivery, particularly the yorker which gained him so many of his 119 wickets on the tour. George Duckworth, the former England wicket-keeper who travelled with the West Indians, claimed that Griffith's yorker was so lethal because so many English batsmen, including Barrington, had switched to an open stance. But Barrington was suspicious of the change of pace which Griffith was capable of producing on the slowest of pitches.

He told friends, 'One minute he's military medium and the next he's through you like a flash of lightning.' The gossip from the England dressing-room failed to reach the newspapers, and it was a year before the Griffith throwing controversy became public knowledge.

Barrington averaged only 27·50 that summer in the Tests, but wasn't the only batsman to be cut down by Hall, Griffith and the admirable Gary Sobers. No other English batsmen made a Test century, and Dexter only managed an average of 34.

Sobers, with his late in-swing, bowled Barrington twice in the Edgbaston Test, for 9 and 1. With a top score of 110 not out that summer, it had not been a profligate homecoming for England's leading professional batsman. And his luck didn't change on the tour of India in January and February, 1964. After innings of 76 not out, 108, 80 (in the First Test at Madras) and 72 he broke a finger trying to catch a slash in the slips off Gaekwad at Ahmedabad, and took no further part in the tour, returning home before the Fourth Test.

He started the home campaign in 1964 plagued by worries about not having scored a hundred in a Test in England. He had made nine centuries abroad, where his strength off the back foot was more use to him than in England, but in domestic Tests the target eluded him. In forty-four innings he hadn't made more than 87, which is the Australians' bad-luck number.

At Headingley in the Third Test against Simpson's Australians, he thought he was about to break the hoodoo when he was 85 in the second innings. After having an appeal turned down for bad light near the close he decided to pad up to a ball from off-spinner Tom Veivers, and umpire Fred Price gave him out – much to his disappointment, because he felt the ball pitched outside the off-stump.

He hesitated briefly before leaving the wicket. In the England dressing-room later his friend Wally Grout came up and said, 'Bad luck, Kenny.' Today's play-backs might well have revealed it was a bad decision. No one will ever know. But his make-up being what it was, Barrington blamed himself. 'I shouldn't have padded up,' he said. England were only 36 ahead with four batsmen out, and on the Monday were bowled out for 229 and Australia won by 7 wickets. He drove home on the Tuesday cursing himself for causing England's defeat.

Before the Fourth Test at Old Trafford he decided to change his routine. Since his Test debut in 1955 he had put the half-crown that Peter May tossed with at the start of that match in his blazer pocket before setting off to play for England. It was his good-luck omen. But this time he left the half-crown on a shelf in his kitchen at Mitcham, and also made sure of his favourite position in the Old Trafford dressing-room – the nearest two pegs on the left side – by arriving two hours earlier than usual.

The pitch was so good that when Simpson won the toss the England players knew the Ashes were lost and the match doomed to be a draw. Simpson and Bill Lawry put on a record 201 for the first wicket before Lawry was run out for 106. 'That's the only way we're going to get anyone out on this pitch,' said one of the England players.

The superbly fit Simpson batted all day Thursday, all day Friday and an hour on Saturday, and his 311 was the highest score at Old Trafford and the longest innings (12 hours 45 minutes) ever played against England. Dexter used seven bowlers including Boycott, but strangely, not Barrington. Grout came in at 652–7 and announced, 'I'm just the man for this crisis!' He swung at Rumsey, hit a catch to Dexter and was out for 0. He walked off grinning.

Simpson's attitude was much more ruthless, much more calculated. Until his final fling on Saturday morning, he took no risks, concentrating on accumulating runs. When he reached his 200 he checked his guard and went on, determined to pass 300. The critics were savage, accusing him of ruining the Test match and insulting the 30,000 spectators who turned up each day. Sir Learie Constantine – whom Ken Barrington was to succeed as cricket commentator in the now defunct *Daily Sketch* – defended Simpson, despite his reputation for advocating attacking cricket. 'It was the only thing Simpson could do,' said Sir Learie. 'His tactics were justified.'

Barrington, a personal friend of Simpson – he even played golf with him on the Sunday rest day – was in full agreement with the Australian captain. 'I would have done exactly the same as he did,' he said. Simpson's declaration at 656–8 meant England had to score 457 to avoid the follow-on.

Dexter, usually a man of few words in the dressing-room before the start of an innings, was as loquacious this time as any soccer manager. 'Now really get stuck in,' he said. 'We've got a long way to go. I don't want heroics. Give them some of their own medicine. You've got to go out there, get stuck in and fight, fight, fight.'

John Edrich's fight lasted only a few minutes before Dexter strode purposefully in to join Boycott at 15–1. The second-wicket stand occupied three hours, enabling next-man-in Barrington to rest his tired legs. Then Boycott was bowled by McKenzie's slower ball and Barrington got up to walk down the stairs and out through the cluster of members in front of the dank, Victorian pavilion to play his 45th Test innings in England. He was much more tense than usual. England couldn't win. It was a holding operation, and more depended on him than on anyone else. 'A shaky start soon sent Barrington into his shell,' recorded the late Harry Gee of the Press Association.

There were frequent consultations between the two batsmen in mid-wicket, with Barrington doing most of the talking, as was his custom. 'Build it up,' he said. 'They'll never get one past you if you bat like that.' And Dexter would reply, 'Yes, don't worry. I shan't do anything silly.' When bad light stopped play England were 162–2, with Dexter, more restrained than at any time in his career, 71 not out and Barrington on 20.

Dexter nearly floundered on Monday morning, twice giving difficult chances to McKenzie at backward short leg. Simpson planned to stop his powerful driving by asking his bowlers to bowl at him around middle and leg, and it worked so well that Dexter was restricted to hitting the ball into the Australian's defensive arc of fieldsmen on the leg side.

When he was 108 Dexter hit a rare ball on the off in the air towards Peter Burge at cover. Burge dived, and scooped it up. Dexter started to walk, stopped and said, 'Was that a catch?' Burge, one of the most sporting of Australian cricketers, said, 'I'm not sure.' Dexter said, 'I'm not sure either.' Sid Buller, the umpire, intervened and said, 'Not out.' Later Buller explained, 'The ball didn't carry, in my opinion.'

Slowly, remorselessly, Barrington edged towards his century. Finally, after three and a half hours, Veivers bowled a delivery wide of the off-stump and he saw the chance to cut. For a batsman who had a reputation for safety first, he was often willing to play that most dangerous of shots, the cut. This time he failed to get right over the ball and it flew to the right of McKenzie in the slips. McKenzie stuck up a hand, but since he was perhaps fielding too close to the wicket, he failed to make contact. Barrington scampered up the pitch, a very relieved man. 'It was one of the most deliriously happy moments of my life,' he said later. The elusive hundred had taken two hours less than Simpson's hundred on the first day.

As he walked back to the crease to resume the contest he told himself, 'Come on now, get stuck in again.' His next target was the 200 mark. Dexter fell at 372–3, bowled by Veivers for 174, but Barrington went on and on, past 200 and on to 256 – his best score, and the highest by an Englishman at Old Trafford – before he was lbw to McKenzie. The critics criticized him for not being more adventurous on the final day, but he explained, 'What was the point? We couldn't win. The match was bound to be a draw. I was so tired I was batting like a machine. I couldn't remember what I was doing. It was as if I was drugged.'

When England were all out for 611 only five minutes remained, and Dexter let Barrington bowl the first over. Simpson cut him for a boundary, and that was the end of the most gluttonously run-gathering Test Match ever played in England. But there was no respite for Barrington and Dexter. They changed quickly and drove the 240 miles to Hove for a Gillette Cup semi-final the next day which Sussex, the holders, won by 90 runs. Dexter, with 84, was man of the match, and Barrington made only 5. Old Trafford had taken more out of him than it had Dexter, both mentally and physically. Dexter was a man who could switch off and turn his mind to many other activities and interests. But Barrington was single-minded. He had endured sleeplessness during his six-night stay at the Lymm Hotel, Cheshire, and room-mate John Edrich had complained about his constant tea-making. By the end of that week he was exhausted.

He was still showing signs of mental tiredness a month later when his benefit match, Surrey *v.* Yorkshire, took place at the Oval. Organizing the benefit with a committee of helpers had taken up most of his time during the year, and now he had the added burden of having to captain the side in the absence of Micky Stewart, who was suffering from a fractured cheekbone and nose after top-edging a ball from John Price into his face.

The above-average Saturday crowd gave him a standing ovation when he came in at 97–2 to join John Edrich. Yorkshire captain

Brian Close allowed him the customary one off the mark, and realizing that he was likely to be more tense than usual, then crowded him with close fielders. Close himself took up a position three yards from the bat at silly mid-off, and Fred Trueman was a yard farther away at short square leg. Ray Illingworth, one of Barrington's best friends and a former room-mate, was bowling from the pavilion end.

Illingworth pitched one on middle and leg, Barrington played half forward and the ball went off bat and pad towards Trueman, who dived to his left, rolled and came up holding the ball aloft in his right hand. Barrington couldn't see whether it was a catch, and neither could the umpires, the late Paul Gibb and Johnny Arnold.

He said, 'Did you catch it, Fred?' And Trueman replied, 'Aye, I caught it, lad. Bad luck.' Barrington thereupon 'walked'. Throughout his career he was a 'walker'. As he said, 'Fred said it was out, and that was that.' He was bitterly disappointed, but the deep sense of honour which was part of his cricketing make-up never deserted him, even in his benefit match when he was determined to make a big score.

In a break for rain on the Monday one of the agency photographers who worked at the Oval said to him, 'How were you out?' Barrington was surprised. 'Caught Trueman, bowled Illingworth,' he said. 'Take a look at this,' said the photographer. He pulled out a photograph of the Trueman catch which showed Trueman sprawled on the ground, left arm trapped under his body and right hand still six inches away from the ball, which was about to hit the ground.

Photographs can lie, but the only assumption that could be drawn from the picture was that Trueman hadn't made a catch as he had claimed. Barrington was too gentle a person to lose his temper on many occasions, but this time he was very angry. He stormed into the Yorkshire dressing-room with the picture and went straight up to Brian Close, the Yorkshire captain, and said, 'Look, Brian, I've always tried to play my cricket in a friendly and sporting manner but this is . . .' The rest was an outburst of abuse which was alien to his character.

Close looked at the photo for some time and said, 'Well, look, Ken, if Fred said he caught it, then he did catch it.' Trueman was also in the dressing-room, a large, square-shaped room with showers and toilets next to a corridor leading to the exit door on the top floor of the pavilion. Barrington turned aggressively towards him, confronting him with the evidence and shouting. It was the first time he had ever had a serious row with a fellow-player.

'I never thought this kind of thing could happen,' said Barrington. 'We've been playing together round the world in Tests for so many years.'

Trueman became angry too. 'Photos can lie,' he said heatedly. 'I know I caught the ball cleanly. I've never cheated anyone out in my life. If there had been any doubt I would have asked the umpire.'

The rest of the Yorkshire players, Boycott, Sharpe, Padgett, Hampshire, Illingworth, Richard Hutton, Binks, Don Wilson and Ryan, were agog. They were used to rows in Yorkshire, but this was different – it involved a player in the other team.

After a few more exchanges Barrington left, but he remained unconvinced that Trueman had caught him fairly. On the Tuesday morning he felt ill and dropped out of the game. It was reported in the newspapers that he was suffering from a chill, but it was worse than that. The pressures of Test cricket, the hard work put in on his benefit and the row with Trueman had left him exhausted and needing a rest.

He sat at home watching the rest of the match on television. Surrey won by 57 runs with John Edrich in charge. The family doctor prescribed a holiday, and he and Ann went to Saltdean for a week, booking in at a modest-sized hotel under Ann's maiden name, Cozens, to avoid being recognized. He wore dark glasses on the beach. At the hotel on the first evening a woman in the bar said, 'You look like Ken Barrington. Have you ever been mistaken for him?' 'Yes,' he replied. 'On quite a few occasions!'

He was back in time for Surrey's final match, against Warwickshire at the Oval, scoring 36 in Surrey's 391–8. Surrey finished fourth, and he came top of the county averages with 60·14 from 1,263 runs. It had been another good year for him, but a further source of anxiety was building up, the spectre of Charlie Griffith. Early in September a team of West Indians arrived in England for a two-match tour, captained by Sir Frank Worrell. Ten of the players had toured England under Worrell the previous year, and the other two members of the party were Roy Marshall, the Hampshire batsman, and Cammie Smith.

Ken Barrington was invited to play in an England XI that was to oppose Worrell's side, but he declined because he refused to play against Charlie Griffith. By this time he was convinced that Griffith occasionally threw his faster deliveries, and it was time a leading player took a stand.

His mind had been made up the previous year during the England second innings at the Oval. With Sid Buller, the umpire who ended the career of Geoff Griffin, standing at square leg, Griffith bowled at fast medium. But after lunch, bowling from Buller's end, he bowled at a much faster pace, and Barrington was certain he threw three deliveries in one over.

Griffith was spurred on by Barrington's rough treatment of him, including 15 in an over with two hooked 4s from bouncers. The first of the three questionable deliveries rose sharply towards Barrington's face, and he just managed to fend it away with a glove. The second delivery, just as fast, found the edge and flew over slips, almost carrying for a 6. The third one was a yorker which grazed his right boot and knocked the stumps out of the ground.

At the Oval, as at other Test grounds, the groundsman usually waters the holes before putting the stumps in between sessions, and that explains why the stumps go flying when hit, unlike in a club or village match. The bowlers are faster, of course, but the cartwheeling of the stumps is accentuated in Tests by this simple ploy. Barrington's stumps were in disarray. On a good batting pitch, on a nice day when it was easy to sight the ball, England's premier professional batsman had been comprehensively bowled for 28 by a yorker when well set. None of the critics then in the tiny Press box under a tin roof to the right of the England dressing-room sensed that there was anything amiss. They merely recorded that Barrington was another victim of the Griffith yorker. But in the dressing-room Barrington was enraged, and the replay on television served only to anger him more, because it seemed to show that Griffith's action at the time of the delivery was unusual, with his left foot splayed towards the off-side and his chest open, the characteristics of the chucker.

Barrington forsook match fees of £100 when he refused to play for the England XI against Worrell's team at Scarborough and Edgbaston. He didn't make the news of his withdrawal public, or his reasons for it, because he feared that some people might say he was frightened of Griffith – not that such an allegation would gain much support among his colleagues and rivals. Throughout his career he faced the world's fastest bowlers without flinching, and never wore the helmet or extra protection which is favoured by modern players. He wore no chest protector or arm protector, only the customary box and thigh pad. Yet he suffered a broken wrist, two broken fingers, five broken toes and numerous chipped bones as well as concussion. His objection to Griffith was that it wasn't fair that a bowler should be allowed to get away with it. To some people it might be said that Griffith's action induced a complex in Ken Barrington's normal placid personality. Perhaps it did, and it was a factor in his subsequent breakdown.

Reporters started ringing his home at Mitcham and asking why he had withdrawn from the England XI. Ann said that he wasn't right after his illness. But the newspapers soon found out. The other England players knew the reason, and the *Daily Mail* sent a reporter to interview him at his home. The subsequent disclosure that he was making a public protest against Griffith's action – the first batsman to do so – caused a furore. Later Richie Benaud, Ted Dexter and Norman O'Neill all said publicly that Griffith was a bowler with a suspect action.

The row caused a breach between Griffith and Barrington, and it was some years before they spoke to each other again. In his prime Griffith was a surly, moody man who was likened to Sonny Liston, but those who met him later in his career said how much he had changed. Griffith still plays club cricket in Barbados, where he is a coach. And these days he is strictly medium pace with no bouncers and no yorkers. A man who started life as a bus conductor became one of his country's most successful fast bowlers – certainly one of the most controversial – and made many headlines but not much money.

Towards the end of 1964 Ken Barrington's career entered a happier period, when he went to South Africa on the last England tour to visit the country which apart from Rugby was soon to become a sporting outcast. England won the series 1–0 under Mike Smith's phlegmatic leadership, and were unbeaten, four of the five matches being drawn. Barrington had phenomenal success, topping the Test batting averages with 101·60 from 508 runs, and also the bowling averages in all matches with 24 wickets at 7·25 apiece. He enjoyed the lavish hospitality, the shooting and the big-game hunting and the time spent round swimming-pools.

With players of the ability of Graeme and Peter Pollock, Colin Bland, Eddie Barlow, Trevor Goddard, the skipper, John Waite and Dennis Lindsay, the South Africans may well have had the better side, especially as none of the England pace bowlers, David Brown, John Price or Ian Thomson, met with much success and Geoff Boycott was forced to bowl 61 overs in the Tests. The series was won in the First Test at Durban when Smith won the toss and batted on a grassless pitch which took spin from the first day. When Barrington inspected it the day before the match he said, 'We're one up already.' England's off-spin bowlers, Fred Titmus and David Allen, captured thirteen wickets between them, and England won by an innings and 108 runs.

Barrington batted seven and a quarter hours for his 148 not out, sharing an unbroken stand of 206 with Jim Parks, 108 not out, which set a record for the sixth wicket against South Africa. His century meant that he had become the first player in the world to score a Test century in every Test-playing country.

The South Africans were non-walkers, and after several of them remained at the crease when England's fielders thought they were out relations between the two sides deteriorated. England's players didn't claim their opponents were cheats, but they thought that they sometimes went beyond the limits of fair play. After Barrington had scored another hundred, 121 in the drawn Second Test at Johannesburg over the Christmas holiday, the simmering row broke into the open when Eddie Barlow appeared to play a full toss from Titmus into his boot, whereupon it carried to Peter Parfitt at slip.

Barlow didn't walk, and umpire John Warner seemed uncertain as the England players appealed. Finally, Warner ruled not out, and Titmus addressed a provocative remark to Barlow. The stocky South African (known as Bunter because of his girth), strode angrily down the pitch, shouting remarks back at Titmus.

Barrington, fielding at mid-wicket, was convinced that Barlow was out. When Barlow reached 50, none of the England players clapped. When he got to his hundred no one on the field applauded.

Barrington dropped him in the slips at 125 – a rare mistake – and at the close of play he was 138 not out, only to fall in the first over the following morning. Later tour manager Donald Carr arranged for Smith to apologize to Barlow for their churlishness in not applauding, and Titmus also offered a token apology for his comments.

But the controversy stayed on the front pages the next day when Barrington was involved in another incident in England's first innings. At 49 Barrington edged a ball from Peter Pollock into Lindsay's gloves, and there was a unanimous appeal. In normal circumstances he would walk, but now he stood his ground, and umpire Warner, aware that the batsman facing him was a walker, said, 'Not out.'

A second or two passed and Barrington set off for the pavilion, sacrificing his wicket to the applause of the 16,000 crowd at Newlands. Immediately his gesture in staying and then walking was seen as the fair man's retort to the 'cheating' Springboks, and J. L. Manning, the liverish columnist of the *Daily Mail*, wrote, 'Barrington's gesture was too ostentatious to be convincing. It smacked of "We chaps know how to play the game, even if you lot don't." '

The South African Rugby Board sent a telegram of congratulations, and Barrington had to explain that he had no intention of ridiculing the umpire. The England players, pressured as they always are by the authorities to do the right thing, became so anxious to observe the spirit of the game that later in England's innings Titmus walked although he hadn't touched the ball with his bat. It brushed his pad, but in the confusion he gave himself up. 'I was in such a state with it all that I didn't know what to do,' he explained.

With no chance of a result in the match Smith put Barrington on to bowl, and he delighted the crowd by imitating Jim Laker's action. Titmus and Allen bowled 112 overs between them and captured only 4 wickets, but Barrington, turning his joke off-breaks prodigiously, proceeded to take 3 wickets in 19 deliveries at a cost of only 4 runs. He bowled Lindsay for 50 with a ball which came back nearly a foot, had Peter Pollock lbw with another delivery which turned considerably and bowled last man Hall for a duck.

One of England's early-order batsmen came up to him after Pollock's dismissal and said, 'For pity's sake. We don't want to have to bat again when there's only twenty-five minutes to go and no chance of a result.'

'All right,' replied Barrington, 'I'll go in to bat.' And he opened the innings with Boycott. Only twenty minutes remained, and he gave the spectators the full range of his batting impersonations, including the Army colonel, W. G. Grace and 'Slasher' Mackay.

Barrington's proud boast that he could read a pitch in advance let him down in the Fourth Test at Johannesburg. A member of the selection committee along with Smith, Dexter and manager Donald Carr, he forecast the pitch would suit England's seam bowlers Ian Thomson and Tom Cartwright because it appeared to have more grass than usual, and a little moisture in it. Smith won the toss, and put South Africa in, and they scored 390–6 and 307–3 declared. Rain, and Boycott's 76 not out in the second innings, saved England from defeat.

There was another controversy when Smith went down the pitch gardening after Waite had gathered the ball, and Peter Van der Merwe threw his wicket down. Umpire Kidson gave Smith out, but Goddard withdrew his appeal and Smith was reinstated. Despite the incidents, the players drank in each other's dressing-rooms, and Smith's team were often invited to the homes of their opponents. It was one of Barrington's happiest tours, certainly in bowling. He took 24 wickets at 7·25 apiece with his best performances against the South African Universities, an aggregate of 9–54, and 7–40 against Griqualand West.

In the match against the Universities he bowled a long hop which skidded along the ground, and the batsman, Mackay-Coghill, appealed against the light. The appeal was turned down, and next ball Mackay-Coghill was caught by John Murray off a perfectly pitched leg-break which turned sharply.

Near the end of the tour Ann joined him, and they planned to stay on after the tour was over for a three-week holiday, but the day before they were due to start the holiday a message arrived saying his mother was very ill. Next day they flew back to London. The much-needed holiday was abandoned, and Barrington's mother (to whom he was devoted) recovered.

Perhaps it was the fact of not having a holiday – which had been prescribed by the family doctor – that was a contributory cause to his failures in the English summer of 1965, which culminated with him being dropped by the selectors for slow scoring against the New Zealanders, who shared the Test programme that summer with the South Africans, the first year of double tours. The innings which earned Barrington dismissal from the Test side was his 137 in 7¼ hours at Edgbaston in the First Test. It was his thirteenth Test century, and he heard that he was being left out as a disciplinary measure on 13 June. The decision embittered him so much that he thought of retiring from the game.

The season began inauspiciously when Crawford White, then cricket correspondent of the *Daily Express*, rang him and asked him whether, in view of the spate of drawn matches in Tests, he would set an example by playing more shots. Conscious of his position as England's leading professional batsman, and concerned about the bad publicity Test cricket was getting, Barrington replied that he would try to score at a faster rate.

In the published interview he was quoted as saying, 'For me, careful cricket is OUT. This year I'm prepared to give it a go with every shot in the book.' Many Test players say things to newspapermen – nowadays for fees of up to £2,000 an article from the tabloid Press – and don't worry about the outcome. To them yesterday's headlines are today's fish-and-chip wrappings. But Barrington being the kind of person he was, he felt obliged to start the season playing in the aggressive manner which marked his early days in Surrey's Second XI. Derek Ufton, the former Kent player, recalls: 'I remember playing with him in a second eleven match and he scored 180 odd in 90 minutes. He was probably a better player then than he was later on in his career when he became more of a grafter. He had all the shots and hit the ball with tremendous power.'

In the Second XI the bowling was less taxing, and when Barrington tried to recapture the abandon of his younger days in the opening first-class matches of the 1965 season he failed disastrously. His scores were 41 not out, 23, 21, 3, 7, 5, 6, 3, 0, 15, 18, 35, and Arthur McIntyre, the Surrey coach, arranged a simulated game for him at the Oval to eliminate some of the faults he had developed. McIntyre told him he was lifting his bat in the direction of gully and coming down across the line of flight of the ball with a bat which was facing mid-wicket. The old worries returned, and it was a jittery Ken Barrington who awaited news of the England team for the First Test against the New Zealanders to be played at Birmingham at the end of May. To his surprise the selectors retained him in the twelve, and before leaving for Birmingham he vowed to make some changes in his superstitious routines.

Changes had worked at Old Trafford the year before, and now he took out a five-year-old MCC cap which he had lying around at home and took it with him as a lucky talisman. On the way to the M1 he called in at Stuart Surridge's sports goods firm to borrow a bat he had scored 2,499 runs with in 1959 to take with him as another talisman. 'We have a big stock of famous bats and this was one of them,' said Surridge. 'It was no surprise to me that he wanted it because he was very superstitious.'

A flat tyre at a service station delayed him, and after losing his way in the outskirts of Birmingham he arrived at Edgbaston just before three o'clock, much later than he had intended. His favourite dressing-room position had been taken by another player, and he saw that as a bad omen. Though he was a senior professional, he would never have thought of asking the player to change places. He upheld the unwritten etiquette of the dressing-room with scrupulous fairness.

When the players inspected the pitch most of them thought the top would break up and it would take spin. Mike Smith won the toss, and decided to bat in the cold, cheerless conditions. Geoff Boycott and Bob Barber put on 54 against the pace bowlers Richard Collinge, Dick Motz and Frank Cameron, and both openers had gone when Barrington joined Dexter at 76–2. With Dexter playing strokes at the other end, there was less pressure on Barrington, and he felt in a slightly more relieved frame of mind.

However, the longer he batted the more his complexes about his poor form overtook any feelings of composure gained by his early mastery of the bowling. At the close of a miserable day's play he was 61 not out in 3¼ hours, having struck only three 4s.

John Reid, the New Zealand captain, set defensive fields with only one slip and a cordon on both sides of the wicket to stop singles, and his bowlers bowled just short of a length. In the inquest in the bar that night none of the other England players were critical of Barrington's performance. They agreed with his assessment that 'the ball hadn't come on to the bat'. Colin Cowdrey's 44 in 90 minutes at the end of a turgid day – described by Norman Preston, the editor of *Wisden*, as 'a charming innings' – had taken some of the pressure off Barrington, just as Dexter had done earlier in the day.

After an interrupted night's sleep Barrington drove to the ground next day determined to keep going, but at a faster pace. It was a bitterly cold day, so cold that instead of the usual cold drinks of orange or lemon, hot coffee was brought out at half-past twelve. Cowdrey continued his enterprising innings until at 85 the ball bounced off his body and rolled back on the stumps. Mike Smith came in, and was promptly leg before to Collinge for a duck. Around this time Smith was known as a 0 or 99 player. He failed at 0 more often than most players – because of his eyesight, said his critics – but he also scored a number of 99s, and numerous centuries.

It was his fourth duck in six Test innings, and his tenth in Test cricket. Like Mike Brearley, he suffered from being classed as just short of Test quality as a batsman, though he was generally acknowledged to be a fine captain. Conservative Prime Minister Harold Macmillan had inspired the word 'unflappable' around this time, and Mike Smith was cricket's most unflappable person. Smith played in all six Tests that summer, and never once reached 50, but such was his popularity with both players and selectors that he was retained as captain in Australia the following winter.

The nadir of Barrington's innings at Edgbaston came when he was 85 not out either side of lunch. He remained scoreless for 62 minutes as 20 overs were bowled, and Reid beat him five times in an over. Barrington came down the pitch to Jim Parks, his partner, and said, 'I can't hit the skin off a rice pudding.'

At lunch none of the other players, or the selectors, were critical, and Smith was non-committal. There were none of the usual 'Well played, Kenny' salutations from his colleagues. As he strapped his pads back on Smith came over and said, 'Try and push it along this afternoon. I would like 450 by tea-time.' Barrington apologized. 'I'm sorry, Mike,' he said. 'But I just can't hit the blasted ball.'

Back in the middle, another twenty-five minutes went by before he scored again, and the comments of the small crowd were increasingly cynical. Once he threw his bat down in frustration. At the other end Parks scored his 34 in almost even time. After $6\frac{1}{2}$ hours, Barrington at last reached his hundred to muted applause. He celebrated by taking 14 runs off an over from the nineteen-year-old off-spinner Vic Pollard, including a drive for 6. He was finally out for 137, caught behind off Collinge, who took 3–63 in 29.4 overs, in $7\frac{1}{2}$ hours. Again, there were no congratulations from the other players, who sensed the mood created by the selectors – namely, that Barrington had overdone the caution. To put his slow-scoring feats in perspective, Barrington's does not appear in a list of eleven slowest Test centuries, ranging from Nazar's 114 in 557 minutes to Greig's 103 in 414 minutes.

That evening after the close of play, Doug Insole, the chairman of selectors, asked Barrington to step out on the balcony of the dressing-room where they could converse without being overheard. 'Ken,' he said, 'I can't say we're very happy about your knock these past two days. Against New Zealand, particularly, we're expected to show the way in attractive cricket.'

Barrington replied that he thought a large total was necessary because the pitch would deteriorate, but accepted that he should have scored much quicker. 'I just couldn't hit the ball,' he said. Insole pointed out that he *had* hit it, but only after reaching his hundred. 'I can only say that to me and the other selectors it appeared as though all you wanted was a hundred, which looks very selfish.'

In no sense was it a row. The two men were former playing colleagues and friends, but Insole saw his duty to the game overriding any personal feelings. 'I can't speak for the other selectors,' said Insole. 'But there is a chance that you might not be required for the next Test.'

Barrington was so downcast that he left Edgbaston without signing the autograph books of the small knot of boys who were waiting patiently for him. Usually he was the keenest signer of all the England players. At the team's hotel at Droitwich he had two half-pints with Fred Titmus and went to bed early, thoroughly dejected, and worried more than he had ever been before about his performance and his future in the game.

Next morning the newspapers featured headlines about 'Barrington's Bore War' and the critics demanded action. Keith Miller, an old friend, wrote in the *Daily Express*: 'Barrington set cricket back to the Dark Ages. His innings was a selfish exhibition, the worst I have seen in this respect. It was a painful crowd-killer and the stuff that is emptying the cricket grounds of England.' The Editor of *Wisden* described his innings as 'tedious' and 'deserving of censure'.

Some of his anxiety was removed when the New Zealanders were bowled out for 116 in their first innings, justifying Barrington's claim that the pitch was below Test standard. Following on, New Zealand were 215–4 by Saturday night, still 104 behind, and England's players provisionally booked out of their hotel on Monday because they expected the match to finish.

However, the New Zealanders proceeded to disprove Barrington's claim that the ball wasn't coming on to the bat by scoring positively even when losing wickets, finishing up scoring 413, their highest total against England for fourteen years. Pollard batted 4 hours for his unbeaten 81, which was compiled at the same pace as Barrington's innings but in a different context. England duly won by 9 wickets, and ten days later Barrington showed what he could do on a flat pitch against Reid's team when he scored 129 not out in 3½ hours at the Oval, hitting twenty 4s, and captured 5 wickets for 88 runs in New Zealand's 422–9.

The Sunday before the Second Test at Lord's he was playing in a charity match for Micky Stewart and a Coventry City footballer at Coventry, and while he was chatting with the jockeys Terry Biddlecombe and Josh Gifford a group of newspaper reporters came up and told him that he had been dropped from the England team as a disciplinary measure. After what Insole had said he expected it, but the news still came as a shock. He was angry more than anything that the information had come from the Press. He felt he should have been told direct by the selectors.

One of the reporters said his newspaper would offer a large sum for an 'exclusive'. Barrington declined. Unlike most of today's cricketers, he had no agent acting on his behalf. His quotes for the newspapers were restrained. 'I am naturally very disappointed but I hope to be playing again later in the series,' he said. Privately, he felt depressed and bitter. After all his service to his country, the bruises he had incurred, they dropped him for one bad performance! In the days that followed he again thought seriously about quitting the game, or at worst going into League cricket.

Stuart Surridge recalls him coming round to his house to talk it over. 'Don't be so silly,' Surridge told him. 'Just get your head down and play sensibly and you'll be back in for the next Test.'

Barrington's mood wasn't helped by the weather in the next two days during Surrey's match against Oxford University at The Parks. In between the showers he bowled 20 overs and failed to get a bat. The critics were pleased that he had been punished. E. W. Swanton wrote in the *Daily Telegraph*:

> Neither the conditions nor the state of the game [i.e. the First Test] remotely justified such a weariness to the flesh and the only conclusion that could be reluctantly drawn was that Barrington put an undue value on getting his hundred. The selectors could not have been provided with a clearer challenge to their authority and their moral courage should be applauded without reserve.

Barrington had become a test case, the first England player to be dropped as a disciplinary measure for making an excessively slow hundred in a Test Match. Insole was quoted as saying:

> I hope he plays many times for England in the future, but not like this. His Edgbaston innings was no good for cricket, no good for the crowd, no good for himself. He admitted that. I made it absolutely clear when I took over what kind of cricket I wanted England to play. Brighter cricket is a cliché I don't recognise. I don't expect a batsman to throw his bat about when the side is 40–4. But when you are 300–4 as England were, that's different.
>
> We talked for half the meeting about this and in the end decided it was the only thing to do. Ken is one of the nicest blokes in the game. He is a good player and has done a tremendous amount for England. People will say "look at his average" but you have to look at figures only in relation to the game. We can talk until we are blue in the face about the right methods of playing cricket and nothing will happen. Only by practical action are we likely to achieve anything.
>
> We have agreed that we have to show the younger players in particular that we are prepared to leave out and discipline a man whatever his status if he does not perform in the proper manner.

The day after the news broke Insole wrote a personal letter to Barrington saying he had acted more in sorrow than anger.

> I hope you will appreciate that no personal animosity whatsoever is involved and indeed we look forward to your performing for England for a long time to come, provided your approach is in tune with ours.
>
> This is not an easy letter to write so I won't prolong the agony. By the time you get this I shall have talked to the Press and I hope that what I have to say to them is reproduced factually and without causing any offence to you.

As sackings went it was a very gentlemanly one, but it left its mark on Ken Barrington. Searching for excuses, he blamed the selectors for picking him in the first place when they knew he was out of form. Then he told himself that they should have taken similar action earlier. He hadn't been the only player to bat slowly in Tests.

After a miserable match against Gloucester at Bristol, when he scored only 7, he returned to the Oval for Micky Stewart's benefit match in-mid-July, a local derby against Middlesex, and playing with and against some of his best friends, some of his inherent cheerfulness returned as he scored 109.

CHAPTER FOUR
Breakdown

Ken Barrington was so despondent about his chances of regaining his Test place in the summer of 1965 that the weekend the team was chosen for the Third Test at Headingley he was playing for Surrey against Yorkshire at Bradford and he left his England blazer behind in Mitcham. Normally he would have taken it with him, expecting to travel on from Bradford on the Tuesday night to join the England party the next day in Leeds.

The evening before the selectors met he was bowled by Richard Hutton for a duck. His scores since his century against the New Zealanders at the Oval had been 7, 5, 60 and 32. On the Sunday he was playing golf when the news came that he was back in the side. He rang home and asked Ann if she could drive North with his blazer and gear. If Dexter hadn't stepped in front of his runaway car and broken his leg, or if Boycott had been fit, he wouldn't have been forgiven so soon, or so he thought.

But the selectors were eager to have him back. The disciplinary action had been forgotten about. Not that he could ever forget it! He celebrated his return with an innings of 76 in a partnership of 129 in 95 minutes with John Edrich which enabled Surrey to beat Yorkshire.

Hoping to change his luck, he borrowed Ron Tindall's bat after Tindall had said what a good bat it was. Denis Compton used to borrow other players' bats, and if it worked for Compo, it could work for him. As he arrived at Headingley for the Wednesday practice session on the eve of the Test he was met by Peter May, one of the selectors. May told him, 'You're too good a player to be left out. Now, forget the past and do your best.' Still bothered by guilt although he had subsequently convinced himself that he had been harshly treated he apologized to Mike Smith, who promptly replied, 'Forget it. It's in the past.'

Next day the weather was cold and miserable and the wind swept across the wide-open terracing at Headingley. On such a day

Headingley is the most inhospitable of grounds, with very little shelter. Southern players are less keen to play there than they are at the London grounds. The crowd tends to be more critical, more demanding. But as the players admit, Yorkshire crowds know their cricket, and are ready to applaud the good things.

After Smith won the toss and decided to bat, Bob Barber was caught off Taylor for 13, and at five to twelve Barrington went in to join Edrich, wearing two sweaters to protect him against the cold. Edrich, dropped for the tour to South Africa earlier in the year, took nearly half an hour to open his score. He felt he was playing for his place, and wasn't going to take any chances.

The pressure was on Barrington, because with Motz, Taylor and Collinge bowling accurately, over after over went by without any runs. Fortunately for his state of mind, the spectators, huddled in their coats and rugs, appreciated the position. Eventually, after twenty-four minutes, he got away with a single. Then came an edged 4 and a sharp chance to John Reid in the gully, which a younger man might have held. At lunch England were 102–1, and Barrington had reached his 50 in only fifteen scoring strokes, including ten 4s.

It was a typically easy-paced Headingley pitch, and after the interval Edrich and Barrington surged ahead, with Edrich overtaking Barrington with a straight 6 off Yuile, the gentle left-arm spin bowler. Barrington accelerated once more, and reached his hundred first in just under 3 hours. Two more 6s by Edrich put the left-hander ahead, and so it went on through a near-perfect day for the two Surrey batsmen.

There were two short breaks for rain, so in 5½ hours England scored 366–1, Edrich 194, Barrington 152. When Barrington was out at noon next day – caught behind off Motz for 163 – the stand of 369 in 5 hours 39 minutes was the best in Tests between England and New Zealand, and only 13 short of England's best-ever second-wicket stand of 382 by Hutton and Leyland against Australia at the Oval in 1938. It was also only 42 short of the highest English stand for any wicket, 411 by May and Cowdrey against the West Indies in 1957.

There were twenty-six 4s, an incredible percentage, in Barrington's 163. And incidentally, a 7, one of the rare occasions there has been a 7 in Test cricket. The selectors smacked him on the back and offered their congratulations, and the rest of the team were overjoyed that he had made such a dramatic comeback.

Among the many telegrams was one from Dexter. 'I've heard of high speed gas, but this is ridiculous,' it said. And MCC secretary Billy Griffith wrote: 'Well done indeed! I imagine we shall have to promote you to Brigadier!' Edrich, striking the ball with immense power, went on to compile the eighth triple hundred in Tests, 310 not out, the others being 334 and 304 by Sir Donald Bradman on the same ground; 365 not out by Sir Gary Sobers; 364 by Sir Len

Left In the Cubs with his younger brother Roy.

Above Ken Barrington in the Territorial Army reserves in 1954. 'We cut short our honeymoon so he could do his two weeks' training outside the cricket season,' said Ann.

Ken Barrington *(kneeling, left)* the footballer with West Reading Football Club, one of several clubs he played for in his career.
Berkshire Chronicle

The start of a great Test career. Trent Bridge, 9 June, 1955. Ken Barrington, aged twenty-four, has joined the list of batsmen out for a duck on their debut. Eddie Fuller was the bowler, a medium-pacer, and Ken was so nervous that he was nearly run out first ball. Peter May sent him back. Barrington played defensively at the next two balls, but off the fourth, a shortish delivery outside the off-stump, he tried a forcing shot off the back foot and edged a catch to wicket-keeper John Waite. Normally a 'walker', he waited for the umpire's finger to go up. 'I was in a right state,' he said afterwards. Four more years were to elapse before he was recalled by England.
Central Press Photos

Throughout his career Ken Barrington was a lover of brass bands. He grew to like military music when a boy at his father's barracks in Reading. Here, on his first tour abroad – to the West Indies in 1959-60 – he conducts the Band of the Barbados Regiment at the Marine Hotel, Barbados. With him is the respected West Indian administrator and club cricketer Peter Short.

Ken Barrington was looked upon as a grafter, but those who played with him in his early days knew him as a hard hitter of the ball, particularly on the leg-side. He has just swung Lindsay Kline, the Australian spin bowler, for four at The Oval in 1961. The wicket-keeper is Barry Jarman, and first slip is a youthful-looking Richie Benaud.
Central Press Photos

Ken was revered in India, and this is one of the many amusing incidents he was involved in during the England tour there in 1961. He has just reached his century in the First Test at Bombay, and a fan has raced on to the pitch to press some money into his pocket. A policeman has chased the spectator, and Ken pretends he is being chased too. His affinity with the crowds on that tour was such that he became a national hero, and he retained his popularity in subsequent visits as England manager.
Planet News

ome familiar faces in Aden Harbour n the way to Australia in 1962. From ght to left: Colin Cowdrey, David heppard, Ray Illingworth, Peter 'arfitt, David Allen, Alec Bedser, the ssistant manager, Ted Dexter, Alan mith, Ken Barrington, Len Coldwell nd Tom Graveney.
entral Press Photos

Ken Barrington was a brilliant slip atcher, and this picture vividly aptures his agility. Easton McMorris, he West Indian opening batsman, has icked a delivery from Derek Shackleton in the Fourth Test at Headingley in 1963, and Ken takes off o hold the ball one-handed close to he ground. The wicket-keeper is Jim Parks.
Sport & General

Duke of Norfolk with the England team in Perth in 1963. Before that date the manager would
ı the middle, but despite his office as Earl Marshal of England, the Duke is relegated to the
ide-left position! The team from back row, left to right, is: Ken Barrington, Fred Titmus, John
ray, Barry Knight, Peter Parfitt; second row, W. Watkins (baggage man), Alan Smith, Geoff
ar, Tom Graveney, Dave Larter, Len Coldwell, Ray Illingworth, David Allen, Sam Cowan,
siotherapist; front row, Alec Bedser (assistant manager), Fred Trueman, Colin Cowdrey, Ted
ter, Brian Statham, David Sheppard and the Duke of Norfolk.

:ting Her Majesty the Queen during the Second Test against the West Indies at Lord's, 1963,
Test that was called at the time 'the greatest ever'. Ted Dexter was England's captain, and the
:r players were Fred Trueman, David Allen, Derek Shackleton and Jim Parks, who was
ing with Ken at the time.
: & General

Was it a clean catch? Or did the ball bounce first? One of the most controversial moments of Ken's career. It is his benefit match at The Oval in 1964, and he plays a delivery from Ray Illingwort square on the leg-side, where Fred Trueman dives to his left and claims a catch. On being told by Trueman that it was a fair catch, Barrington walked. A photographer later showed Barrington picture which seemed to prove that the ball bounced before Trueman caught it. Ken said at the time, 'Fred honestly believes he caught it but the picture supports my view that he was wrong'.
Central Press Photos

The end of Ken's highest innings, 256 in the Old Trafford Test against Australia in 1964. Grahar McKenzie is the bowler, and Ken is out lbw trying to turn the ball to leg. The wicket-keeper is the late Wally Grout, and Bobby Simpson – who scored 311 in Australia's innings – is at first slip
Central Press Photos

Ken and Mike Smith, the England captain, record messages to send home to their families from Australia in 1965.

Agony! John Price has just rapped Ken on the inside of the knee in a county match at Lord's in 1966. Luck wasn't going Ken's way at this time. He made a duck in the first innings, his third first-baller in a short space of time, but he recovered well in the second innings, and was 20 when felled by 'Sport's' delivery.
Sport & General

Above left Ken Barrington misses a ball from Peter Parfitt which no doubt prompted some mickey-taking remark from Parfitt. Looking pensive behind the stumps is another lifelong friend, John Murray. The match was at The Oval in 1967.

Central Press Photos

Above right Close of play at Headingley in 1965 during the record-breaking stand by Ken and John Edrich. Ken made 163, and Edrich 310 not out.

Patrick Eagar

If Ken Barrington hadn't been a professional cricketer, he might well have become a professional golfer. He played off a low single-figure handicap, and was sometimes capable of beating Ted Dexter, perhaps the best of the cricketer-golfers of his era. His partner on this occasion was Alec Bedser, former Surrey team-mate and England selector. Bedser retired in 1982 as chairman of the selectors, but is still actively involved in cricket administration.

The Yorkshire Post

Hutton; 337 by Hanif Mohammed; 336 not out by Wally Hammond; 325 by Andrew Sandham; and 311 by Bobby Simpson.

None of those other players played and missed as much as Edrich! But that was his style. Often he looked crab-like and inelegant, but when he hit the ball it stayed hit. Not so stylish as Barrington, he had many of his partner's qualities, particularly in regard to temperament and willingness to keep fighting.

Edrich was on the field for the whole duration of the match as England, 546–4 declared, went on to beat the New Zealanders, 193 and 166, by an innings and 187 runs. Lord Nugent, President of Surrey, sent a telegram saying: 'I hope you repeat the dose in the Gillette Cup semi-final against Middlesex.'

That match was played the following day at the Oval, and Edrich, 71, and Barrington 68 not out, answered his lordship's pleas on another superb batting pitch. Middlesex made 250–8 in their 60 overs, with Barrington capturing 3–41 in a rare spell on bowling in a one-day match, and Surrey reaching their target for the loss of 5 wickets. He said later that it was not far short of being the most exciting and enjoyable game of cricket in which he had ever taken part.

The Final against Yorkshire at Lord's on 4 September was much less pleasant for Surrey. On a soggy, wet ground Yorkshire won by the huge margin of 175 runs, with Geoff Boycott making the highest individual score in a Gillette Final of 146 before being caught by Stewart Storey off Barrington's bowling. Barrington hadn't wanted to bowl. 'Not my wicket, captain,' he told Micky Stewart. The game started ninety minutes late because of the heavy overnight rain, and might not have started at all if the Lord's groundstaff hadn't borrowed the Surrey CCC drying machines. 'We should never have loaned those machines,' said a Surrey player.

The second Test series that summer, against Peter Van der Merwe's South African side, the last Springbok side to tour England before the apartheid bar went up, was much more demanding of the England players. Indeed, the South Africans won the series 1–0 through their victory (by 94 runs) at Trent Bridge in the Second Test, a match that was dominated by the Pollock brothers. Graeme scored 184 runs in his two innings, and Peter collected 10 wickets for 87 runs in 48 overs. Several hours after the match was over, some of the celebrating Springboks went out on the pitch and relieved themselves on it!

Barrington made 1 and 1 in that Trent Bridge Test, but his innings of 91 in the First Test at Lord's, the hundredth between England and South Africa, had been one of his best in England. From 88–4, England pulled round to 338, with Barrington the inspiration. Lord's was packed with 26,000 people – 5,000 of them sitting on the grass, which is now prohibited since the pitch invasions of the West Indies years – and they revelled in some outstanding cricket, not least in the fielding department.

Colin Bland, the amazingly fast South African cover fielder who was arguably the greatest fielder of all time, brought constant applause with his brilliance, swooping on the ball like a hawk, and more often than not knocking the stumps flying with his fast, flat – almost baseball-style – returns.

Barrington was one of his victims. Nine short of his hundred, he played a delivery from Jackie Botten, the medium-pace bowler, in the direction of mid-on, and started running as he was finishing his shot. Halfway down the pitch he saw that Bland was racing in on the ball from squarish mid-wicket. From thirty yards and square to the wicket. Bland threw and knocked all three stumps down from thirty yards. Barrington was out by an inch. Later in the same innings Jim Parks was run out by Bland.

South Africa, 120–4, were in danger of defeat in their second innings, but Bland, 70, enabled Van der Merwe to set a target of 191 in four hours. Edrich was struck on the head by a Pollock bouncer and retired hurt, and the rest of the batsmen – including Barrington with 18 – showed no capacity to go for the runs against accurate seam bowling, so that the First Test ended in a draw. The Third Test at the Oval was also drawn, although England – needing 109 in 85 minutes when rain wiped out play on the final day – might just have won with six wickets still remaining. Barrington's contribution in a high-scoring second innings was a confident 73.

He was close to his thirty-fifth birthday when in November 1965 he left Heathrow with the MCC party for the tour of Australia. As he had toured Australia before, the trip was less stimulating to him than it would have been earlier in his career. He wasn't becoming blasé. He was still excited by the prospect of playing on some of the world's best batting pitches, but the sharp edge was missing. There were other worries. His father-in-law was seriously ill, and he didn't like leaving Ann behind to cope. On arrival in Perth a letter awaited him saying his father-in-law had died. He missed the first up-country match in Western Australia because of 'flu, and for the same reason had to drop out of the first serious match against a Combined XI after scoring 3.

Once the party arrived in Adelaide – one of his favourite venues in Australia – his mood and his fortunes changed, and he made 69 and 51 against South Australia, followed by 158 against Victoria in Melbourne later in the month. His approach to batting seemed less inhibited, no doubt encouraged by Billy Griffith, the then MCC secretary who managed the tour. Griffith was given overall powers by MCC to make sure that England played positive cricket. With a batsman of such an aggressive style as Bob Barber, Mike Smith's team was able to match the scoring rate of the Australians. In the field, however, they were criticized for not taking enough chances. According to the critic E. M. Wellings, Smith was 'a spent force as captain'.

Once Australia batted into the fourth day of the First Test at Brisbane there was little chance of a result. Barrington lasted 3 hours for his 53 in the first innings, and when England were immune from the possibility of defeat he struck 38 in only 54 minutes in the second innings.

The Second Test at Melbourne – also drawn – was notable for Barrington having to don the wicket-keeping gloves when Jim Parks went off ill, the second time he had filled the role, the first being in 1961 when John Murray retired hurt. The first ball bounced out of his gloves – much to the amusement of his colleagues, who ribbed him unmercifully. But Simpson and Lawry batted so soundly that hardly a ball passed the bat. He did, however, make a straightforward catch off the bowling of Barry Knight.

The Third Test followed in Sydney three days later, and saw Bob Barber play one of the great Test innings, 185 in just under five hours. It enabled England to win by an innings and 93 runs on a pitch which helped the spinners. For once Ken Barrington played almost no part in his team's success. He was out for 1, caught McKenzie bowled Neil Hawke.

England had only to avoid defeat in the remaining Tests at Adelaide and Melbourne to win back the Ashes, but Smith's players batted badly at Adelaide and lost by an innings and 9 runs, despite Barrington's 60 and 102. Fred Titmus, with 53, was the only other player to pass 50.

It might have been different had Cowdrey not been run out for 38 in the first innings when he was batting safely with a seemingly immovable Barrington. As Barrington hit the ball towards Hawke at mid-on and waited a yard or two down the pitch to see if the stroke was beating the fieldsman Cowdrey suddenly set off on a run. Hawke picked up and returned to Keith Stackpole, the bowler – now a TV commentator – and Cowdrey was easily run out. Afterwards Cowdrey explained he thought he heard Barrington say, 'Come on.' In fact, wicket-keeper Grout had said to Hawke, 'Watch the one.'

After 3 hours 20 minutes at the crease for 60, during which time he was loudly barracked, Barrington was lbw to Doug Walters, the nineteen-year-old new discovery of Australian cricket, one ball after he had doffed his cap to his critics. By the end of the match Barrington and the other England players were thoroughly depressed. The opportunity to lift the Ashes had gone. A winter's hard work had been carelessly thrown away.

Barrington was tired and weary and ready to go home. He found it harder to concentrate at the wicket, and when the final Test began at Melbourne on 11 February he was in a thoroughly depressed state of mind, which wasn't helped by England losing two wickets for 41 after Smith won the toss. Boycott, after taking sixty of the first eighty deliveries bowled (to the dismay of his more dashing partner Barber), called for a run and ignored Barber's 'No!' Barber was run out, and Boycott fell 5 runs later, caught at slip off a slash.

Barrington was in no mood to play a long innings, and when he joined Edrich he had what was for him the strange idea that England couldn't win, so what did it matter? For the first time in his career he was less than fully prepared mentally to play a long, fighting innings. The result was staggering: he proceeded to play the most sensational Test innings of his career, hitting 115 off 122 balls in 2½ hours, the fastest hundred of the series. It won him the Lawrence Trophy for the fastest Test century scored in 1966. Lord Chobham, who was to make the presentation at a ceremony in London, couldn't believe that the recipient was Barrington. 'You don't want me,' he said. 'You want Trevor Bailey!'

The barracking of the Australian fans played a part in Barrington's amazing transformation that day in Melbourne. He admitted afterwards that he had lost his patience with them. 'I said to myself, if Keith Stackpole pitches the next one up I'll have a slog at it,' he said. Stackpole's next delivery wasn't pitched up, but he still swung at it like a village-green tail-ender. He put so much power into the shot that it soared high into the air and dropped 110 yards away in the members' enclosure. It was a bad shot, one of the first deliberately bad shots he had ever played in a Test match, but it achieved the desired result.

Grout, standing behind the stumps in his last match for Australia, said, 'You drunk or something, mate?' 'Well,' replied Barrington, 'it's probably my last Test in Australia. Anyway, I'm fed up with all this pushing and prodding.'

In Stackpole's next over he nearly hit another 6, and having scored 63 in two hours, he went to 102 in only 21 deliveries. The shot that earned him his century was the most spectacular of all. Ninety-four not out, he decided in advance that it would be very satisfying to reach three figures with a 6. He had done it twice before in his career. Now for the hat-trick! Tom Veivers, the off-spinner, bowled around middle and leg, and Barrington was already in position to smash the ball straight.

It went low and very hard, like a golfer's tee shot which doesn't quite get into the air but still goes a long way. It was, he said afterwards, the finest 6 of his life. After tea he was caught by Grout off Walters. The stand with Edrich – who made 85 before becoming another victim of Walters – put on 178 in even time. His innings was in vain, however, because with Bob Cowper scoring 307 the match ended in a draw. Grout's farewell to his old friend was: 'I'm glad you don't always bat like that, mate.'

Once more he finished top of both batting and bowling, 464 runs, average 66·28 and two wickets, average 23·50, in the Tests, and was also top of both batting and bowling in the other matches, 946 runs, average 67·57 and 6 wickets, average 24·83.

E. M. Wellings thought Bob Barber should have been bowled more, but though Barber had many more overs than Barrington – 176 to Barrington's 32·4 – he took only 10 wickets at 87·30 apiece. Barrington should have bowled more, not Barber, or so it seemed. Recognizing that he had done his fair share – indeed, more than his fair share – of the work, and was now feeling the strain, Billy Griffith and the tour committee decided to let him go home and forgo the New Zealand section of the tour.

He arrived home close to exhaustion, but was only able to get a few weeks' rest before starting pre-season training with Surrey. Since becoming an England regular in 1959, he had toured with the MCC every winter except 1960–1, when he went on a Commonwealth tour, and cricket had been an almost all-the-year job. He worked out that he had spent a whole year out of the previous seven playing in the tense atmosphere of Test cricket, and he was feeling the strain.

In addition, there was the undercurrent of criticism in the Press. Most of the journalists were his friends, but they didn't hesitate to criticize if he failed to produce good figures. Few professional sportsmen are under such close scrutiny from the media as cricketers. They are on television live for much of the day, and experts on both TV and radio analysed their every move. As happened during the 1981 England *v.* Australia series, it is easy for the players to become resentful of criticism. Some of Ian Botham's team became so upset that they decided to reply, and Bob Willis, the vice-captain, said in an interview at Headingley, 'The standard of cricket reporting has never been lower.' Mike Brearley, reinstated as captain in place of Botham, said he wouldn't attend interviews if the Press didn't change their approach. Fortunately for the game, the damage was repaired by the end of the series.

Barrington was tolerant of criticism of his batting on most occasions, but in 1965 one attack – on his standard of fielding now he was thirty-five – riled him more than any other. If there was one aspect of his game in which he had pride, it was his fielding. He told colleagues, 'I'd flatten that fellow if I met him!'

It was an untypical response, but other cricketers have felt the same way about criticism. Kim Hughes, the Australian captain in England in 1981, appeared to have an excellent relationship with the Press, both English and Australian, but criticism of his team's batting at Headingley and Edgbaston – one critic wrote, 'his team showed the character of melting ice cream' – incensed him so much that at the team's farewell dinner in London at the end of the tour, he said, 'If people said things to your face that these critics wrote, you would deck them!'

Peter May quit cricket earlier than most people expected, partly through illness and partly through the perpetual criticism which was souring his cricket. Sir Len Hutton was another great player who suffered. Ken Barrington refused to let the critics get the better of him, but at the start of the 1966 season the worries were building up, especially since Charlie Griffith was arriving with the West Indies team.

Barrington's meeting with Griffith in the First Test was being billed as cricket's most controversial confrontation: the dreaded chucker against his leading critic. Would Charlie try to knock his head off? Would Ken have to retract? Outwardly Barrington showed no sign of being concerned by the impending meeting, but inwardly it had affected him. He wasn't frightened, but he was a man who found controversy distasteful. He was a person who liked to be liked, a man who liked other people. He wasn't a Tony Greig or a Dennis Lillee, hard-headed personalities who enjoyed having feuds with opposing players. His style was to have a laugh and a joke with opponents, not a curse and a scowl.

His growing complex about Charlie Griffith was just one factor in his downhill rush towards a nervous breakdown. He viewed the start of the 1966 domestic season with no enthusiasm. Unseasonal snowfall had caused the postponement of outdoor practice at the Oval, and the players had to go to the Crystal Palace National Recreation Centre for indoor nets. In the early matches he found it hard to concentrate. Instead of being tensed up before an innings, he felt listless and uncaring.

Too much all-the-year cricket with its accompanying pressure – much of it self-inflicted because of his sensitive nature – and the Griffith affair had weakened his natural toughness. For the first time in his career (discounting the isolated occasion of the Melbourne hundred) he didn't care about his batting or what was wrong with it.

He became increasingly irritable and hard to live with, snapping at team-mates and loved ones. He found it impossible to relax, and more alarming than anything else, started to get the shakes. His hands would start trembling, and there was nothing he could do about it.

His early form with Surrey was not too bad, and an unbeaten 103 against Northants at the Oval convinced the selectors that he was still the Ken Barrington of old. No one, not even his team-mates, suspected he was about to crack up. He was duly chosen for the First Test at Old Trafford, and Griffith, looking more morose and moody than ever, ignored him when they met. Facing a total of 484, England started disastrously, losing Colin Milburn for a duck when he pushed a delivery from Wes Hall straight to Lance Gibbs at cover, and was sent back by Eric Russell at the other end.

When Barrington came in at 11–1 Hall and Griffith were hardly warmed up. He took guard and played defensively for a short time before he prodded tentatively at a straight delivery from Griffith and was caught and bowled for 5. Up on the balcony, some of the other players noticed he had hopped about more than usual when facing the then world's fastest bowlers, but they saw no sign of impending trouble. In the second innings he lasted longer in making 30 runs.

Griffith – not so lethal as he had been in 1963 – was scrutinized several times from square leg and point by umpires Charlie Elliott and Sid Buller, but they could see nothing amiss with his action. He was no-balled nine times, but only for over-stepping. With the attention of the cameras on him, and the Barrington allegations fresh in everyone's mind, he had passed his first test.

Back home in Fetcham, a fraught Ken Barrington went to see his doctor. 'What you need is a holiday,' he was told. It was the familiar reply of the doctor faced by a patient suffering from stress. A supply of tranquillizers was prescribed, and Barrington took those instead, not the holiday. He continued playing, and just before the Second Test at Lord's (for which he had been retained) he was involved in some extraordinary scenes in Surrey's first county match played on a Sunday, on 12 June.

The match was against Kent, and an 8,000 crowd was at the Oval. Barrington angered them by batting even more slowly than usual after coming in at 70–3, and didn't manage a run in the final 25 minutes, by which time the crowd were streaming home. His 68 that carried on into Monday lasted 3½ hours, and must rank as one of his worst innings.

Surrey's second innings of 229 was the top score in a low-scoring game played on a dreadfully slow pitch, but the spectators, and some Surrey committee members, didn't feel that the pitch was a sufficient excuse. As he came off a member sitting in front of the dressing-room shouted, 'That was disgraceful, Barrington!' Instead of ignoring the man, Barrington stopped to argue with him, and Arthur McIntyre, the club coach, came down to pull him away. As the two men walked up the steps to go into the dressing-room there was a shout from behind them 'Wait until Charlie Griffith gets hold of you!'

The Oval has long boasted some of the most destructive barrackers in cricket. Crowds are usually so small there, except on Sundays or during Tests, that the players can hear most things that are said. Barrington wasn't the first to be angered by them, nor will he be the last.

The Second Test was a splendid contest, with England putting up a much better performance before eventually drawing. But for Ken Barrington it was six days of agony. He was bowled by Sobers in the first innings for 19, and yorked by Griffith, feet all askew, for 5 in the second innings. It was unusual for him to be bowled twice at any level of cricket, certainly in Tests. *Wisden* recorded: 'There was no excuse for Barrington's performance.'

Still, no one knew the facts. His colleagues thought he was just going through a bad patch, and would pull out of it as he had done so many times before. In four innings he made only 59 runs against the West Indies, and the critics began to doubt the wisdom of retaining him in the side. 'You are only as good as your last innings and Ken's last one was a disaster,' wrote one.

To the surprise of some observers, Barrington was kept in the side for the Third Test at Nottingham. Before starting the lonely, 150-mile drive to Trent Bridge from his home he consulted his doctor again, and was prescribed some stronger tranquillizers. He was looking so queasy after breakfast at the team's hotel that Alec Bedser, one of the selectors, said, 'Kenny, I know you pretty well, and we've got the impression lately that you're not quite yourself. Is anything wrong?'

Barrington explained that he was under the care of his doctor, and hadn't felt well for weeks. 'Well I don't know,' said Bedser. 'I don't think you can play, the state you're in.'

Doug Insole, the chairman of selectors who had had the task of explaining that he was likely to be disciplined for slow scoring the year before, now intervened. He gave the distraught-looking Barrington a lift to the ground in his car, and on the way said, 'There's a place for you in the team if you want it. You are the only person who can tell if you are well enough to play. The decision is yours, and we shall accept whatever you say.'

All kinds of thoughts must have gone through Barrington's mind. Would they say he was dropping out because he was petrified at facing Griffith? Would he be letting the other players down? Would he ever get back in? Finally he said, 'Doug, I don't feel I could do justice to anyone if I played. It's better I sit this one out.'

Insole sympathized, and he was taken back to the hotel to collect his car for the long ride home. Meanwhile his replacement Russell failed, recording scores of 4 and 11 in the problem position of Number 3. Secluded at his home in a quiet part of the suburb of Mitcham, Barrington discovered there was no respite. The tension seemed worse than ever, affecting his neck, back and shoulders.

Ann, who fielded all the Press inquiries with stoical calm, had to massage his neck for long periods. At night he found it impossible to sleep, and the doctor virtually ordered him to go away and take a holiday. Ann drove him to a hotel in Bournemouth where he tried, unsuccessfully, to wind down.

He was out of the game for three days, but it should have been longer. He was still jittery when he returned to the Oval at the end of July. Surrey wanted him to play in a three-day match against the West Indies, but he declined. Instead he played several matches for the Club and Ground and the Second XI, without much success. He was still too tense, and when he was out for 5 against a South African touring side called Willows he threw his bat down and said, 'I might as well give up this bleeding game!' Arthur McIntyre took him to the committee room for a drink to calm him down.

The following week an innings of 103 against Kent Second XI at Greenwich convinced him that perhaps he hadn't lost his form after all. By the beginning of August he was ready to return to the first team in a match against Essex at the Oval. His form continued to be erratic, with knocks of 76 at Cheltenham, 50 at Eastbourne and 57 not out at the Oval against Gloucester, interspersed with three first-ballers. In his first eighteen years in the game he had only been out first ball twice.

His rebirth came at Old Trafford in the final match of the season, when his 117 not out in nearly 6 hours after Surrey were 20–4 brought a smile back to his face. Despite all his troubles, he still came second in the Surrey averages that season, with 40·34 from 928 runs, and even more surprisingly, fourteenth in the national batting averages. With no winter tour, he felt in a much better frame of mind, and resolved to strive to continue his Test career against weaker opposition, India and Pakistan, in 1967. At thirty-six, he still felt he could do it.

CHAPTER FIVE

Retirement

One of the questions in a poll organized by the Advisory County Cricket Committee, forerunners of the Test and County Cricket Board, in November 1966, and addressed to all 150 capped cricketers in the country, was: 'Do you enjoy playing county cricket?' To the surprise of the people who drew up the questions, seven players replied No. One of them was Ken Barrington.

The ACCC was about to consider the David Clark Committee Report on the future of the game which recommended two new Leagues, one for a four-day championship match programme in mid-week and the other for one-day matches at weekends, and they wanted the opinions of the players as a guideline. Barrington, who started playing professional cricket when grounds were still moderately filled, wrote copious notes in his letter of reply explaining why playing in front of a handful of spectators no longer held any appeal for him. He said the game had become too defensive, ruled by medium-pacers on pitches which discouraged stroke-play. Some members of the committee found a certain irony in the fact that a player dropped for slow scoring in Tests should find his job dull and boring!

But Barrington's motives were impeccable. He could have given skimpy replies, as indeed had most other players, but he cared about the future of cricket so much that he wanted to play his part in seeing that changes were made. He was in full agreement with the Clark proposals, except that he wanted two one-day matches played at weekends, not just one. He was one of the original advocates of Sunday play. In those days the only games played on Sundays were Cavalier matches and benefit games. Most of his ideas – like the appointment of a full-time marketing expert at Lord's – were subsequently adopted, but the main proposals of the Clark Committee, that there should be two new leagues, were defeated by ten votes to one, with the other counties abstaining.

The news that Barrington had said he didn't enjoy playing cricket leaked to the Press, and he had to explain his views in detail. 'I didn't say it because nervous stress had taken away my appetite for the game,' he said. 'It was because the way the game is now played in most county matches, it's a bore to everyone, players and spectators alike. When I was ill I went to watch some games but I couldn't stick it. I walked out.'

He started the 1967 season, having rested throughout the winter, in a better frame of mind than for years. His opening innings, 26 in the Parks at Oxford, was unexciting, but he was so consistent in the weeks that followed that two months went by before he was out for less than double figures. He made 62 for Surrey against the MCC at Lord's, 63 not out and 95 against Warwickshire, 41 and 60 against Hampshire and 84 against the touring Indians. Any fears that he might not regain his Test place soon disappeared as the runs piled up. Brian Close, appointed England captain for the Fifth Test against the West Indies the year before, retained the post, and headed a familiar batting line-up of Boycott, Edrich, Barrington, Graveney and D'Oliveira in the First Test against a weak Indian side at Headingley.

Every batsman qualified to play for England in the country would have been overjoyed to play against the Indian opening attack, which consisted of two gentle medium-pacers in Guha and Surti. Ten minutes after lunch, Surti was struck on the leg while fielding close on the on-side, and didn't bowl again, and Bedi – who had bowled only 15 overs – also withdrew with a leg-strain. Only Chandrasekhar and Prasanna offered a challenge on a good batting pitch, but their overs cost nearly 3 runs apiece as the England total went higher and higher.

Barrington thought another Test century was on its way until he was run out at 93. Boycott went on to 246 not out, his highest score, but his methods were criticized by Press and selectors alike, and he was left out of the Second Test as a disciplinary measure. Boycott trod on the ball, and didn't field until the fifth day, and when England needed 125 to win in the second innings Edrich opened with Barrington, whose brisk 46 won the game with ample time to spare.

At the start of the Lord's Test which England won by an innings and 124 runs Barrington had a new target in mind, his first Test hundred at cricket's headquarters. In the absence of Boycott he again opened with Edrich, and was just 3 runs short of his objective when Chandrasekhar bowled him. Chandrasekhar, whose bowling arm was slightly withered through his having contacted poliomyelitis as a child, bowled leg-breaks and googlies – mainly googlies – at a much faster pace than most spin bowlers, and England's batsmen were always wary of him.

Barrington revealed the extent of his eased mental state in the equally one-sided Third Test at Edgbaston, when he struck Prasanna and Bedi for 6 in his first innings, 75. England's master batsman was back at his best, averaging 64·80 in the three-match series. His performances in the Pakistan series which followed were even more remarkable, an average of 142 from 426 runs, with scores of 148, 14, 109 not out, 142 and 13 not out.

A new opening partnership of Colin Milburn and Eric Russell was tried in the First Test at Lord's, but Barrington was virtually in the role of opener again because Milburn was out for 3. Confronted by medium pace and spin again, Barrington played with such confidence that he raced past his hundred – his first in ten years of trying at Lord's – and reached 148 before Asif Iqbal had him caught behind by Wasim Bari. Barrington was a supremely happy man that night. From having doubted whether he had a future less than a year before, he was now back in control as England's top professional batsman.

The selectors could even forgive him taking nearly 7 hours to score 109 in the Second Test at Nottingham on a rain-affected pitch. A heavy storm saturated one end of the pitch two days before the match started, and just as it dried out on the Sunday another downpour got through the inadequate covers again during the rest day. As Pakistan had been dismissed for 140 – they had such a strong batting side that Majid was Number 6 and Asif 7 – Barrington felt it was necessary to occupy the crease, and did so, making nearly half of England's winning total of 252–8 declared.

It was his first Test hundred at Trent Bridge, and he followed it with his first Test hundred at the Oval in the Third and Final Test, an innings of 142 in nearly six hours. So, in one prolific summer, he completed his cherished ambition of making Test hundreds on all the major Test grounds.

He was an automatic selection for the winter tour of the West Indies, the last tour he undertook. He packed his bags with unusual excitement. The thrill of going abroad with England to one of the most pleasant parts of the cricketing world outweighed any fears that it might leave him tired and exhausted as the previous Australian tour had done.

There was just one fear in his mind . . . would Charlie Griffith still be as fast as he was in England? His reception from Charlie preyed on his mind, he admitted, and though he tried to laugh it off, it was a worry. Everywhere he went, hotels, airports, cricket grounds, friendly West Indians came up with a smile and said, 'Charlie's waiting for you, man. He'll kill you!'

Griffith didn't play in the opening match against the President's XI in Bridgetown, Barbados. The opening bowlers were Winston English and the white all-rounder from The Wanderers, Richard 'Prof' Edwards, and Barrington ran himself out for 1 in the first innings and made 53 not out in the second. The first meeting with Griffith (who was now thirty, and no longer at his peak) came in the First Test in Port of Spain. Colin Cowdrey, replacing Close (who had been stripped of the captaincy after his altercation with a spectator at Edgbaston), won the toss and batted on a superb batting pitch.

Wes Hall, aged thirty-one and also in decline, was hit for four 4s in the opening two overs by Boycott, and the spinners Gibbs and Holford were bowling when Barrington came in at 102–2 to join Cowdrey. The beautiful ground of Queen's Park was filled to capacity with 30,000 spectators, and many of them chanted 'Griffith, Griffith' as Barrington strode towards the middle.

Gary Sobers, the West Indian captain whose leadership qualities came some way short of his qualities as a player, probably made a mistake by not introducing Griffith into the attack right away. When he finally signalled Griffith to bowl Barrington had played himself in, and was well into double figures.

Griffith made a play of marking out his run with long, deliberate strides while Barrington stood in his crease trying to appear indifferent. The first ball went off without incident. Then as Griffith came running in to bowl again Barrington pulled away from the wicket, a gesture which always annoys fast bowlers.

Barrington did so because he felt there was too much noise from the crowd, and it was affecting his concentration. When Griffith bowled his second ball it was a fearsome delivery, straight and on a length. Barrington blocked it. Once more that over Barrington jerked back and stopped Griffith in his run-up, adding to the bowler's annoyance.

Neither man spoke, although Griffith appeared to be cursing to himself. At the end of the over, some of the tension had left Barrington. The first part of the trial was over. He had survived. The next over from Griffith was equally fast and hostile, but again Barrington played safely through it. Griffith bowled five rapid overs before Sobers was forced to take him off.

At the interval Barrington said, 'That's a weight off my shoulders, I can tell you!' He was so relieved afterwards that he was able to reach his hundred with a 6. His innings of 143 may not have been technically correct in some aspects, but as a test of character it proved one of the most important in his career. The Griffith bogey was ended.

Once he misjudged a bouncer from Griffith, and, attempting to duck under it, was hit a painful blow on the shoulder. But that didn't worry him. The runs kept coming. West Indian crowds may be noisy and distracting but they understand cricket, and the fans that day gave Barrington's innings the acclaim it deserved. Near the end of his 6½-hour marathon, an incident happened which brought the feud between them to an end.

Barrington was backing up as Griffith bowled, and accidentally caught the Barbadian fast bowler in the throat with his elbow. Griffith collapsed in a stunned heap, and one of the players who helped him to his feet was . . . Barrington. 'I'm sorry, Charlie, it was an accident,' he said. Those were the first words between them for more than four years. Realizing that Barrington was anxious about him, Griffith thawed, and later began joking with his old adversary.

Griffith was to have him lbw in the Second Test at Kingston for 13, a game that was interrupted by bottle-throwing, and his absence through injury in the Fourth Test at Port of Spain – won by England by 7 wickets after Sobers, in a moment of recklessness, decided to set England 215 in 2¾ hours – probably cost the West Indies the series. Griffith was unable to bowl in the second innings, and Sobers only had the spinners Gibbs and Rodriguez and occasional bowlers Carew and Butcher to back up his own bowling.

After making 206 in his first two innings, Barrington added only 82 in the remaining five, and he came fifth in the averages with 41·14 – by modern standards still a commendable figure.

In the final weeks of the tour the mental pressures had built up again, and he was needing two sleeping tablets a night to obtain rest. If he didn't take his pills he didn't sleep. Even with the aid of pills, he was still waking in the middle of the night. He was so worried that he asked Les Ames, the England manager, to arrange a check-up at a hospital in Bridgetown. The doctor found nothing wrong, but repeated what he had been told in England: 'You need to get away from cricket and have a holiday.'

By the time the Australian series was starting in England in 1968 he was suffering from back trouble, and had to drop out of the First Test at Old Trafford, Bob Barber taking his place. The pain affected his hip and pelvic area as well, and in June he had a manipulative operation which only partly eased the discomfort. His early scores were mediocre, with only one 50 before he was chosen for the Second Test at Lord's.

Coming in at 147–3, he played circumspectly before he was hit on the finger and retired at 61. He resumed his innings, and was out for 75, his highest total of the season, just 3 runs short of the Australian first-innings total of 78. With fifteen hours lost through rain, there was insufficient time for England to bowl Lawry's side out a second time, and the game ended in a draw.

Any feeling he might have had that this would be another high-scoring summer was soon dissipated by Eric Freeman's break-back at Edgbaston in the Third Test which saw him depart for a rare Test duck. His figures in the Fourth Test at Headingley – 49 and 46 not out – should have earned him a place in the Final Test at the Oval, but to his dismay they didn't. Three matches had been drawn and one lost, and the selectors wanted a more attacking line-up to square the rubber, and with England winning by 226 runs, the selectors' decision was vindicated.

He told the Press, 'I'm naturally disappointed but I'm confident I can fight my way back into the side.' He was to be proved wrong.

The season was disastrous for him, with no centuries and only 671 runs, average 20·96 for Surrey, The last first-class innings he played was at the Oval in early September against Hampshire. After being run out for 0 in the first innings he scraped and prodded to reach 8 in the second when he mishit a double-bouncer from the Antiguan Danny Livingstone and was caught by Richard Gilliat.

As he came into the dressing-room he threw down his bat and said, 'That's it, that's my lot.' And it was too. He had two invitations to play abroad that winter, one in Israel with the Bournemouth 5705 Club (5705 being the Jewish Year when the club was formed) and the other in a Double Wicket tournament in Melbourne. He enjoyed the trip to Israel, and found himself being appointed Honorary President of the Israel Cricket Supporters' Association.

The Double Wicket contest was played at the St Kilda's Oval, Melbourne in early October, and his partner was Colin Milburn. Their first opponents were Rohan Kanhai and Charlie Griffith. By this time Griffith was a friend, not an enemy, and the fact that he was in opposition didn't create an extra pressure. Milburn and Barrington won, and back in the dressing-room Barrington suddenly said, 'I don't feel too good. I think I've caught the sun.'

Milburn saw his white face, and immediately came to the conclusion that his friend and partner was unwell. 'What do you mean, sun?' he said. 'There isn't any. It's been cloudy all day.' Milburn called a doctor, and the doctor asked for an ambulance. Ken Barrington had just had a mild heart-attack, and he was rushed off to hospital.

It was 9 a.m. and Ann Barrington was still in bed when the phone rang at the family home in Burney Close, Fetcham. 'It's Bobby Simpson,' said a voice. 'Ken's been taken ill and he's in hospital. I'll ring you back when there's more news.'

Ann Barrington chain-smoked for an hour, then the phone rang again. 'It's advisable you come out,' said Simpson. She was able to get a flight later that day, and left immediately. Harry Secombe, hearing the news on the radio, sent a huge basket of fruit and flowers.

Thirty hours later she arrived in Melbourne and was driven straight to the hospital where her husband was wired to an electrocardiograph. 'Hello, darling,' said Ken, 'don't stay with me too long. I know what that flight is like.'

'When he said that,' Ann recalled later, 'I just broke down. It was so like Ken to be in pain himself and all he could think of was me.'

He spent two weeks in hospital before being allowed to return to England. The specialist said he saw no reason why he shouldn't continue to play cricket, but he would need regular check-ups. Meanwhile smoking was right out, and he was advised to go to bed early. The couple came back to England in the *Canberra*, relaxing on the sun-deck all day, chatting and reading. Perhaps, as E. M. Wellings once said, if England cricket teams had travelled to and from tours in that leisurely way fewer cricketers would break down.

Surrey still thought he would play a few more seasons because he had talked of doing a Jack Hobbs and playing well into his forties. But in January 1969 he announced on BBC TV that he was retiring from the first-class game. 'I haven't just had to think about myself, but about Ann,' he said.

He wanted to stay in cricket, however, and a way was found when a friend fixed him up with a job commentating on cricket for the *Daily Sketch* in succession to Sir Learie Constantine – later Lord Constantine – the great West Indian cricketer who had sometimes been a critic of his batting. Instead of being in the middle when the 1969 season started, he was in the Press Box. Although he was later to be admitted as a card-carrying member of the National Union of Journalists, I wrote his column for him each day. He was as meticulous about that as he was about everything else in his career.

He used to talk with the players over lunch, and come back with an envelope covered in notes which I translated into passable English. His views about players and how they played were always constructive, never destructive. And his relations with the other critics, some of whom had been vitriolic in their criticism of him when he was a player, were first-class. He was a forgiving man, a man who never bore grudges.

For fifteen years he and Ann had tried for a family, and now their wish was granted. On 16 November 1969, two weeks before his own birthday, Ann gave birth to a 6lb 1oz son at Epsom District Hospital, but the child, christened Guy Kenneth, developed breathing difficulties, and had to be transferred to the Queen Mary Hospital at Carshalton.

There followed an anxious week before the doctors confirmed that he was out of danger. Ken Barrington busied himself with fatherhood, with running a garage (which was officially opened by Harry Secombe in company with several other friends from the Lord's Taverners, including Ian Carmichael, Bernard Cribbins and Cliff Michelmore in 1971), and with his sports-clothing business. And of course there was his journalism with the *Sketch*, which merged with the *Daily Mail* in 1971.

He still hankered after closer ties with cricket, however. In 1975 he managed a tour for Derrick Robins in South Africa, and just before the team returned he heard that he had been appointed a Test selector along with Sir Leonard Hutton, Charlie Elliott and Alec Bedser. He did the job so conscientiously and efficiently that the Test and County Cricket Board asked him to be manager of the England party for the 1976–7 tour of India, Sri Lanka and Australia. He was an ideal partner for Tony Greig, the England captain, and for the first time in five ventures since the War, England were successful on Indian pitches, winning 3–1. The Centenary Test in Melbourne, however, was lost by 45 runs.

Barrington was retained as manager when England toured Pakistan and New Zealand in 1977–8, this time with Mike Brearley as captain. With only one victory in six Tests, England failed, and the trip was full of problems for Barrington. Brearley broke an arm, and was replaced in New Zealand by Boycott, who never really got on well with Barrington.

The most testing moments came in Karachi, when the England team had a meeting and issued a statement saying they were opposed to playing with players who were members of the Kerry Packer World Series Cricket. The decision was taken as a threat that they would withdraw from the Test if Packer players Mushtaq Mohammed, Zaheer Abbas and Imran Khan, who had flown in from Australia, were included in the Pakistan side.

Barrington rang Donald Carr, secretary of the Test and County Cricket Board, at Lord's for advice, and spent forty-five minutes talking to Carr and Doug Insole, the Board chairman. He was in an impossible position. Carr and Insole said the England players were contracted to play and would have to fulfil their contracts. But they were in London. Barrington was the man on the spot, and he couldn't insist that the players go out and play. To everyone's relief, the Pakistan selectors decided not to include the Packer players in their side, and the game went ahead.

The 1978–9 trip to Australia, when he accompanied the team as Doug Insole's assistant, was far happier, and England beat a Packer-denuded Australian side 5–1. Barrington was immensely popular with the players, and there were some uproarious moments, one of the highlights of which was a Christmas Day fancy-dress party when he appeared dressed as a colonel. Boycott was a half-naked hula-hula girl, and Insole was disguised as Inspector Clouseau.

Regular Saturday-night sessions on England tours are one of the ways of relieving the boredom and of improving team spirits, and Barrington had been on so many tours that he was able to provide the inspiration for many of the rituals. In the nets he was an invaluable member of the group, organizing, coaching and cajoling. But Brearley was reluctant to allow his players to undergo too much coaching. His theory was that having reached Test standards, players didn't need regular coaching.

By this time Barrington virtually had a job for life as cricket manager of England tours abroad, and he went Down Under the following winter, 1979–80, as Alec Bedser's assistant. The influence of Packer was seen wherever England went, and it was a miserable tour, Australia winning 3–0.

According to the vice-captain, Bob Willis, Brearley wasn't in accord with Bedser for much of the time. Barrington, who was closer to the players, was the intermediary. Bedser, said Willis, was one of the old school who believed in hard work, particularly in the nets, and was always saying, 'In my day . . .' That was a trap which

Barrington never fell into, although he agreed with Bedser about the virtues of hard work. There were frequent disputes, with umpires, with officials and with opponents.

It seemed to Bedser and Barrington that Packer cricket had introduced many unwelcome features into the game, and the Englishmen, notably Brearley, were labelled 'whingeing Poms' when they expressed their disquiet about the many innovations. The experience failed to lessen Barrington's enthusiasm for touring abroad with the England party, and he confidently expected to be appointed in a similar capacity for the 1981 tour of the West Indies. It was an acute disappointment to him when Alan Smith was named as manager and no assistant was appointed.

According to his friends, he took it personally. 'What have I done wrong?' he asked. Officials of the Board tried to assure him it was an economy measure. The Board couldn't afford the extra place on a tour which was expected to bring in little money.

Ian Botham was the captain as Brearley couldn't go, and it was that appointment more than anything which persuaded the Board to reverse its decision and invite Barrington to accompany the party as assistant manager. Botham made representations himself, and so later did Alan Smith. Barrington probably got on better with Botham than with any other administrator at that time. He was his mentor, and Botham looked up to him and respected him.

The Caribbean tour was fraught with problems, and Barrington was more concerned than anyone, although Smith was the man in ultimate control. In Guyana, when Robin Jackman was ordered out because of his South African connexions, he was edgier than almost anyone else in the group. At one team meeting he surprised some of his colleagues by suggesting that the team should have armed protection.

John Woodcock, the correspondent of *The Times* and editor of *Wisden* in succession to the late Norman Preston, said at fifty Barrington looked in the top three of the batsmen in the touring party, and definitely the outstanding leg-spin bowler. His capacity to work out with the players in the nets was astonishing. No one could equal his exuberance. But often it was impossible to find suitable practice facilities, and this brought its frustrations for him.

Just before his death in Bridgetown he had some heated words with Boycott on the subject. However, he was a happy man when Ann joined him for the Third Test in Barbados in early March. Ann came out with a friend and his wife, and the four of them enjoyed the 85-degree, balmy heat of the Bajan beaches and the dinners on the jetty of the Holiday Inn Hotel. England were decidedly losing the match on the Saturday when they returned and went for a quiet dinner.

It didn't worry him because he accepted – as everyone did – that the West Indians were a far better team. Retiring at 10.30 for a reasonably early night, he laughed and joked about a hat Ann had bought, frolicking with it on while he undressed. He got into bed, and before either of them could get to sleep he uttered a sound which Ann knew at once meant that he had been stricken by a heart-attack, the heart-attack she feared might happen after his first warning in 1968. He wasn't able to say a word. It was a massive attack, and within a minute he was dead.

Bernie Thomas, the England physiotherapist, was in the next room with his wife, and was still awake. He raced in when Ann raised the alarm and tried vainly to resuscitate him, using a ventilation tube to pump air into his lungs while Joan, his wife, pushed his chest. But there was nothing he could do. A local doctor was summoned, and was in the room within minutes. All he could do was agree to write out a death certificate.

Downstairs the journalists in the lobby knew that something had happened, and soon they learned the sad news. It hit them as hard as it was to hit the players later, because he was their friend too. To a man they agreed to keep the news back for several hours until Alan Smith had contacted the housemaster at his son Guy's school.

The ambulance came, but the lift was too narrow to take a stretcher. The body had to be carried down the stairs. Some days before the body of a young supporter from England who died in a swimming-pool after drinking had been stolen from the local mortuary, and there was some reluctance to take Ken's body to the same place. There was no room on a plane until the following Tuesday, but the airlines made every possible sacrifice to ensure that a place should be found on the next day's flight, and it was. Ann returned to England on the same flight.

Though it was a Sunday, there was no time for the players to grieve because the match was continuing, but before play began they lined up for a minute's silence. Most of them were crying, and so were many people in the ground that day.

Woodcock perhaps summed it up better than anyone in his dispatch. 'When they heard the sad news', he said, 'countless people in Barbados thought they had lost a favourite friend. So stunned were the England players that their hearts were no longer in the game. Quite simply, a light went out in many places and the sadness showed on many faces.'

A light went out all round the cricketing world.

PART TWO
RECOLLECTIONS

David Allen

The former Gloucestershire off-spin bowler captured 122 wickets at 30·96 apiece in 39 Tests for England between 1959 and 1966.

Kenny became something of a national hero when I toured India and Pakistan with him in 1961–2. He scored slowly in most of his innings, but got the huge crowds on his side with his antics. In the opening match in Poona against the Combined Services he drove the first ball of an over bowled by a slow left-arm spinner straight at a fielder at extra cover who was wearing a turban.

Next ball he again drove at the same fielder. And once more the fielder made a good stop, to the delight of the 25,000 crowd. The third ball was also played in the same direction with the same result. Kenny played the next three deliveries at the gentleman in the turban, and when he made his sixth and final stop Kenny took off his gloves and went over and shook hands with him. He had played the ball deliberately in that direction to amuse the crowd!

When he was barracked he put his fingers in his ears. He imitated 'Slasher' Mackay's walk and gum-chewing antics. 'Slasher' had been out there the year before, and was very popular.

When he reached his century youngsters ran on to the pitch with sweets, rupees and garlands of flowers. He played the next ball with the garland of flowers still around his neck, before taking it off and handing it to the umpire.

One of the best stories about him was about Frank, the man from the High Commission. Some of us were having a walk one night when we got lost and found ourselves outside the house of this man from the British High Commission. He took us home, and we invited him down to the nets the next morning as a reciprocal gesture.

He said he was a bit of a leg-break bowler, and Kenny was always interested in leg-break bowlers. Next day he duly turned up in his whites and joined us in the nets when Kenny was batting. None of our bowlers – Butch White of Hampshire, Alan Brown of Kent, Barry Knight of Essex, Dave Smith of Gloucestershire or myself – could get the ball past Kenny's bat, but when Frank bowled Kenny played down the wrong line and was bowled. It pitched middle and hit middle, but Frank said it was a leg-break.

When it was Frank's turn to bowl again Kenny edged one to where first slip would have been. Frank became more and more excited about his prowess as a bowler. The England bowlers hadn't made an impression on Kenny, but he'd dismissed him twice in two balls! Kenny never let on that he was playing him along, but it certainly made Frank's day!

Kenny had a vast mail-bag in India. Most of the writers wanted his autograph or a souvenir, but he also had a few proposals of marriage. One lady wrote: 'I have a proposition for you. Accept me as your wife. I want to marry you. I await your reply while you make centuries in Tests and think upon my proposition as well. Thousands of kisses. Only yours.'

Another story I remember about him was when the MCC were playing in Cape Town in 1964. It was a match against Western Province, and Kenny batted most of the first day and was 90 not out. Don Carr, the tour manager, wasn't too pleased at the way he was batting, and told him to get a move on in the morning.

When play resumed Kenny reached his hundred with a straight-driven 6 off the bowling of Kelly Seymour, the Western Province off-spin bowler. As he played the shot he turned and waved his bat in the direction of the pavilion as if to say he was taking note of the manager's advice.

Les Ames

The former Kent (1926–51) and England (47 appearances) wicket-keeper was manager of the MCC tour of the West Indies in 1967–8. Ames scored 37,248 runs in his career for an average of 43·51, and his record of 127 dismissals in a season in 1929 has never been approached by an English wicket-keeper. He now lives in retirement in Canterbury after being secretary of Kent.

We won that 1967–8 series 1–0 when Gary Sobers declared at Port of Spain in the Fourth Test when no one really expected him to call a halt. Colin Cowdrey, then captain, was a bit doubtful about going for the target of 215 in 2¾ hours, but Ken, Tom Graveney and I all urged him to give it a go. We said even if we started badly, there was no time for us to be bowled out.

By joining in the successful effort to persuade Colin, Ken did himself out of an innings, because Tom Graveney and Basil D'Oliveira were promoted above him and he didn't get in. I think Gary was banking on Willie Rodriguez taking some quick wickets. Willie spun the ball a lot, and was quite quick through the air. In the match against Trinidad he took 6–51, getting Ken caught and dismissing Tom Graveney the next ball.

Anyway, Willie bowled an awful lot of muck – too many long hops, most of it – and had to come off. Gary had to use Carew and Butcher, who weren't regular bowlers.

Then there was that time in the Kingston Test when the bottles started coming on and I went out and told the players to come off. The police started using gas, and it blew back into our faces!

Ken often said he wasn't well on that trip. In Barbados he complained of pains in the chest and we took him to a doctor who could find nothing wrong with him. Later that year, of course, he had his first heart-attack.

Dennis Amiss

The Warwickshire batsman averaged 46·30 in 50 Tests for England, many of them played in company with Ken Barrington.

Some of my funniest memories of Ken occurred when I was standing at the other end in Tests when the light was getting bad. He was an expert in pretending that he could hardly see the ball. So much so that the umpires would often come off for bad light.

How he did it I don't know, but the faces he pulled and the way he would play and miss on purpose were a hilarious sight. Even the umpires would have a smile on their faces, and found it very difficult to take offence at this great character at the other end.

I suppose a lot of people thought Ken played a great part in influencing my batting technique while playing for England in the 1960s and 1970s. As I had played with him at the start of my career, he obviously helped me tremendously.

He said that if you wanted to play regularly for England you had to cut out a lot of shots, and therefore reduce the number of chances of getting out, thus becoming an accumulator of runs rather than a natural stroke-player. That was Kenny's way of playing at international level, but he could play all the shots with tremendous power when he wanted to.

Certainly a bit of his technique at top level rubbed off on to me, as I wanted to play cricket for England as long as I could. Apart from his coaching, and trying to put an old head on young shoulders, he was always by your side when things went wrong, and I can remember him coming to me on occasions after failing in a Test Match and saying, 'Never mind, Den, far worse things can happen. You can still go home to see your wife and family. They still love you!'

John Arlott

The broadcaster and writer on cricket. He now lives in retirement in Alderney.

It was the last day of the match. Of course, it would be. The game had run until well after six. Of course, it would. The car would not start. Of course, it would not. Lifting the bonnet was like flying a flag of distress; apart from the radiator cap and the oil-gauge, what it revealed was meaningless.

The consequence – abandoning the damned thing until a local garage, probably not to be contacted until next day, could collect it, then waiting while it was repaired and making arrangements to collect it with a Test match only a day ahead – piled heavily on the skull. Then, all at once, a cheerful, semi-Cockney voice lifted the depression.

'Hello, mate. What's wrong then, eh, won't she go?' It was Ken

Barrington, rolling along with his bag, all toothily cheerful and grinning.

'You don't know too much about it, do you?'

'No, nothing, Ken,' I said. 'Move over, then.' Apart from human beings, cricket was by far his first major enthusiasm, but motor-cars were unquestionably the second.

There followed a dissertation on that particular car, its engine, its shortcomings and merits, and an examination of what seemed to be the present problem. A near-by bench was requisitioned as a resting-place for screws, nuts, washers and the other objects gradually exhumed from the innards of the mechanism. The light began to go.

A suggestion that it would be a good idea to ring the AA or a garage met with: 'No, don't worry. By the time they get here I shall have it done.'

The light failed. A torch was produced. Car-owner humbly brought beer from near-by bar. Beer ignored now by deeply involved mechanical investigator.

It took a solid hour and a half. Then, face suffused in triumph, the technician tugged the starting wire and everything burst into action. Then the beer could be poured down with the air of one who had earned it.

Would he come into the pub now and have the other half? And wash the oil off his hands? Already, though, he was swabbing the grime with a cloth and petrol. No, no, it was too late and he had far to go. Farther, in fact, than the beneficiary of his skill.

'Please?' 'No, another time.' Spluttering, respectful gratitude. 'So grateful. What would I have done without you? What can I do?'

'Nothing, mate,' he said. 'Just don't give it another think.'

Kind as they have ever come. There were better batters, though not many if they were playing for your life. But surely, none who was so well liked by so many. Dear old Ken.

Geoff Arnold

The 37-year-old Sussex bowler played with Ken Barrington at Surrey from 1962 until Ken's retirement in 1969. Arnold, who played in 34 Tests for England, left Surrey in 1977. Out of the cricket season he works as a sales executive.

Kenny was very superstitious, and my main memory of him is watching him sitting just inside the door of the home dressing-room at the Oval waiting for his turn to bat.

He had this routine of putting down his bat and laying down his gloves in the same way every time. He had this favourite position, and would sit there, puffing away at countless cigarettes until it was his turn to go in.

He would crack a few jokes, but never seemed completely relaxed.

Even after all the years he was in the game, he was still nervous before he went in.

He followed the same routine in the dressing-room. He put his left sock on first, his left boot on first and his left pad on first. And he always carried the half-crown that Peter May tossed with in his first Test in 1955 in his blazer pocket as a good-luck token.

Wherever he went he would have a favourite corner of the dressing-room which he had used before and made his own, and used to be upset if someone else got it first.

On the morning of every Test Ann used to send him a good-luck telegram which he would put in his hip pocket and keep there for the whole of the match. In 1964, when he was becoming a bit obsessed about not making a Test century in England, he asked Ann to change the contents of the telegram to try and change his luck, so Ann sent a new message which read: 'Vincit qui patitur, love Ann.'

Not being a Latin scholar, he didn't know what it meant. He got his 100 all right and went on to score 256, his highest Test score, at Old Trafford. When he got home Ann translated it for him. 'He who endures, conquers,' it said. He certainly did that!

Alex Bannister

The former Daily Mail *cricket correspondent and distinguished cricket journalist is now retired. Alex went on countless overseas tours with Ken Barrington, and shared many amusing experiences with him.*

England couldn't have had a better ambassador abroad than Ken Barrington. In South Africa he ended gamesmanship and bickering in a Test by leaving the wicket when he could have remained. In the West Indies they admired his tenacity and the way he laughed with them. In Australia they acknowledged a fighter on the field and a friend off it. In India and Pakistan he was a king.

Touring India with Ken was like being on the right hand of a dearly loved Viceroy. His playing successes there only partly accounted for his massive popularity and postbag. Indian crowds were quick to sense his naturalness. They adored his humour, and sought his friendship. One letter reached him in an envelope bearing the one name: Ken.

Before the days of anonymity behind helmet and visor, Ken WAS and LOOKED a batsman as did Sir Jack Hobbs, Wally Hammond and Sir Don Bradman even in the act of walking to the wicket. The titans created an aura by their very appearance, a fact which those who saw Hammond leave the wicket gate at Lord's in the crisis at Lord's in 1938 will never dispute.

I felt the same presence of greatness one morning in 1961 at the Brabourne Stadium, Bombay. In those days players and visiting Pressmen lived in the pavilion in rooms overlooking the ground, rather like occupying a small suite on the top balcony at the Oval. One was awakened at sunrise by the chatter of thousands already in the ground and the *pop pop* of the motor roller.

At the fall of the first wicket, at a healthy 159, I chanced to see Ken emerge from the opposite door. Perfectly turned out, he was in absolute control of himself, exuding calm assurance. If ever a batsman seemed certain to make a big score it was Ken.

He duly scored his century, 151 not out – one of four centuries in the first four Tests in Pakistan and India – and that evening soon after the close of play he was displaying more classy footwork on the improvised dance floor in front of the pavilion.

Looking on, one of the Indian bowlers said to me, 'When you see Mr Barrington coming to the wicket the heart sinks. He is a jolly fellow, and I like him very much, but I think we see too much of him at the wicket!'

In the days before modern hotels and European food, Ken's presence in a touring team was a godsend, for he had patience and humour. Once in a small up-country town in Pakistan he was urged to take the wheel of a dilapidated coach and drive the team to the ground.

The drive was not free from incident. First, he took off some brickwork surrounding the hotel, and after successfully avoiding the straying pedestrians, goats, motor-cycle rickshaws and dogs he became jammed between two brick uprights serving as an entrance to the ground. The team had to leave by an emergency exit at the back of the stuck-fast coach!

His appointment as manager in India in 1976–7 was an inspired one, and he was privately proud, as he had every right to be, of his status. Sitting in the Taj Mahal Hotel, Bombay, overlooking the archway known as the Gateway to India, Ken turned to me and said, 'My father, who was in the Army for twenty-eight years and was in both Great Wars, went through there as a private soldier on the way to the North-West Frontier. And here am I in one of the top hotels in the world and manager of the MCC!'

As manager in India, Sri Lanka, Pakistan and New Zealand, and as an assistant in Australia and the West Indies, Ken served England as he did as batsman and Test selector, with pride, honesty, unfailing good humour and high ability. If there is any small comfort to be gained in his untimely death it was that he died doing the job he loved, and Ann was with him.

Players are the first to see through artifice and insincerity, and they were quick to accept him as 100 per cent genuine. One of his more endearing traits was to appreciate the problems of the modern player, and not to fall into the trap of believing the best belonged to the past. I never once heard him pull rank, boast of his achievements or bear a grudge.

Considering his stature and record of a Test average of 58·67, bettered only by Sir Don Bradman, Herbert Sutcliffe, Eddie Paynter, Graeme Pollock and George Headley, Ken's humility was quite exceptional.

It is perhaps a measure of his ability that pundits still argue that he could have been even greater had he not stifled some of his strokes in the cause of 'percentage' batting. I discussed this point with him when we sat together at the farewell dinner to the Gillette sponsorship before the team left for the West Indies in 1981.

'I think if I began all over again I would be more relaxed,' he said. 'I might not have ended with quite so many runs, and I would certainly have had less stick from the critics. But, on the other hand, I might not have been as useful to Surrey and England!'

What needs to be remembered by any critics of his methods is that he batted at a most difficult period. Not only were home pitches often poor, but bowlers plugged away at inswingers, or fired outside the leg-stump.

The best batsmen were cramped and often wrongfully blamed for slow scoring. I am sure he was overworked at home, and the best of Barrington, which could scarcely be improved upon by any of the world's batsmen, was seen away from his native conditions.

Jack Bannister

The ex-Warwickshire bowler, who is secretary of the Cricketers' Association and cricket writer for the Birmingham Mail.

When I was in Barbados in March 1981 I walked out to the middle with Kenny to inspect the pitch at the Kensington Oval before the four-day match between England and Barbados.

'Look at that,' said Kenny. 'You don't see pitches like that any more. They always used to be like that. There's an inferior difference in pitches all over the world!'

Bob Barber

The former Lancashire and England left-hand opening bat who played 28 Tests between 1961 and 1968, often with Ken Barrington. Bob Barber was also a member of the exclusive Leg Break Bowlers Union.

Kenny was known as a very sound player, but a man who did not normally demonstrate his significant skills. I am one of those who wished that he had been allowed to relax more.

Playing in Johannesburg in 1964, I was enjoying a partnership with Ken, and reached 97. I remember walking up the wicket to him and saying, 'I'll finish it with a six or get out.' He chastised me for my irresponsibility.

I dragged a wide ball on to the stumps and was out for 97. Later

Ken reached 94, and then proceeded to complete his 100 with a six over the sight-screen of a very long boundary. What this illustrated, I think, was that he had tremendous ability which was not always apparent.

Alec Bedser

Alec joined the Surrey staff with his brother Eric in 1938, and later became one of the county's greatest bowlers. His record of 236 wickets in 61 Tests was unequalled, until subsequently bettered by Fred Trueman, Derek Underwood and Brian Statham. He played with Ken Barrington, and also worked with him as a selector, and until 1982 was chairman of the selectors. Few people have served the game of cricket more devotedly.

Ken was a marvellous chap, very conscientious in everything he did. If he said he would see you somewhere at ten o'clock, he was there on the dot. If I asked him to go a long way to watch a player he would go without complaint.

He was good in his assessments of players, and made many good points at our meetings. His opinions of batsmen were in many ways influenced by his own approach as a player. He felt that it took a long time to mature into a Test player, and he was always reluctant to push a youngster in before his time. In that sense, he tended to play a bit safe.

He was so conscientious, so eager to meet every demand, that I often felt he undertook too much. And he was an awful worrier!

I've never met anyone who was more meticulous. He was meticulous about everything, his appearance, his gear, his car. We often used to have a laugh about the way he insisted on parking his car a long way away from where he was intending to spend the day. 'Less risk of it getting scratched there,' he excused himself.

He was a great loss to the game because he had so much enthusiasm and energy. We'll miss him, Eric and I, and so will everyone else in the game.

Richie Benaud

The former Australian captain and all-rounder is now a commentator with the BBC and a business-man in Australia. Benaud took a record 248 wickets for Australia in 63 Tests, and was rated one of cricket's finest captains.

In 1960–1 Kenny and I went on a Ron Roberts tour to South Africa and Rhodesia, and it quickly became obvious to me that Kenny's main interests, next to his love of cricket generally, were leg-spin bowling and playing golf.

We did a lot of both together. We used to have competitions in the nets, like seeing who could land the ball on the same spot most times, or stop a batsman scoring. I taught him to bowl the flipper, which is a back-spinning leg-spinner which comes back a bit from the off and tends to keep low and skid through.

Clarrie Grimmett invented it, and Bruce Dooland, who played for Nottinghamshire for a time after the Second World War, passed it on to me. It is bowled with a leg-break action, and comes from the bottom of the hand when the wrist is turning at the point of delivery, not the top, as happens with the leg-spinner and googly.

It is a very intriguing ball, and it got me a lot of wickets. In one match in Rhodesia on that tour I took 9–16 against a local side, and eight of them were out to the flipper.

Bruce Dooland used to have a long run when he played in Australia, but when he came to England he cut it down, and concentrated on disguising his hand before he released the ball so that the batsman couldn't see what was happening, whether the ball was coming out of the top of the hand or the bottom. The batsman could see that something was going on but couldn't pick it out clearly. This was one of the reasons why I chopped my own run-up down to six paces.

Kenny used to bowl off the same kind of run-up, just a few paces. I told him it had taken me a year to learn the flipper and a whole year went by before I used it in a match. After our spell in Rhodesia he picked it up quickly, and was soon pitching it in the nets.

The following season in England he was full of his new discovery. 'It will revolutionize my bowling,' he told Tony Lock. One day Surrey were playing in a county match at the Oval and he told the other players he was going to unveil his flipper.

He told Tony Lock, 'Go to leg-slip, that's where the catch will come.' Lockie started to walk towards leg-slip. 'No, up a yard,' said Kenny. 'The fourth ball is going to be the flipper, and I want you a bit closer because he'll nick it to you.'

Kenny bowled his first three deliveries. Then the fourth . . . a full toss which went straight in the direction of the batsman's head without pitching! I can't remember who the batsman was, but he stepped inside the line and smashed it past Lockie's ear for four. The umpire signalled four, and Lock just stood there, saying nothing.

At the end of the over the field changed over and an embarrassed Kenny said, 'Sorry, Lockie, it slipped.'

Lock replied, 'Marvellous! It took Richie Benaud twelve months to master the flipper, and you perfect it in one match!'

Bowling the flipper puts a great strain on the shoulder ligaments and tendons, and that was why I had to give it up in the 1961 tour of England when I hurt my shoulder. The pain went right through my arm into my fingers.

Kenny went on and bowled a lot more flippers, and bowled them very well. I always thought he was a very good leg-spin bowler who would have taken many more wickets if he had the opportunity to bowl more often.

He was unlucky in that he played in a Surrey side that was very strong in bowling, and wasn't needed much. Also, leg-spin was never very popular in England. They used to tell him to concentrate on his batting and have a few overs from time to time to keep his hand in.

As he didn't bowl regularly, he often used to be a bit nervous when he first started a spell, and sometimes bowled a few loose deliveries, but that was understandable. Your palms get wet and you can't hold the ball properly. I thought Kenny was a fine bowler . . . whatever Lockie may have thought about his flipper!

Don Bennett

The former Middlesex all-rounder is now Middlesex coach.

Kenny was manager of a Derrick Robins tour of South Africa in 1975, a trial run for him becoming manager of the England team. One day we met these two chaps from the rag trade who invited us to play golf.

We were taken to the Mowbray Club for a foursome. The rag-trade chaps were fair golfers, but not in Kenny's class. While we were waiting to start Kenny said to me, 'Shall I give them the Colonel bit?'

I said, 'Why not? It should be fun.' So when he teed up for the first hole Kenny did his impersonation of a colonel. swinging his club with stiff arms and mishitting the ball. His drive didn't go too far. Our opponents probably thought they were on a good thing when Kenny said, 'Do you think we ought to have something on the round?'

They mentioned money, but knowing they were in the cloth trade, Kenny suggested a suit. Once the bet was struck Kenny started playing properly, and we each won a suit!

He was a very good golfer. He was down to a five handicap at the time, if I remember right. Like everything else he did, he worked hard at it to become good.

Jack Birkenshaw

The Worcestershire, and former Yorkshire and Leicestershire, all-rounder.

In my Leicester days we were playing against Surrey, and we had a chap named Tommy Thompson playing for us, an off-spinner.

After being on the field about half an hour, Tommy crashed into a boundary fence and hobbled off the field, not to be seen again by the Surrey players until he emerged near the end of our second innings with a brief to smash the wicket up as it was beginning to turn.

We assumed he would be fairly subtle about the job, but proceeded to stop play while he banged the pitch with his bat on a spinner's length!

Tommy managed about 20 with the bat before being out and retiring to the pavilion where he stayed while we went out into the field. Eventually he managed to get him on to field for about five minutes while someone went off to change his boots.

He took up a position just behind square leg as Ken Barrington took strike. The bowler bowled a very short delivery which Ken pulled like a tracer bullet towards square leg. Tommy emerged from behind the umpire and dived full length to his right to take a really magnificent catch.

Ken couldn't believe it, but had to go, and as he passed me at mid-on said, 'If you can only get that bugger fit he'd be a world-beater!'

Geoff Boycott

England's leading run-scorer in Tests, who played many times with and against Ken, and went on numerous tours with him.

The Colonel made a million contributions to team morale. Like that time in Port of Spain on what was sadly to be his last tour. During the team dinner a phone rang and Geoff Miller answered it.

'Call for you, Colonel,' he said. 'Battoo Brothers.' Ken took it, wondering what new problems could have cropped up with the team's transport arrangements.

'Hello, hello, Mr Barrington. Battoo Brothers here,' said a voice rather more music-hall Pakistani than West Indian. 'I am afraid we are having problems with the taxis for the morning. A lot of people have arrived in Trinidad and our cars are going to the airport to pick them up. But we can spare you one taxi at 6.45 a.m.'

Ken put the phone down with a sign. 'Gawd help us,' he said. 'We want four taxis at 8.30 a.m. and they say we can have one at 6.45. Don't know what the 'ell it's coming to. One ruddy problem after another. What good's one ruddy taxi at that time?'

The first caller seemed to have been afflicted with a fit of giggles, and a second rang five minutes later. 'Call for you again, Colonel, Battoo Brothers.'

'Hello, Mr Barrington. Yes, we have some good news. We have now available two taxis for the morning. The only thing is that they have been involved in a collision.'

Ken put his hand over the mouthpiece. 'What do you make of that? Two taxis, and they've ruddy well run into each other! What a palaver.' Speaking into the phone, he said, 'Yes, thanks for your help. Do the best you can.'

The Colonel was used to problems, and half expected them every time the phone rang. Perhaps that was why he hadn't noticed that most of the team were purple-faced with suppressed laughter, that the rest seemed acutely aware that something was going on without quite knowing what, and that Messrs Dilley, Bairstow and Gower were absent from the room in relays.

The phone rang again. 'Mr Barrington? Yes, it is us again. You will be pleased to hear that we have found an eighteen-seater bus to transport the team tomorrow.

'There is a minor problem, though, because we are short of spares. For a start, we are in need of a steering-wheel.'

'Stone me,' said Ken, as the phone clicked dead again. 'Ruddy bus here with no steering-wheel! Fancy having a bus with no steering-wheel! How the hell are we supposed to get away in that! I dunno, one problem after another. . . .'

The phone rang yet again. 'If that's for me I'm not in,' he said. 'Buses without steering-wheels, what next?'

Battoo Brothers again. 'Mr Barrington? Good news! We have the steering-wheel.'

'Thank Gawd for that,' said the Colonel.

' . . . but I am afraid the bus has just crashed into the two taxis we found for you.'

The Colonel began to relay the message to the team when a light dawned in his eye. 'Wait a minute! This ruddy fellow from Battoo Brothers has a Yorkshire accent! Where's Bairstow?'

Ken was a very relaxed, amusing character when he retired, the complete opposite of what he was like when he was a player. I don't think I've played with someone who was so tense. Before he went in he would sit there chain-smoking away, and he didn't like anyone larking about in the background. He would soon get upset if they did.

You need to concentrate, but I felt he was too tense about his cricket and that wasn't helpful. He was cocooned in a shell of concentration. Too much really.

When he retired he was a different person. If you saw him in the nets, bowling away and loving life, you thought 'There's a man who is enjoying himself'. He was full of enthusiasm, and loving every minute of it.

Mike Brearley

The England captain when Ken Barrington was manager or assistant manager or merely a selector.

Ken was a lovely man. I remember some of his remarks. 'On a good pitch, you should lace up your boots and book in for bed and breakfast.'

'Make him [the batsman] push forward a bit. Pitch it there and you will have him in two man's land.'

Donald Carr

The secretary of the Test and County Cricket Board and former player and captain with Derbyshire. He went on two tours with Ken Barrington, the MCC 'A' tour of Pakistan in 1955–6 and the MCC tour of South Africa in 1964–5.

I was batting with Ken in a minor match in Lyallpur, and I thought we needed to speed things up a bit. I said, 'Let's go for the quick singles', and he said 'yes', he would. He ran one or two and then he chopped a ball to gully's right hand and shouted, 'Come on, Skip!'

I set off, although there didn't seem much chance of making it, and as I approached the other end I saw Ken diving back into his crease! The wicket-keeper had the ball in his hand, and with Ken face downwards and obviously not in a position to do much running, I decided I would have to try and make it back to the other end, racing the ball as the keeper lobbed it back to the bowler.

I somehow managed to get in before the bails were removed, and turning round, I saw Ken dusting himself down as he got to his feet. A little shamefacedly, he said, 'I think I ought to get a run for that because you covered the distance both ways!'

He said it in such a nice way that I couldn't help but shriek with laughter. He had this sense of self-preservation when he was batting!

Then there was the occasion when I was manager of the MCC touring party in South Africa in 1964–5 when we were playing Western Province at Cape Town and Ken had been batting about four hours for 80 odd not out. At the close of play I told him he ought to get on with it in the morning and said, 'I bet you can't score those extra runs for your hundred in the first ten minutes of play. I'll bet you a rand.'

'Done,' he said. Next morning I arrived fifteen minutes after play started, and when I looked at the scoreboard number 4 was showing 101 not out. He'd won his bet. Apparently he was 94 not out with a few seconds remaining when he drove a 6 straight back over the sight-screen. It proved he could do it when he wanted to! He then proceeded to bat another hour for 12!

One of the outstanding memories I have of Ken was the partridge shoot I went on with him in Pakistan while on tour there with the MCC 'A' team. A couple of local lads had gone shooting the day before, and bagged 280 birds. They said, 'Why don't you all come? We will supply the equipment.'

There were only enough guns to enable two of us to share one gun, which no one minded. Kenny, with his military upbringing, showed the others how to handle a gun, looking expertly down the barrel as he lined up one or two likely targets.

The locals took us to a field which they said was full of partridges, and they crossed to the other side to start the beat. Kenny had one of the guns, and the players who weren't armed stood some way away.

Just as we were about to start, a rather large hare came into view, and Kenny became very excited. 'It's mine!' he said, lining it up in the sights of his gun. As the hare raced across the field he followed it through the sights, trying to make sure of a hit. Within a matter of seconds he was pointing his gun in the direction of the other players whom he hadn't seen and I shouted, 'Get down!'

Kenny was vainly trying to squeeze the trigger, not realizing that the safety catch was still on! The hare escaped, and so did the players, I was relieved to discover! When we eventually got going we fired three hundred barrels between us, and although the sky was black with partridges, we bagged only thirteen of them.

Kenny was like Royalty in India and Pakistan. They revered him there, and I remember when he had to come home early from Pakistan in 1961–2 because of a broken finger, Air India laid on VIP treatment for him. I went to meet him at Heathrow along with Ann, and we were ushered into the VIP lounge for drinks. Kenny was taken through to the lounge from the plane without having to undergo the usual formalities, and we spent an hour drinking with senior Air India officials before we set off home.

Gubby Allen, who was then President of the MCC, and Billy Griffith, the secretary, were in India at the time negotiating over a tour, and the following week they returned to London Airport and again I had to go to the airport to meet them. This time there was no red-carpet treatment, and Gubby and Billy had to queue up along with all the other passengers. I told them how Kenny had been received the previous week, and they saw the funny side of it.

I first played against Kenny at Brock Barracks, Reading, when he was about eighteen. He was playing for a regimental side, as his father was in the Royal Berkshire Regiment and I was playing for a side my brother, Major Douglas Carr, took down there. I had been in the Berkshires myself, and so had my father.

Kenny came on with his leg-breaks, and I thought he was dynamite. One of the best young leg-break bowlers I have ever seen. He quickly ran through some of the old gents in our side and ran another one by a mile.

After Kenny had retired he said to me on several occasions, 'Is there anything I can do for cricket? The game has been so good to me I want to put something back. I'll do anything, even act as baggage man.'

He was desperately keen to do something. He had a deep love of the game, and wanted to stay in it. It had been his life. Cricket made him, and he would always be indebted to it.

There had been suggestions that a full-time coaching job could be found for him – well, not quite full-time, but on a more permanent scale than hitherto. I think he would have done it extraordinarily well because he got on so well with the players. They could laugh at him because of the things he said and did, but he could still command their respect.

Len Coldwell

The former England and Worcestershire swing bowler now lives in Teignmouth, Devon.

When I toured Australia with Ken in 1962–3 we went on a night-time kangaroo shoot with Fred Trueman, Ken and some locals. Ken, Fred and myself stood in the back of a truck armed with ·303 rifles and a 12-bore shotgun, and the driver picked out the kangaroos in a spotlight.

Fred gave us all the chat about his shooting experiences in Yorkshire, but hadn't managed to hit a single kangaroo. Mind you, it wasn't easy, as the truck was travelling at speeds up to 40 m.p.h.

You can imagine we gave Fred a bit of stick, especially as he had the shotgun. Eventually the driver picked out a rabbit in the spotlight and called to Fred.

Fred turned quickly and let go both barrels about three inches from Ken's nose . . . and missed again. Ken jumped off the truck, walked out to the rabbit which was sitting on its haunches, picked it up and brought it back to hand to Fred. 'Here, mate,' he said. 'It's easier than trying to shoot one!'

When I was told that my wife had given birth to twins Ken used to come and sit next to me and say he was going to eat and drink the same as me.

'I've been trying for a family for years,' he said. 'And all I can do is fire blanks.' I was pleased to hear that he succeeded soon after he retired from cricket.

Denis Compton

Compton's record of 5,807 runs from 78 Tests, average 50·06, was very similar to Ken Barrington's. Now with a London PR company, Denis also writes for the Sunday Express.

I played with Kenny in his first Test in 1955. It was against the South Africans, who had a very strong bowling side. He looked a very good player, and it was a mystery to me why the selectors dropped him.

He made a duck in his first innings at Trent Bridge, but he wasn't the only player to start his career in Tests with a duck. At Lord's in the Second Test he made 34 and 18, and we thought that would be enough to keep him in. But he was left out, and didn't play a home Test for a further four years.

When he got back in, against India in 1959, he made sure they weren't going to drop him again by scoring four successive half-centuries. He was unlucky that he made his start against such a good side as the South Africans.

Peter Heine and Neil Adcock were two very fine opening bowlers who could be very nasty propositions. They were quicker than any bowler in the England *v.* Australia series in England in 1981. And as for Hugh Tayfield, who had Kenny caught in his third Test innings at Lord's, I don't think the South Africans have produced a better off-spin bowler.

Ann told me that I used to be her hero before she got married, and when they moved into their first house there was this picture of me on the dressing-room table. 'What's that doing here?' asked Kenny.

'He's my hero,' said Ann. 'We're not having that,' said Kenny, and he tossed it away!

Later, when I became friends with Ken and his wife Ann, I presented Ann with a signed photograph of myself to replace the one Kenny threw out.

Alan Connolly

The former Victorian, Australian and Middlesex pace bowler played in 29 Tests in the Sixties. Connolly now runs a plumbing and gas-fitting business in Melbourne.

Though many miles apart for most of our lives, Ken and I never lost the tremendous comradeship that developed from a mutual respect for each other's abilities in our respective departments of the game of cricket. Our stock greeting, even before we said 'hello', was 'Which way did it go?'

That referred to the time when I strangled his wicket in the first innings of the Headingley Test in 1968 when he was on 49. I still consider it the prize among my 102 Test wickets. Ken always asked me throughout the years, and the last time was at Lord's in the Centenary Test in 1980, which way the ball went and how it got through.

My answer was always a rather vague one, as whenever one was bowling to Ken there was never a big enough gap to shoot a garden pea through, and this occasion was no exception. For my part I was denied the pleasure of seeing the off-stump go.

The first clue I had that I bowled him was the roar of the crowd, and then I saw a gleaming white stump lying on the turf some ten yards back, near the feet of wicket-keeper Barry Jarman.

Perhaps one day I might see an ancient film and so be able to understand what happened. But until then it will appear that it will have to stay 'Which way did it go?'

Bernie Constable

The former Surrey batsman played for Surrey in 1938–64. He now works as a carpenter near his home in Hersham.

One year we were playing against Yorkshire at Headingley and it was very dark. Peter Loader was batting, I think, and I was sitting next to Kenny in the dressing-room.

After a while someone said, 'It's getting a bit lighter.' Kenny said, 'It's not getting brighter. That's the moon coming out.'

I always think about that, especially when it's a dark and miserable day. Kenny always had something funny to say because he was that type of bloke.

I used to try and help him when he first joined the staff in 1948 because I joined as a leg-spinner, just like he did. We all tried to help each other, but cricket is an individual game where you work out your own salvation.

He had his own ideas about the game, like his open stance with his left foot pointing towards mid-on. I was the opposite. I had my left foot pointing to extra cover, looking right over my left shoulder.

Colin Cowdrey

Cowdrey's aggregate of 7,624 runs in 114 Tests, average 44·06, was the highest of any English player until Geoff Boycott surpassed it. Ken Barrington's aggregate of 6,806 from 82 Tests, average 58·67, put him fifth in the list behind Boycott, Cowdrey, Hammond, and Hutton.

Cowdrey, aged forty-nine, is now a business-man in the City of London. His Test career ran almost parallel to Barrington's, although it started a year earlier and finished five years later.

'The Colonel' was always a bit of a worrier, even when he was playing well. I recall an occasion when we were batting together in a Test Match at Port of Spain – it was a third-wicket stand of 135 – and I said to him, 'Are you free for an hour?'

He said, 'What do you mean?' 'Well,' I said, 'I thought we might pop down the town and have a pot of tea together.' He laughed, and it helped break the tension.

Whenever I batted with him after that I would repeat the conversation, and it would be the private joke between us. A variation was me saying to him, 'Feel like a game of golf?' He always responded to that one. He loved playing golf.

Geoff Boycott was sharing a room with him on that tour, and I remember he asked if he could be shifted to another room because Kenny kept waking him up. Kenny was an awful sleeper. He was down to four hours a night around that time. He would order a pot of tea at 4 a.m., another one at 5 a.m. and a third at 6 a.m. Poor

Geoff complained that he'd had three cups of tea before breakfast, and it was too much for him.

Dennis Cox

The former Surrey all-rounder joined the Surrey staff at the same time as Ken Barrington in 1948, along with Alan Brazier and Derek and Ron Pratt. Dennis left the Oval in 1959, and is now managing director of an import company.

Soon after we joined the staff we were playing together in a second-eleven match against Gloucester at Bristol. The first night someone arranged to fix us up with tickets for a variety show which featured Phyllis Dixey, the striptease artist.

Ken was seventeen at the time, and a bit gauche. We'd been sitting there, impatiently waiting for Phyllis Dixey to reveal all, when THE moment was about to arrive. Suddenly, Ken got up and started pushing past us. 'Got to get an ice-cream,' he said.

Another time, I remember playing against Kent with him at the Oval, and Ted Witherden was batting for Kent. Ted always played the same way – nicks and edges, and hardly a shot worth remembering.

Ted had been frustrating us for a long time when the skipper asked Ken to have a go with his leg-breaks. Ken used to be very nervous when he came on, and his first ball was a rank bad long hop. Ted smashed it straight at a fielder, and was caught.

Ken bowled some terrible deliveries that day, and finished up with five wickets for not very many. I was slightly older than he was, and he always treated me with respect.

When he became England's leading professional batsman, and later a selector and England manager, he still showed the same courtesy and respect. If he saw me he invited me into the committee room. He never changed, or lost touch with his old friends. He was a man of great humility.

Ted Dexter

Played in 62 Tests, many of them as captain. Dexter's 70 in England's first innings in the 'Greatest Test of All' in 1963 against the West Indies at Lord's is still considered by many spectators who were there to be the finest innings played at cricket's headquarters in post-War years. Ken Barrington, with 80 in the first innings and 60 in the second, was England's top run-scorer in the match.

One Kenny Barrington story lingers on . . . when I captained MCC in Pakistan in 1960–1. Kenny was leaving the hotel to walk to the ground one morning when he was stopped by a young lad wanting his autograph.

Kenny was immaculately attired, as he always was. The crease in his flannels was just right. The shirt was ironed and pressed, so there wasn't a crease to be seen. He was 100 per cent determined to do everything right.

He took the boy's book and fountain pen and tried to write. The pen wouldn't work. 'It won't write,' he said. 'Needs some more ink.'

'It does write,' said the boy. 'No, it doesn't,' said Kenny, handing it back. 'No, no,' said the boy. 'It will. Let me show you.'

The boy shook the pen . . . and ink splattered down Kenny's shirt and flannels. He stood there in disbelief. 'It couldn't happen,' he said. 'I've travelled seven thousand miles, done my best to look smart and look what you've done to me!'

Kenny was marvellously popular on that tour. The fans loved his by-play and antics on the field. They really took to him.

John Edrich

The Surrey and England left-hand batsman shared countless partnerships with Ken Barrington, at both county and Test level. John scored 5,138 runs in 77 Tests at an average of 43·54, and came only three places behind Kenny in the list of leading England run-getters.

John is now a successful business-man and a former Test selector.

I was one of many players who were run out by Kenny. There ought to be a club for us all! I'm afraid he wasn't the greatest judge of a run.

One year we were playing in a county game against Somerset, and I was 99 not out. I played a maiden from Fred Rumsey, and he played the first ball of the next over towards third man and shouted something as he moved down the pitch.

I couldn't understand his Berkshire accent, and probably he couldn't understand my reply in broad Norfolk, and the result was that he finished up down my end after saying, 'Come on then, if you're coming.' In fact, I wasn't coming. I was run out by the length of the pitch . . . one short of a hundred.

The first time I went to India, in 1963, Kenny acted as my personal adviser, as he had toured there before. He knew all the pitfalls, he said. 'You will find that nothing works,' he said.

When we disembarked off the plane at Bombay we were escorted to an air-conditioned bus – no windows – and driven off to the Brabourne Stadium, where we were quartered. Everything seemed to go off quite well, and I thought that Kenny had been exaggerating.

'I can't understand it,' he said. 'The place seems to have changed since I was last here.'

We went to our room, and he lay on his bed for a while reminiscing about things that had gone wrong on a previous tour. 'I think I'll have a shower,' he said. He was a great one for having a shower.

He stripped off, went to the bathroom and stood under the shower.

As he pulled the device above his head, the whole lot crashed down on top of him. 'Hello,' he said. 'We're back to the India I know and love.'

We had many wonderful times together over the years, and many laughs. Even if he hadn't had that heart-attack in 1968, I don't think he would have played on much longer.

Mike Edwards

The former Surrey batsman who was on the Oval staff between 1963 and 1974. He is now senior sixth-form tutor at Tulse Hill School, London.

We used to call Kenny 'Mr Punch' because of his long hook nose, the way he said things and the way he whacked people . . . all in good fun, I must add! 'That's the way to do it,' he would say. He asked you what you wanted, the six-incher, the punch that travelled six inches, or the twelve-incher.

The other players used to rib him a lot, particularly 'Ob' Long. One day at Lord's Ken had a go back, grabbed hold of him and hoisted him up on the dressing-room pegs on the wall. 'Ob' was literally hanging there on his sweater.

'Ob' was quick-witted and could get his quips in first. Kenny's response was usually a whack. One of the funniest incidents concerning him was the time a TV crew came down the Oval to do a commercial with Kenny as the star. The commercial was advertising Right Guard, the BO people. Kenny came in all sweating after scoring a hundred, and they filmed him as he came off the field.

Then they filmed him a bit later coming out of the shower with a towel round him. He only had a couple of simple sentences to say. Something like, 'After a long innings I get it right, I use Right Guard.' He tried it a few times, but they weren't satisfied. His intonation wasn't right. They tried it a few times more. Still it wasn't right.

Luckily, it was raining heavily and we didn't have to go back on the field. We spent all morning watching this going on, and we were rolling about with laughter. These TV people are sticklers for getting it done the correct way, and they kept insisting on a retake. Twenty, thirty times Kenny did it before they finally agreed to call a halt.

Kenny was very apologetic to the rest of us. 'Don't worry, I'll get you fixed up with some Right Guard,' he said. But he never did!

A tidy, orderly man himself, he wouldn't tolerate people who were scruffy or untidy. Anyone who didn't measure up to his standards used to get a rocket from him. Or a whack!

Just after he scored that 256 at Old Trafford in 1964 he played in a county game at the Oval against Nottinghamshire, and was going well for another big score when I was called upon to field substitute for Notts.

Geoff Millman, the Notts captain, put me at mid-wicket, and when Kenny was 118 not out he hit a steepler on the leg side and I dropped it. Notts weren't so worried about those things in those days!

Anyway, next ball he pulled a hard one in my direction, and I dived and just got a hand on it but couldn't hold it. Kenny caused a lot of amusement by waving his bat at me and directing me to another position. He went on to score 207!

John Emburey

The England off-spin bowler went on tours of Australia, 1979–80, and the West Indies, 1980–1, when Ken Barrington was assistant manager.

Kenny was a great man to have in the dressing-room. He was always cheerful, always optimistic and never criticized anyone. You knew he was on your side all the time. He was the best encourager I knew, and no one could ever fill his role. His death was a terrible loss to the English team. We couldn't believe it when we heard the news.

I'll always remember how he used to 'read' wickets. He usually took a penknife and a ball with him out to the middle to probe around and test the bounce. In Australia and the West Indies he used to say, 'That one's a jaffa. You can book in for bed and breakfast on that and still be there tomorrow morning.'

Godfrey Evans

The former Kent and England wicket-keeper played ninety-one times for England. His career in Tests was ending as Kenny's was just starting, but he remained a friend of Kenny's. He still keeps in touch with Test cricket by acting as advisor to Ladbroke's.

Kenny used to like coming to the Ladbroke's tents at the Test grounds for a little punt. Not a lot, but just enough to give him an interest. He would ask Ron Pollard, one of our directors, if he could have slightly better odds, and thinking that perhaps Kenny could supply some useful information that might be useful when fixing the odds on cricket, Ron used to oblige.

Unfortunately, Kenny never did supply any information! Kenny did accumulators, and though he came up occasionally, I wouldn't say he was a good tipster. He certainly wasn't on cricket.

He used to have a bet on what the number of runs scored in a session would be, but he was usually off target. I used to say to him, 'If you can't get that right, how can you select the right team?' We had many laughs together.

Although our careers didn't overlap by many years, I did play against him several times. In one match, Kent *v.* Surrey, Surrey only needed 4 to win when they came out for their second innings. Kenny opened, and someone else kept wicket. I fielded at mid-wicket.

The bowler bowled a long hop, and Kenny pulled it – he was a very good puller – straight at me, and I managed to push it up and catch the rebound. It was going like a rocket!

'What did you do that for?' he said. 'Anyone else would have let it go at this stage of the game. You've ruined my average!'

In those days he was something of a striker of the ball, a player who used to go for his shots. But being dropped firstly by Surrey and then by England made him change his approach. He began to accept that the only way to keep his place was to become consistent and score lots of runs, so he cut out a lot of shots and became a percentage player.

One of my early matches against him was for the MCC against Surrey at Lord's. Kenny was nervous when he came in at 6 after I had stumped David Fletcher and Peter May. I said, 'Good morning, son.' And he replied, 'Good morning. I'd better not move my foot, had I?'

'It might be a good idea to remember that,' I said. A few overs later he forgot his own advice, and I stumped him for 8 off Alan Oakman!

Laurie Fishlock

The former Surrey batsman (1930–52) now lives in retirement at Cheam, Surrey.

The first time I played with Ken was very early in his career when I was running the Wimbledon charity match at Merton. We were short on the morning of the game, and Andy Sandham suggested I give Ken – who was a young lad not long on the staff – a game.

We had such a powerful batting side that I had to put him well down the order, so I thought I would try and give him a bowl later in the other team's innings.

'Here you are, son,' I said. 'Have a bowl. You'll tidy this lot up.'

'But I'm a batsman,' he said. I had some difficulty persuading him to come on. At first he wanted to bowl seam because he'd started as a quick bowler. 'No, you'll do better throwing it up to them,' I said.

I think he was a bit nervous about his leggers even in those days. Anyway, he came on and bowled quite well. I can't remember if he got any wickets. He wasn't a bad bowler, you know. I retired shortly after that and didn't play with him again, but I met him on the golf course a few times when we played together in the Surrey Cricketers' Golfing Society.

One of the first times we played together was in a tournament at Sunridge Park, Bromley. He got behind some trees and asked me what club he ought to take. I said a seven, and he hit so hard it cleared the trees, the green and everything else. 'I don't think I'll be taking your advice,' he said. I didn't realize he could hit a ball so hard. He was a big hitter on the golf course. He was a lovely person: a real comic.

Dave Gibson

The former Surrey pace bowler is now the club's coach.

Kenny was a great eyebrow-raiser. Any time we went out to inspect a pitch he would look at it, poke it about and turn round, eyebrows raised and say, 'How do they expect people to bat on that?'

Most batsmen moan about pitches, but Kenny was worst than most. If the ball didn't bounce the same six times an over the pitch wasn't a good one in his eyes.

One of his party pieces in the dressing-room was his drum act with a chair. If any military music came on the radio he would grab hold of a Bentwood chair, stick it between his legs, put half a dozen coins on it and start beating it with his hands.

The chairs had a plywood seat, and the noise from the coins bouncing up and down sounded rather like a real drum.

Alf Gover

The former Surrey pace bowler took 1,555 first-class wickets between 1929 and 1948. Now seventy-four, Alf still coaches in his cricket school in Wandsworth. He is a Past President of Surrey.

Ken was a wonderful mimic, and I always remember that story from the MCC tour to Australia in 1962–3 when Billy Griffith was manager after the Duke of Norfolk had to return home.

The Test in Sydney was being played when I visited Australia, and I called in to see Ken and some of the other players I knew. The dressing-room at the Sydney Cricket Ground is in two parts, and if you are in one section you can't see who is in the other section.

After the day's play Billy Griffith came up to me and said how pleased he was to see me. 'I don't mind you coming into the dressing-room at any time,' he said, 'but I would appreciate it if you asked me first.'

'I haven't been in the dressing-room yet,' I said. 'Yes, you have,' said Billy. 'I distinctly heard your voice.'

Then I realized what had happened. Ken Barrington was giving his Alf Gover impersonation. He used to do it brilliantly, down to the exact intonation of my 'old boy' pet phrase.

There was an occasion on a subsequent tour when he rang Geoff Boycott and, using his Gover voice, proceeded to interview Boycott about how he was faring on the tour. I was doing some journalistic work for the *Sunday Mirror* at the time.

Ken was so convincing that Boycott never suspected he had been duped. Next day in the dressing-room Geoff asked Mike Smith, the skipper, for advice on how to deal with Press inquiries!

As a skinny boy, Ken came to my school for us to have a look at him. He fanced himself as a bowler in those days, but Andrew Sandham, the Surrey coach, said, 'He'll never make a bowler. But batsman, yes. He's a good prospect.'

So it turned out. He had a great career for Surrey and England. He loved the game, and was a wonderful person.

Billy Griffith

The former secretary of MCC was manager of the England tour of Australia, 1962–3.

I had the greatest possible admiration for Ken Barrington. As a member of a touring team, he was my number one selection because he was always terribly helpful, full of jokes and good humour, and a very fine player with it. A manager needs a player like that on a long, arduous tour.

Bill Hunt

Cricket-lover from Corfe Mullen, Wimborne, Dorset.

During the South African season 1957–8 Ken went to Cape Town as a coach as a replacement for Eddie Watts. The late Ron Roberts was covering the Australian tour of South Africa at the time – Ian Craig was the Aussie captain – and one day at Newlands Ron asked me if I had seen Ken.

I duly located Ken – whom I had met previously – and asked him to speak to Ron. It transpired that there was a message for Ken from Surrey, asking him to spend as much time as possible while in Cape Town developing his spin bowling. Apparently Tony Lock's knee was causing him problems, and Surrey thought they might have to use Ken's leg-spin more the following English season.

A few days later at Newlands I saw Ken playing in a match, and he spent a lot of time bowling. I looked up *Wisden* the next year, and I noticed he bowled only 99 overs in the 1958 season and took only 4 wickets. Lock must have been pretty fit, because he bowled 723.5 overs and took 114 wickets! I suppose leg-spin was not fashionable, even in 1958!

Ray Illingworth

The former Yorkshire, Leicestershire and England all-rounder played in sixty Tests, many with Ken Barrington. Illingworth is now manager of Yorkshire.

I shared a room with Kenny on three tours, including the Duke of Norfolk's tour of Australia which gave birth to the famous Duke story.

Kenny was a bad sleeper, and one night he lay wide awake in the early hours, getting in a real state. Finally he decided to call the Duke, who was the team manager, to ask if he could have some sleeping tablets.

The Duke was a bit annoyed to be woken, but said, 'Come on down to my room, Barrington, and I'll give you some.' Kenny was so relieved that the Duke had been able to do something for him that he went straight off to sleep while the Duke sat up waiting in his room for him to collect his pills.

Kenny never seemed able to overcome this sleeping problem. He used to worry a lot, particularly in Tests. I must have been a good sleeper, because I used to sleep through most of it.

Doug Insole

The former Essex and England batsman, former chairman of the Test selectors, is Chairman of the Test and County Cricket Board's cricket committee and one of the most influential voices in world cricket.

Ken Barrington was as likeable a man as anybody is ever going to meet. As my collaborator in management on the tour to Australia in the winter of 1978/9 he was tremendous value, both as colleague and as friend.

He was also one of the great scroungers of our time! If I wanted supplies for consumption by the lads in their rooms, Kenny would know just the man. He played golf with a bloke in Melbourne, and told me afterwards that he had been promised an ample supply of crayfish when we got to Perth.

I allowed myself a guffaw or two, partly because Perth is about 1,500 miles from Melbourne, and why should a philanthropic fisherman from Perth be playing golf in Melbourne? Whatever the explanation, there appeared one day at Perth a mass of crayfish. We had them boarded out in the mini-refrigerators that were in all our rooms and on two evenings, washed down with donated wine and eaten with mayonnaise and salad, they provided us with superb if messy suppers.

The Colonel had done it again! He revealed after a few glasses of wine that it was the only occasion that he had ever played a 'customers' game' at golf.

His golf was something that Kenny took very seriously indeed, but it was the subject of some hilarity within our touring party. Very early on, while Ian Botham still had his injured arm in a sling following a mishap at home, the two were talking about a 'blood match' that was to take place at some stage of the tour. I was even invited to name the course. The talk went on endlessly for weeks on end with much huffing and puffing until eventually the match was played and Ian Botham won on the last green. The Colonel conceded grudgingly that the winner had played well, but reckoned his handicap was phoney!

Ken's sometimes excessive caution at the crease was not apparent in his performance in the casino. In Tasmania he conned Bob Willis, Bob Taylor and me into putting up 25 dollars each for him, 'the great expert', to play the tables. 'I'll make it last all evening, manager,' he said. 'We'll have a bit of fun.'

Within twenty minutes he had blown the lot. Totally convinced that he had found the answer to all our problems, he bunged the last 60 dollars on the red all in one go, and when he lost, grinned from ear to ear and offered by way of apology that well-worn cliché, 'You can't win 'em all, manager.'

We slunk out, skint, and sought solace in our team room with a glass of orange juice and a fifteen-year-old recording of *Dixon of Dock Green* on the telly. It was worth 25 bucks to be able to remind him of his indiscretion at regular intervals over the ensuing weeks.

The Colonel's gambling instinct came out too in his affection for the 'trots', races for horse-drawn buggies which are a big deal in Australia. He always organized the tickets and the meal, 'on the house' as he put it. He was not allowed to forget an occasion early in the tour when, due to a monumental miscalculation on his part, we found ourselves obliged to pay for our food, and then, taken unawares, had to have a whip-round to raise the cash and save our embarrassment.

It was therefore no more than poetic justice when one or two of us, heavily jet-lagged, fell asleep over our food just as the Colonel was reaching the punch-line of one of his more scintillating anecdotes about the glorious Oval era of the 1950s. His reputation as the most palpably boring raconteur in the Southern Hemisphere was thus established beyond all reasonable doubt.

I happened to arrive in Australia in 1968 on the day that Kenny suffered his heart-attack. I went to Melbourne to visit him, and he ordered me a cup of tea from the nurse as if he were staying at Claridges. He said he knew that he wouldn't play again, but that he wanted somehow to stay in the game.

I told him that cricket needed people like him if he was prepared to play a part, and that we could certainly use his experience on the selection committee. For a year or two afterwards I pursued him, but he was writing for a national newspaper (the *Daily Sketch*).

Then, finally, he gave up his Press involvement and became a selector, and later a manager. He was a great cricketer, but most of all he was a great friend, and he is sorely missed.

Robin Jackman

Joined the Surrey staff in 1965, and in 1980 was the most successful bowler in England with 121 wickets. His success led to him being chosen for the tour of the West Indies and ultimately to his deportation from Guyana, after it was revealed that he had coached and worked in South Africa.

I still have a baggy old pair of trousers which Ken Barrington sold to me for £2, second-hand, in 1965. I keep them because they are comfortable and I can get my thigh-pad on underneath. They've been darned countless times and don't look too good, but they serve the purpose. The Surrey lads are always taking the mick out of me about them.

When I first went to the Oval in 1965 I remember being in the bath after practice one day, and Ken was in the shower and he had quite a long chat about the game and how to succeed. Ken said the only way to get to the top was to work hard, and he mentioned the names of a few players who had dropped out of the game because they didn't put enough into it.

I always remember that conversation. It had a great influence over me. I worked hard, and I did make it. Ken was a great encouragement to the younger players. He would always take time to talk to them. He was a very humble man, a man who was a credit to the game.

There was another occasion, shortly after I joined, when he asked me to bowl to him. He was going through a bad trot, and we went to the nets and had a session, just me and him.

'If you see anything wrong, don't hesitate to tell me about it,' he said. He was a famous England cricketer, and I was a junior new to the game. I thought that was remarkable, really.

On the 1981 tour of the West Indies there wasn't really much to laugh about but there was plenty of humour, as there usually is when you're up against it. In Guyana we couldn't find a decent practice pitch, and Ken's job was to try and find one. Most days he would come in and say, 'I've got one. Just the job for you blokes.' But invariably it would fall through or it wasn't good enough. It became the joke in the party.

'Found a practice pitch today, Kenny?' the players would say. Eventually he did find one, and it was a good one. But we were about to leave the country by that time.

John Jameson

The former Warwickshire and England opening batsman is now a coach at Taunton School.

No batsman likes being run out, and Kenny was no exception. I remember playing with him in a second-eleven game when he was trying to get some match practice after breaking a toe.

The fellow at the other end called him for a bad one, and he was run out by a long way. As he left the middle he said, 'Amateurs!'

[*Footnote: Ken Barrington was run out 21 times, out of the 695 times he was dismissed during his career.*]

Brian Johnston

The much-loved BBC personality and commentator went on many tours with Ken Barrington.

Ken and I had a standard greeting when we met. I used to say, "Hello, Barrers' and he replied, 'Hello, Johnners, how's your right tit?'

It started when we played a charity match together at Stellenbosch in South Africa in 1965, Mike Smith's tour when England won 1–0 against a very good Springbok side.

I was keeping wicket, and Ken was bowling his leggers, and there was a fair amount of bounce in the pitch. He bowled, the batsman played and missed . . . and so did I. The ball bounced so high that it hit me on the right tit!

We had some great times on that trip. Ken was in his element, impersonating an Indian colonel and W.G. Grace when he batted, and Jim Laker when he bowled. He had Jim Laker off perfectly. He was a different person abroad. Always clowning and trying to amuse the crowd. The spectators loved him.

In the Third Test at Cape Town, which ended in a dull draw, he came on late in the South African second innings and took 3 wickets for 4 runs. I always felt he would have taken many more wickets if he had been used more.

South Africa made 501 in their first innings, with Eddie Barlow making 138 and Tony Pithey making 154. That was the Test which had the 'walking controversy'. There was an appeal against Eddie for a catch, but he stood his ground.

When a similar thing happened to Ken in England's first innings when he was 49, Ken walked. Ken was one of the last of the 'walkers'.

England kept the South Africans in the field for 11½ hours while scoring 442 in their first innings, and it was really a most boring Test match. Ken enlivened it with his bowling impersonations, and when he came out to open in the second innings with Geoff Boycott with half an hour remaining he treated the crowd to his full repertoire of Indian colonel and W.G. Grace acts.

In another Test, when Ken completed a century, I said, 'He is batting well now. But he had a bit of luck early on. He was dropped when two.' A woman wrote in deploring the carelessness of the modern mother!

Pauline and I were personal friends of Ken and Ann. I think Ken may have suspected he was living on borrowed time after his first heart-attack in 1968, and though he was very careful after that he enjoyed life immensely.

I bought cars from him, and you knew you were never going to be swindled. Just before he went to the West Indies he was bringing a car over for Pauline when he rang up and said, 'It's caught fire!' He was a lovely man.

Frank Keating

The Guardian *sports feature writer and author was born in 1937, and has been Fleet Street's Sportswriter of the Year, and also Columnist of the Year. He wrote a book,* Another Bloody Day in Paradise, *about the England tour to the West Indies in 1981, and this is what he wrote about Ken Barrington the day Ken died.*

He was the players' man, both spiritual and temporal. Each morning he gave them all their individual alarm calls. In the nets he bowled at them and followed through to cajole or advise with tiny hints of technique; always a smile; always relishing the day like mustard. Perhaps he knew there wasn't all that much time. On match days he was for ever lifting spirits and humping kit. In the evening his boys would gather themselves and a few beers around him and listen to the tales of long ago when cricket tours might have been to other planets for all these new jet-aged players knew.

Ken Barrington had done it all. The first of his twenty centuries for England had been here at Bridgetown. For a dozen years, till a first warning heart-attack in 1968 when doctors ordered him to take off his pads, he had squared his shoulders, jutted his jaw and come back for more; he was England's rock-solid, often unconsidered trellis around which the public's favourite fancy Dans and flash Harrys entwined their colourful summer blooms.

He was invariably up the other end, grim and determined as he conscientiously swept the stage for the entrance of the Mays and Cowdreys and Dexters and Graveneys, the last great quartet of the golden line of legend. They would not have done even half as much without Barrington.

I will never forget the mid-summer Monday in 1963 during that second Test match of unremitting tension at Lord's, the only time I saw Frank Worrell, remember. But if I couldn't recall his innings (to my shame) I can still see Kenny there. In the last innings England, needing 233 to win, lost Stewart, Edrich and Dexter to the blazing fires of Griffith and Hall with only 31 scored. Barrington and Cowdrey dug in and ducked and battled it out on into the afternoon. They were on the point of swinging the match with an epic stand when a withering delivery from Hall broke Cowdrey's forearm. Crack! At once Barrington, in answering fury and spontaneous hate, struck Hall for venomous one-bounce fours over mid-on.

The rage was on him in manic defence of his wounded officer – but then just as suddenly he took breath, tapped his gloved fist on his chest to relieve the palpitations of anger, calmed his soul to concentrate, and turned to stand again to see out the day in England's cause.

They always called him the Colonel, as befitted a soldier's son. But he was more of a kindly sergeant-major – without any bark or bite, mind you, just a large beak and larger beam. He first signed for Surrey as a leg-break bowler, but they soon realized that he had too much grit and guts to stay long messing about with his twiddly stuff. In the end it was a grim business he had worried and worked himself into. But after his ticker first complained at the unrelenting life at the top, he emerged to everybody's astonishment and joy from behind the ropes with one of the loveliest, hail-fellow natures that could be imagined. He built up a successful Surrey motor business, then asked if he could be of any more help to cricket.

As you know, we logged his malapropisms; some pinched-lip types thought we were sending him up. He loved it, and laughed back at himself. 'Well, Frank, you all know what I bloody mean, don't you?' And sometimes they were quite ingenuously perfect. Now his boys had to breakfast and prepare for a Test match only with the faith that he will 'sleep like a lark' in eternal peace.

Roger Knight

Captain of Surrey since 1978. First joined the Oval staff in 1965, made his debut in 1968 and left in 1970 to join Gloucester. He played for Gloucester until 1975, when he joined Sussex. Returned to Surrey in 1978. Now a schoolmaster at Dulwich College.

I played one or two second-eleven matches with Ken when he had his breakdown in 1966, otherwise I never played many games with him. One match sticks in my mind, a game at a very inhospitable ground. There were iron bars across the windows in the dressing-rooms, and he caught the mood of the place right away when he said, 'Cor, this place is like Parkhurst Prison!'

He was a legendary figure at the Oval at that time, but I remember he had no 'side' about him. He was the same to the junior players as he was to the senior staff and committee men.

When I became captain in 1978 he was always ready to offer advice when it was wanted but he would never push his opinions on me. I had a lot of time for him. He was an impressive person.

Alan Knott

Kent's record-breaking wicket-keeper, whose 263 dismissals in 93 Tests was a world record.

I remember Kenny as a great encourager of younger players. 'Deadly' Underwood and I were youngsters when he was in his prime, and he was always giving us advice.

He had the great ability to see the funny side of any situation, and didn't mind laughing at himself. I batted with him briefly during the Headingley Test in 1968, after which he was dropped for the second time for slow scoring.

He was giving it the grind in front of a big Saturday afternoon crowd. Alan Connolly was swinging it about all over the place. Kenny told me not to worry. 'No one else is getting any runs,' he said.

He would say things like: 'At this rate, this bat will do me for the next ten years.'

He was very strict. 'Deadly' and I were late for practice one morning, and he gave us a right rollicking. He was like that as a senior pro. Everything had to be right and you had to be on time. If you had a broken lace, he'd have a go at you.

Jim Laker

Laker's career at the Oval between 1946 and 1965 overlapped Ken Barrington's. In that time he took 1,944 wickets at a cost of 18·40. His feats for England were legendary – 19 wickets in a Test at Old Trafford in 1956 at a cost of 90 runs, and 193 wickets in 46 Tests at a cost of 21·24.

Shortly after visiting the West Indies early in 1981 Jim Laker needed surgery after falling ill, and to the delight of his many friends made a full recovery. He was one of Ken Barrington's closest friends.

Ken was a bit of a tapper in his early days. He was a bowler who liked batting, and used to score a lot of runs in Second Eleven and Club and Ground cricket.

In 1954 he was brought back to the side after being dropped, and he and I put on 198 for the eighth wicket, seven short of the county record set by Tom Hayward and Len Braund in the 1890s. I made a hundred – one of two I made in my career – and he scored his maiden hundred.

It was a greenish pitch, and I joined him when Surrey were about 70–6 and he was 30 not out. 'I'll have a belt now,' he said.

I told him to get his head down, and he did. There were a number of occasions in the next few years when I had to tell him not to throw his wicket away.

Being left out after his Test debut in 1955 changed his attitude. He realized that if he were going to play regularly for England he would have to score runs consistently, so he started eliminating the risky shots and became a different player.

I got to know him well from his early days at Surrey because I used to give him a lift to Paddington Station most nights. He didn't have a car in those days, but he soon saved up and bought a second-hand banger. He used to spruce it up and treat it like a Rolls-Royce.

He was the most orderly and meticulous person I ever knew. To watch him pack his long, old-fashioned cricket bag was truly an experience. Everything would be immaculately laid out, the shirts and trousers looking as though he had just taken them out of the laundry.

Most of us used to throw our things in the bag and rush off, but not Kenny. Everything had to be in its place. Nothing was too much trouble. He took great pride in all his possessions, and looked after them.

Micky Stewart tells that story about the time he called at Kenny's house in Mitcham. Kenny was a great do-it-yourself man, and was up a ladder stripping some wallpaper.

'Hello, decorating again?' asked Micky. 'No,' replied Kenny, 'we're moving house tomorrow.'

That little house in Mitcham was where he changed his approach to batting in the early Sixties. I know how it happened because I called round and he explained why he was changing to a two-eyed stance.

He was concerned about the imminent trip to Australia, and felt that Alan Davidson's bowling from left arm over the wicket, with its mastery of in-swing, would be a problem.

With the aid of two kitchen chairs and a broom-handle, he proved to me that he could counter Davidson. A lot of other players tried to copy him, but didn't have the same success. His tactics certainly worked. He finished top of the England averages with 582 runs for an average of 72·75. Davo was top of the Australian bowling averages with 24 wickets, but he only got Kenny out twice in the series.

Kenny was proud that everything he achieved in life – which was quite considerable – came through his own hard work. His fierce determination, his guts and bravery, were always evident. But most remarkable of all, and something so rare, he didn't make a single enemy on the way. Many hard-bitten old pros openly cried when they heard the news of his death.

Peter Laker

Cricket correspondent of the Daily Mirror, *who went on most of the overseas tours when Ken Barrington was either manager or assistant manager. Ken was famous for his malapropisms, his unintentional misuse of the English language. It was one of his funniest features, endearing him to cricketers all over the world. The stories about his* faux pas *are legion, and Peter Laker, one of his best friends, was the leading authority.*

One of the ones I liked best was Kenny's comment to Mike Brearley after a particularly torrid day against the Australians' fast bowlers. 'It's a good job we had those helmets,' said Kenny, 'otherwise there could have been some fertilities!'

Or the one at a reception in Pakistan when the players crowded round a buffet. 'Look at them,' he said. 'They're like a plague of lotuses!' He told the story of some crowd trouble in Bangalore. 'It was all right, though,' he said, 'because the police had sent in to mingle with the crowd two hundred plain-clothes protectives.'

One day he was helping Mike Hendrick with his bowling in the nets. Mike was bowling too short, and Kenny told him to pitch it up more, which he did. 'You've got the batsman in two man's land now,' said Kenny.

One of his favourite phrases was 'he didn't know whether to stick or twist'. When we were in the West Indies in 1981 I asked the manager Alan Smith whether he could comment on the Trevor Chappell underarm bowling incident in Australia. 'Sorry,' said Alan, 'I can't comment on that.'

I asked Kenny if he would like to say something. 'Oh no,' he said, 'I think I'll twist on what the manager said.'

His usual reply when asked if he had had a good night's sleep was: 'Not half, I slept like a lark!'

In Australia Kenny umpired a practice session under lights and gave three batsmen out lbw. 'It caused a commotion, I can tell you,' he said. 'It raised a few eyelashes.'

We were at a function on the same tour, and Sir Don Bradman was sitting with us at the same table. Kenny was telling a story about how someone came through some doors into a bar. He wasn't sure of the right word. 'You know,' he said, 'those sling doors.' The Don was rolling about with laughter!

After one of the England bowlers had bowled well in a Test, he said, 'That was good bowling on any side of the fence.' On another occasion he said, 'That was good bowling in anyone's cup of tea.'

Kenny was telling a story about Charlie Griffith once, and he said, 'The ball came at me like a high philosophy bullet.'

When the England team was at Heathrow before the 1981 trip some of the lads were ribbing Kenny about his cars, and the way he insisted that everyone should buy British. Graham Stevenson said he had a Japanese car because it was more reliable.

'You!' said Kenny. 'You're like a kamahari pilot!' One breakfast-time in the Hilton Hotel in Port of Spain, Kenny was sitting with Bernard Thomas, and had difficulty in reading the menu in the half-light. Bernie suggested he borrow the glasses of a man who was sitting at the next table.

Kenny took his advice and asked the man if he could borrow his glasses. The man was only too pleased to oblige. 'Here,' said Kenny, 'you need good eyesight to see through these!'

There are always practical jokes on cricket tours, and one I remember about Kenny was at Hyderabad in 1978 when Wasim Bari insisted on batting on against England until twenty minutes before the close of the next to last day, enabling England to bat out the final day and avoid defeat.

I wrote out a dummy Telex message saying that Ken Barrington, the England manager, had described Wasim's refusal to declare earlier as the biggest act of cowardice he had encountered in his long career in cricket. I took it to Kenny later and said, 'I couldn't find you earlier, but the lads told me this was how you felt, so I sent it off.'

Kenny's neck shot out as it often did in moments of crisis. 'I didn't say this,' he said. 'But the lads said you did,' I said. 'Ah well, I might have said it privately, but I don't want that published.'

'Can we not stop it?' 'Sorry,' I said. 'It's too late. It's in the paper by now.' Anyone else would have lost his temper, but Kenny was such a gentleman that he kept reasonably calm. 'What can we do to stop it?' he said. In the end Terry Brindle of the *Yorkshire Post* and I couldn't help bursting out into loud guffaws, and Kenny realized it was only a joke.

Later Terry typed out another message saying the future of the tour had been put in jeopardy by critical remarks made by Ken Barrington. Kenny grabbed it and tore it up. 'You don't know these blokes out here,' he said. 'They might not see the joke!'

Once he was showing some of us some old pictures of his younger days, black hair standing up. 'I look like one of those Guardsmen outside Buckingham Palace,' he said. 'What's it they have on their heads? Fuzzbies or something?'

When it was raining hard, as it does in those hot countries, he used to say, 'It's coming down like pea-pods!'

Tony Lewis

The former England and Glamorgan captain is now a broadcaster.

I was interviewing Kenny on *Sport on Four*, and we were talking about some of the peculiar grounds we had played at in our careers.

I'd just reached the point where I was relating the story of the time I played at Ebbw Vale when sheep came on the pitch when Kenny said, 'That's nothing. I was playing in Israel once when suddenly this woman carrying her shopping walked right across the thoroughpath!'

We both had a good laugh, as I'm sure the listeners did. Kenny had this endearing habit of mixing his words up, but no matter how distorted his comments, the truth always came out and everyone understood him.

There was that time in Sydney when he invited me into his bedroom for a cup of tea and a chat. He fiddled about with the seams of some cricket balls as we talked about the modern preponderance of fast bowling, and the West Indian quartet of Colin Croft, Andy Roberts, Mike Holding and Joel Garner in particular.

'It's like putting all your eggs in one summer!' he said.

I chuckled. The word he should have used was 'basket', but when I thought about it, 'summer' was probably more appropriate.

David Lloyd

The Lancashire and England left-hand batsman.

Ken was manager of the Derrick Robins XI which I captained in 1976. The one thing that sticks in my mind was that every wicket we played on in South Africa was referred to in the same way by Ken.

'If I was batting on that I'd book in for bed and breakfast,' he said, meaning they would never get him out, and none of us would argue with that.

He had some hilarious team meetings. He'd tell us that he had 'taken care of this and that, bits and pieces, and odds and ends'. We would all say 'thanks', not knowing what he had been talking about!

Peter Loader

The ex-Surrey fast bowler who played thirteen Tests for England between 1954 and 1958. He now runs a mini-bus firm in Perth, and commentates on cricket for a television company.

Kenny was a very talkative fellow on the field. There was one game, against Hampshire, when he was fielding in the covers and another talkative character, Bernie Constable, was mid-wicket.

The batsman was a bit of a hitter. I can't remember his name. Kenny said, 'I've played against this fellow before in the second eleven. He's very good on the off. You'll need another one on this side.'

Bernie interrupted. 'He's stronger on the leg. You'll need another fielder this side.' Stuart Surridge, the captain, looked up in the air and said, 'I don't know what has come over my side. They're all going mad.'

I just carried on bowling, disregarding both bits of advice! Kenny was just making a name for himself in my final years at the Oval.

He was a very superstitious person. Before going in he used to lay out his gear on the shelf in the players' room – his gloves, his cap and his packet of cigarettes all in the neat line.

If someone disturbed his row of possessions he would get very angry. And woe betide anyone who tried to nick a cigarette! The rest of the players used to tease him a lot.

Arnold Long

The former Surrey and Sussex wicket-keeper retired at the end of the 1980 season. He played for Surrey between 1959 and 1975, and knew Ken Barrington as a friend and colleague. He is now a director of Arnold Long and Co. Ltd, insurance brokers.

Kenny had a wonderful personality, but there were times when he became annoyed. One of them was during a Bank Holiday game against Nottinghamshire at the Oval when I came on as substitute and dropped a catch off his bowling at square leg. The batsman was Cyril Poole. Kenny had a right go at me! He took a great pride in his bowling.

The time he was really upset was when Fred Trueman 'caught' him in his benefit match against Yorkshire in 1964. Kenny was 8 when he played a ball from Ray Illingworth towards FS – Trueman – at short leg and FS dived and claimed the catch. Kenny was a walker, and he walked when FS said he'd caught it.

But the newspapers published a picture the next day which showed the ball falling out of FS's hand. It looked a bit suspicious, and I don't think Kenny took to that too kindly, especially as it was his benefit match.

Kenny had a fetish about medium-pacers. If anyone was going to tie him down it was a medium-pacer. And his pet hate was Brian Crump, the little seamer who used to play for Northamptonshire. Crumpy became a nightmare to Kenny. He probably got him out more than any other bowler.

'Oh, Christ, not him again,' Kenny used to say. Crumpy used to tie him down by moving the ball just a bit off the seam. He'd whack Kenny on the pads, and Kenny used to say, 'I wish I could get you on a flat pitch out in Australia, I'd see you off!'

In English conditions Crumpy was a very effective bowler, and he could bat a bit too.

Kenny was a compulsive talker in the slips. We used to have this discussion about which golf-club we would use to hit the ball over certain landmarks at the Oval. Kenny always said he could hit an iron-shot over the gasworks if he had the ball teed up high enough.

If things got a bit dull we would gee him up with remarks like,

'What iron would you take to put it over Archbishop Tenison's School?' and things like that. He was an expert on aeroplanes, and would identify for us every plane that flew over the Oval during play.

He was very strong, with big shoulders and forearms. I think that was why he hit the ball so hard. Dave Sydenham, the left-arm bowler who played for us, was always geeing Kenny up, and Kenny used to threaten him and say, 'I'll give you the six-incher.' Meaning the knock-out punch which travelled just six inches.

One day they were larking about at tea and Kenny actually did give him the six-incher. He caught Dave on the shoulder, and when we went out after tea Dave couldn't bowl!

Another memory I have of Kenny is the pride he used to take in his cars. At one time he used to have two cars – a brand-new Rover and an Austin Cambridge. If it was raining he wouldn't take the Rover out of the garage!

Ken Barrington's benefit in 1964 raised £10,656. His first charity match was attended by just 29 people, and he lost money. But like everything he did, he worked hard at it, and by 1964 standards £10,656 was a considerable amount for a cricketer's benefit.

Ken Mackay

The Australian all-rounder whom Ken Barrington was always mimicking. 'Slasher' – so called because he was primarily a defensive batsman – was one of the leading characters in world cricket between 1956 and 1961 when he played 37 Tests for Australia.

During the Fifth Test against England at the Oval in 1961 I plugged through 68, and I received a rare compliment from Ken.

His frequently expressed admiration for my bowling was never so eloquent as when he turned to Wally Grout during one of my overs and said, 'Is it Slasher's birthday, Wal? He bowled me a half-volley!'

Ken and I were in agreement about walking. Many batsmen claim that by staying they are merely compensating for earlier or future wrong decisions. Ken and I argued with some Australian officials about the ethics of walking when Ken was in Australia with Ted Dexter's side in 1962–3. They maintained that the batsman should act only on the umpire's decision. If he knew he had touched the ball and was given not out he should, according to them, remain at the crease.

Ken's comment was typical of him. 'If I stayed at the wicket when I knew I had touched the ball, I couldn't possibly enjoy any runs I might make later,' he said.

In my last Test in Adelaide in 1963 I had to open the bowling with Graham McKenzie because Alan Davidson was injured. My first ball was to the Rev. David Sheppard, an outswinger which the Rev. nicked straight to Richie Benaud in the slips.

The ball popped out of Richie's hands towards Bobby Simpson at first slip. Bobby dived at it, but Wally Grout went over the top of him and caught the ball inches off the ground. A great juggling act!

Ken was the incoming batsman as the fielders (who were all sprawled on the ground) sorted themselves out. As Ken got to the pitch he looked at them and said, 'You fellas should be on at the Palladium!' To me Ken Barrington was a great bloke as well as a fine cricketer.

Robin Marlar

Former Sussex captain and now cricket writer of The Sunday Times.

I first met The Colonel when I was at Harrow School. Tom Barling, the former Surrey player who was the coach, invited one of the ground-staff lads down to show us how to bowl leg-breaks.

It was Ken Barrington, and I remember he bowled us all out in the nets that day. John Thicknesse of the *Standard* was there that year, and Kenny bowled him a few times too.

Peter May CBE

Born in Reading, as was Ken Barrington, and played for Reading Cricket Club, as Barrington did, before becoming established as a professional at the Oval.

He was eleven months the senior. They came from different backgrounds and made it to the top by different routes. May, more gifted, was possibly England's finest all-round post-War player, scoring 4,537 runs for England in 66 Tests, in 41 of which he was captain, a world record. May retired at the age of thirty-three, a rare case of a player quitting when still at the height of his powers. He is now a successful business-man, chairman of the Test selectors and Past President of the MCC.

I was at the other end when Kenny made his debut for England at Trent Bridge against the South Africans in 1955. With half an hour to go, we were 200–2, and I was batting with Denis Compton, Kenny was number five in the order.

At nine minutes past six, Denis was lbw to Neil Adock at 228–3, and in came Kenny. He was obviously very nervous, and pushed his first delivery into the off-side and tried to run. There was no run, and I sent him back.

Off the fourth ball he received he tried to force a shortish delivery from Eddie Fuller on the off-side off the back foot and edged a catch to John Waite, who was standing up. Like many more very good

Test players, Kenny had started his international career with a duck. Perhaps I should have run that first run!

It was mentioned that perhaps I should have asked Frank Tyson, the nightwatchman, to come in and not Kenny. It was a debut for me as well, as England captain. But I always felt nightwatchmen were something of a myth. If you look at it logically, a nightwatchman is more likely to get out than an accredited batsman, and if he does get out, you are back to square one.

A good player should be able to go out and face the final overs. I was never one for using nightwatchmen.

It was me who persuaded Kenny to field close to the wicket. He was an exceptionally fine catcher. When he started at Surrey he was an outfielder with a very good arm, but one day I said to him, 'Why don't you try fielding close?'

He made such a good job of it that he never looked back. He held some terrific catches in the slips. The first season he made the change, he took sixty catches.

Arthur McIntyre

The former Surrey wicket-keeper, coach and manager, who now lives in retirement at New Milton, Hampshire.

One day Surrey were playing in a Bank Holiday Monday fixture against Nottinghamshire at Trent Bridge, and in those days – the Fifties – they always had a military band playing during the lunch interval. Kenny and I were not out at lunch, and when we came out for the resumption Kenny said, 'Come on, Arthur, let's march them out.'

So we marched out to the wicket like soldiers with our bats over our shoulders like rifles. The crowd loved it. But they didn't like it quite so much when both of us went on and scored centuries!

I was responsible for Kenny being promoted from four or five to number three in the order. When I took over from Andrew Sandham as coach at the Oval in 1958 I suggested he ought to bat higher up because he used to get in such a state while waiting to bat. He would sit smoking away and chewing gum and often would be reading the paper upside down! With less time to wait when he went in three, he wasn't so nervous.

He was always very appreciative if you could point out deficiencies in his technique. In 1965 he was having a bad run, and just before a Test he gave up a day off to come to the Oval to try and sort things out. He practised on a pitch at one end of the square and David Sydenham, who bowled left-arm over the wicket, bowled him three times in an over with well-pitched-up deliveries.

I told him I thought he was taking his bat farther to the off-side with every tap as he waited for the bowler to come in, tapping his bat impatiently on the ground. He had opened up his stance, and that accentuated what was wrong. He was picking up his bat towards gully and coming down across the line of the ball. He was very grateful for my advice . . . and proceeded to score 137 in 7¼ hours at Edgbaston, and was dropped as a disciplinary measure by the selectors!

He was just the same at golf. I played with him in his early days, when he first played the game as a 24-year-old with a 24 handicap. He picked golf up very quickly, and in a few years became a very good five-handicap golfer. He often said he would have liked to have been a pro, but I don't think he had the temperament for that. I couldn't imagine him sinking a ten-foot putt if there was £10,000 on it!

I remember one of his early games at Wimbledon Park. We were playing a couple of chaps, and they had to give Kenny a few shots because he was playing off 24 at the time. At the first hole, a dog-leg to the left, Kenny hit a huge shot right over the trees and it landed on the green. It must have gone all of three hundred yards. The other fellows were livid, and they kept moaning about his handicap right through the round.

Kenny could hit the ball big distances, usually accurately, but he never worried about his ball. He would always say, 'Where's my tee?' He never liked losing his tee.

Colin Milburn

The England opening batsman was a playing contemporary of Ken Barrington's. 'Ollie' was one of the most exciting batsmen produced in the post-War years, but his Test career was cut short at the age of twenty-seven when a car crash cost him the sight in one eye. He had played in just nine Tests.

I was with Kenny when he had his first heart-attack. I was partnering him in a double-wicket contest in Melbourne in 1968. We had just beaten Charlie Griffith and Rohan Kanhai. Suddenly he went white as a sheet.

The next thing, they'd taken him off to hospital for tests and he was all wired up when I went to see him. If you can have such a thing as a good heart-attack, then this was a good heart-attack. It wasn't very severe. Just a warning.

The doctors told him to slow down, and he took their advice. He never played first-class cricket again, although he made a full recovery, and was superbly fit.

It was two years or so before he started playing the odd charity match. He played more golf. He was a golf nut. I don't really know why he was struck down. He was so active and fit. But he did worry a lot about cricket. He'd worry about all kind of things.

He was a great averages man. He would worry about getting out. He'd worry about his average. He used to think that if you averaged 45 you were a better player than someone who averaged 35. I didn't agree with that. You could get a few not outs and boost your average and a lot depended on the conditions and the state of the game. I don't think averages tell the whole story, but Kenny thought they were important.

That day in Melbourne Charlie Griffith didn't try and bounce him although he bounced one or two at me. Kenny had this thing about Charlie. In 1966 he was quoted in a newspaper article as saying that Charlie's action was suspect. At Trent Bridge we were in the dressing-room when Doug Insole came in and said, 'Kenny's not playing.'

I was amazed. Physically, he looked in great shape but he got himself into a bit of a state about Charlie. He let it get him down, and he didn't play for a month. He wasn't frightened of Charlie. He was as brave a player against fast bowling as you'd ever seen. But the situation got on top of him. He was that type of person.

When he met Charlie later he got on well with him, and they were great mates. Kenny got on with everyone. He was a bloke who didn't have a single enemy.

Charlie's all right. In 1963 and 1966 when he toured England you couldn't speak to him, he was so moody. He had this outsize chip on his shoulder. A terrible fellow he was then!

Wes Hall was the life and soul of the party and Charlie just sulked. Now Wes is an MP in Barbados and has sobered down a lot, whereas Charlie has come right out of his shell and is a great bloke now.

Even after he retired, Kenny worried about cricket, and when he became assistant manager to the England team he did the worrying for the players. He had this father-son relationship with them. I was in Barbados when he died. That day he had bowled in the nets for an hour, and looked so fit for his age. He was fantastic for a fifty-year-old.

I was staggered when I heard the news. I shouldn't think there has been a more popular cricketer. He was so funny when he wanted to be.

Keith Miller

The great Australian all-rounder now works in public relations in Newport Beach, New South Wales, Australia.

Although I knew him for years, I'm buggered if I can think of a solitary thing to say about him except saying as we all do that he was a beaut bloke.

Alan Moss

The former Middlesex and England bowler played nine times for England between 1956 and 1960.

We were coming back from the West Indies in 1960 and landed at New York to find that we had a seven-hour wait and a change of aircraft.

We eventually took off in a Comet. I was seated – goodness knows why – next to the manager, R. W. V. Robins, and Kenny was seated behind me. The aircraft took off as steeply as I have ever gone into the air, but at the same time it seemed to be screwing its way into the sky and Kenny leaned forward to me and said, 'For goodness' sake, Mossy, go and see the pilot and tell him to do the loop-the-loop and get it over and done with.'

This really typifies to me Ken Barrington, because although he didn't like flying, he could still see the funny side of things.

John Murray

A former England and Middlesex wicket-keeper whose 21 Tests between 1961 and 1967 were played with Ken Barrington in the same side. For a short time 'J.T.' was a Test selector with Ken.

The 'Colonel' bit started in 1964 in Rhodesia, the last MCC tour there. We were at a cocktail party at this military club enjoying a drink with some of the officers when I stepped back to allow a lady to pass. I stepped into a lily pond . . . miraculously, my gin and tonic was still upright in my hand as I landed.

Kenny shouted, 'Sergeant-Major!' And I shouted back, 'Sir!' Kenny was the Colonel, and I was his Sergeant-Major. Kenny had a great time talking about his Army experiences at that party.

It came from his father. His father was a professional soldier and Kenny knew all about serving in the Army. During his National Service he rose to being a lance-corporal in the Berkshire Regiment in Germany, but he never made the rank of colonel!

We had so many laughs together, particularly on tours. There was that time we were staying in a Retreat in Kanpur, a marble building which had every kind of luxury, including a swimming-pool equipped with a wave machine, but unfortunately no water.

Not being able to use the pool, we had to seek other ways of filling our time. We were lounging around one day when a couple of porters came in and Kenny said, 'Do you have a snooker table?'

The men couldn't understand. 'You know, snooker,' said Kenny, and he demonstrated a snooker shot. 'Ah yes,' said one of the men. He went off and a little later came back with one of those air spray guns which he started pumping furiously.

Another story I remember about Kenny was the time we were

On the way to recovery from a heart-attack in Melbourne in 1968. The card that Ann is holding up was sent by Charlie Griffith, an old adversary from the days when Ken said his bowling action was suspect. In his later years Ken was a firm friend of the Barbadian fast bowler.
Sun Pictorial, Melbourne

Ken and Ann looking at an X-ray taken after his heart-attack in 1968. They are on a balcony at the empty Oval, his second home.
Central Press Photos

Alec Bedser, chairman of the selectors, makes a point to his fellow-selectors as they sit on the top deck of the pavilion at Lord's. Between Bedser and Ken are Sir Len Hutton, former captain of England, and Charlie Elliott, the ex-Derbyshire batsman and Test umpire.
Central Press Photos

A meeting with the then Prime Minister James Callaghan in Pakistan in 1977. The England players are Mike Brearley, the captain, and Bob Willis. Ken was the England manager.

›nning the gloves for a net with the England players at the Nursery, Lord's, in 1980. It was one of : last occasions he batted at cricket's headquarters. He delighted in practising with the England ıyers. He worked as hard as any one of them, though he was twice their age. He loved batting and loved bowling. Notice the immaculately pressed shirt. Ken Barrington never went near a cricket ch unless he was smartly attired.

:ick Eagar

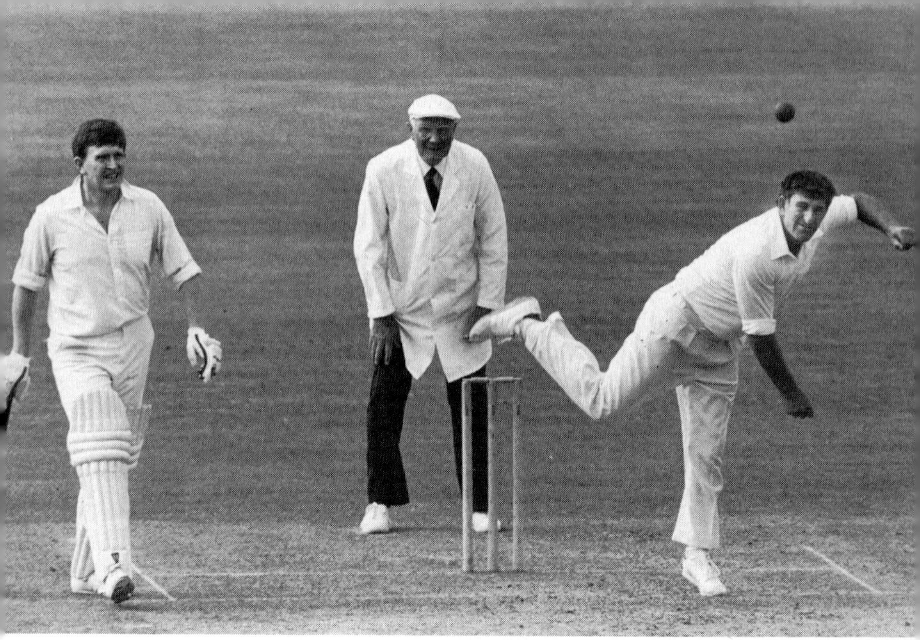

The last time he bowled at The Oval . . . for the Old England XI against Old Australia in 1980. He bowled seven overs and failed to take a wicket, but the spin and guile was still there. And there wasn't much wrong with that action! The batsman is Keith Stackpole and the umpire John Langridge.
Patrick Eagar

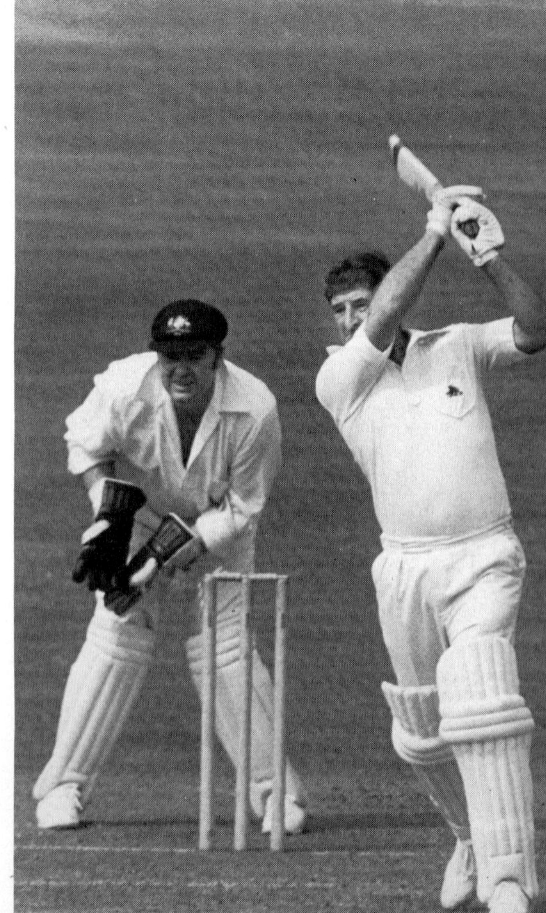

Hitting out in the Old England *v*. Old Australia match at The Oval. Ken made 45 before being caught by Neil Harvey off the bowling of Grahame Corling. Barry Jarman is the wicket-keeper.
Patrick Eagar

:lectorial conference at the Nursery before the start of play in the first one-day international
nst the West Indies in 1980. Alec Bedser and Charlie Elliott join Ian Botham and Ken as they
uss which player to leave out.
:k Eagar

› record-breaking England batsmen. When Ken managed the England side that toured
istan and New Zealand in 1977-8, Boycott was the vice-captain under Mike Brearley, and took
: when Brearley broke an arm in Pakistan.

Ken dealing with an inquiry from the freelance cricket writer and broadcaster Henry Blofeld in Nagpur on the 1976-7 tour of india.
Patrick Eagar

The England side that toured Australia in 1979-80. Back row from left to right, John Emburey, Ken, Phil Edmonds, Bob Taylor, Graham Gooch, Geoff Boycott (significantly the only player without his track-suit top), Mike Brearley, Bob Willis, Mike Hendrick, Chris Old, Geoff Miller, Ian Botham; front row, Doug Insole, manager, Clive Radley, Derek Randall, Roger Tolchard, Bernard Thomas (physiotherapist), David Gower and John Lever.

Ken fulfils an ambition at a fancy-dress party in Australia in 1978 when he assumes the role of drum-major. Next to him in the helmet is Mike Hendrick, and in the background Roger Tolchard and Bob Taylor.

Surveying the luggage as the England team prepare to make a hurried departure from Guyana after 'The Robin Jackman Affair' in February 1981. The players with Ken are Mike Gatting and David Bairstow.
Patrick Eagar

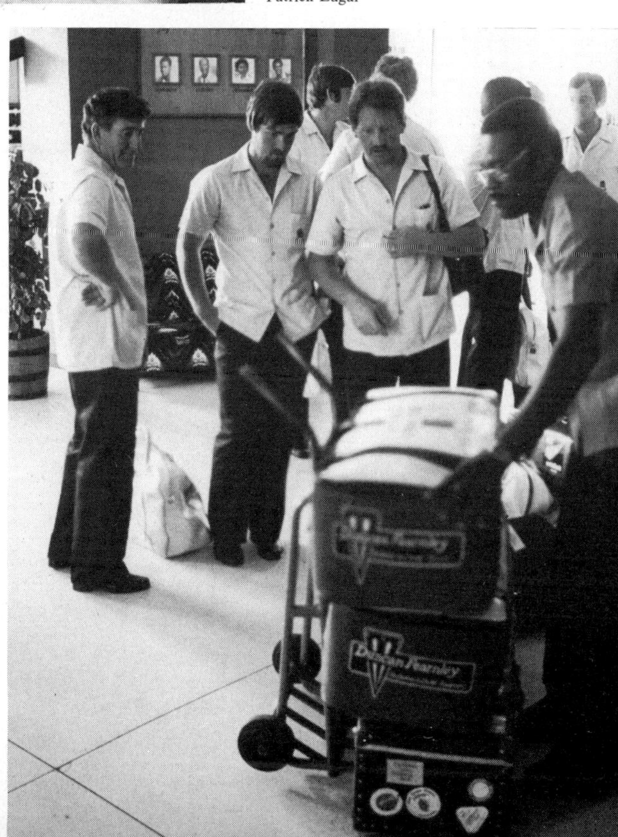

The England and West Indies teams, plus officials, bow their heads as a minute's silence is observed at the Kensington Oval, Bridgetown, Barbados, the day after Ken died. Most of the players were deeply moved, and their hearts were no longer in the game.
Patrick Eagar

Ann with the handsome cup, named after Ken, which the Lord's Taverners are presenting each year in their national Under-13 competition.
Daily Express

playing in Adelaide and he had been batting all day and was about 70 not out. It was very hot, about 110 degrees.

Fred Titmus went out to join him in the middle, and Kenny said to him: 'It's perishing hot out here, Fred. We've got to cut out the quick singles.'

'Okay,' said Fred. 'We'll cut out your quick singles.'

Alan Oakman

The former Sussex and England all-rounder is now coach of Warwickshire.

The game was Surrey *v.* Sussex at the Oval, and John Snow was playing one of his first matches for Sussex. Snowey took a wicket, and in came Ken Barrington.

After facing a few deliveries, Ken turned to Jim Parks, who was keeping wicket, and said, 'I thought this chap was supposed to be quick.'

Jim didn't say anything, but at the end of the next over Alec Bedser, then a Test selector, arrived on the balcony. We told John Snow that he ought to try and impress Alec, and John's next three overs were about the quickest overs he bowled that season.

Halfway through this blistering attack, Kenny turned to Jim Parks and said, 'I thought you were supposed to be a friend of mine. In fact, I've decided you are a——.'

The other recollection I have of Ken was him agreeing to be photographed batting like W.G. Grace. We managed to get a very old type of cricket cap with a very tiny peak, stuffed a pillow down his trousers (which were held up by a tie), provided him with a beard and he proceeded to give a hilarious exhibition of batting like the Grand Old Man.

I was laughing so much that I wouldn't have been able to hold the ciné camera steady had it not been on a tripod. I still have the film, but unfortunately Kenny never saw it.

Ken Palmer

The former Somerset and England all-rounder is now a Test umpire. Palmer, a medium-pace bowler, was a bowler Ken Barrington always respected.

Somerset were playing Surrey at the Oval, and conditions were helping Bill Alley and me. The ball was doing a bit both ways, and Kenny kept playing and missing. He was missing up to four deliveries an over, and was becoming more and more exasperated.

Bill was really bowling well that day. Finally, at the end of another over during which he had been unable to put bat on ball, Kenny came down the pitch to Bill and offering him his bat, said, 'Here, you bat and I'll bowl!'

Another funny story I remember about Kenny was when I played against him for the MCC against the England touring party in July 1963 at Lord's. I was fielding in the slips next to Colin Milburn, and Kenny was having a hard time against Derek Shackleton.

Shack was a master at moving the ball late. There was no one better in the game than him when it came to moving the ball about. Poor Kenny couldn't hit the ball off the square, hard though he tried.

Suddenly we heard this booming voice from the pavilion balcony. 'Hit out or get out, Barrington,' it said. We looked up and saw it was Lord Nugent, President of the MCC!

I don't think Kenny was too pleased. He gave his lordship a bit of a stare!

Peter Parfitt

The former Middlesex and England batsman now lives and owns a pub and restaurant in Earby, Yorkshire.

John Murray, Fred Titmus and I went on a number of tours with Kenny, and when we played against each other the following season we would always have a natter.

One game Kenny came in and as he took guard, said to us, 'If you've got anything to say, say it now because I want to concentrate on my batting.'

Fred came up to bowl . . . and proceeded to bowl him round his legs. Kenny was a wonderful character, and I always enjoyed playing with and against him.

Another story I recall about him was the time when we shared a room on a tour of India. We were staying at a hotel in Old Delhi, and when we got to our room to inspect the beds we found that they sagged in the middle.

'Can't have this,' said Kenny. 'We'll have to get this changed.' He sent for the bearers and explained what he wanted: a hard, firm bed. Everything takes a long time to happen in India, and when we came back from the day's play Kenny found his bed was boarded up. They'd nailed boards across it! If I remember right, Kenny spent the night sleeping on his mattress on the floor!

Jim Parks

The former Sussex, Somerset and England wicketkeeper-batsman went on several tours with Ken and played with him in many Test Matches.

Ken was a very nervous character, and most times when he came into bat wouldn't speak to anyone until he had got into double figures.

He would then turn round and say good morning to everyone.

I remember one Sussex *v.* Surrey game at the Oval when he came into bat and struggled to make runs. I talked to him from behind the stumps non-stop without getting a response.

Eventually Ken turned to the umpire and said, 'Can't you stop this so-and-so talking while I get some runs?'

I was with him in India, where he used to get the crowd going with his imitations, and I remember the time in Cape Town in the 1964–5 tour when the Test was drawing to a quiet close. Ken decided to entertain the crowd with his Jim Laker impersonation, and proceeded to take 3 wickets for four runs in 3.1 overs.

As he bowled them out so quickly, about twenty minutes' batting time was left, and Ken was persuaded to do his 'Colonel' act. He padded his stomach, put an MCC tie round his waist and went out and did his famous net act in the middle, scoring 14 not out and delighting the crowd.

Kenny was one of our greatest post-War batsmen. Certainly overseas there was no one to touch him in my time, and his tragic death was a terrible loss. I can't think of anyone with more enthusiasm for the game of cricket.

Pat Pocock

The 35-year-old Surrey off-spin bowler is one of the characters in the modern game. Known as 'Percy', Pocock is a distant descendant of W.G. Grace's mother. He is one of cricket's great raconteurs. Many experts say he was unlucky not to have played more than 17 Tests. He made his Surrey debut in 1964, and had four seasons with Kenny before the Melbourne heart attack ended Kenny's first-class career.

There are loads of stories about Kenny, but the one I like the best is the bee story. Kenny was bowling in a county match, and a bee kept buzzing around his head. He kept flicking it away, and after a while he managed to stun it.

Kenny wasn't bowling very well at the time, and the interruption came as a relief to the fielders who were having to chase about retrieving the ball.

As the bee lay on the ground Kenny said, 'What are we going to do with it?' He didn't want to kill it. One of the umpires had a piece of paper in his pocket and said, 'Here, pick it up with this.' Kenny duly picked it up and said, 'Now what are we going to do with it?'

Bernie Constable, who was fielding some way away, shouted, 'Stick it down on a length. It will be quite safe there!'

I always had the same conversation with Kenny on the field. He used to say, 'It is turning?' 'Yes, it's turning,' I replied. 'Are you spinning it?' he asked. 'Yes,' I said. 'I'm spinning it.'

'What the hell for?' he said. Probably an even funnier story than the bee one was in Jamaica when I toured the West Indies with him in 1967–8. It was an uproarious incident if you were actually there.

Kenny was lying on the treatment table having some treatment, and unbeknown to him, Colin Milburn had left a big wad of sticky chewing gum on the couch. Kenny didn't realize it, but the chewing gum had stuck to his testicles, and by the time he got up it had set hard.

He had no idea what it was, and feared the worst. I can always remember him sitting in the bath with a pair of nail clippers in his hand trying to cut it off!

Most of the Surrey players had stories about batting with him. In one game Kenny was 159 not out and he was batting with Stewart Storey. Micky Stewart, who was captain at the time, wanted a faster scoring rate, and sent a message out to the batsmen to get on with it.

Kenny and Stewart had a chat, and Kenny said, 'You'd better have a go because I'm not timing it very well!' Stewart hadn't got many, and Kenny was 150 not out!

I had a similar experience with him myself in my first championship game. 'Cha Cha' Forbes was bowling and I got an edge to third man to get off the mark. Kenny was 177 not out at the time.

We had a chat and he said, 'Are you going to stay with me until I get my 200?' 'Yes, I'll try,' I said. Anyway, I didn't face a ball after that as he proceeded to reach 200.

When he reached his target he said, 'All right, you can have a go now!' I'd faced one ball in my debut innings and he was 200 not out!

John Price

The former Middlesex and England pace bowler played fifteen times for England between 1963 and 1972.

Middlesex were playing Surrey at Lord's in 1966 and Ken was in the middle of one of his first spells, during which he collected three first-ballers in three weeks, more than in the previous eighteen years of his career.

He was out first ball in the first innings – much to his disappointment – and in the second innings was going much better, having reached 20, when I hit him a painful blow on the inside of the knee and he collapsed in agony.

He didn't get much sympathy from his many friends and England team-mates in the Middlesex side. John Murray said, 'It's that bugger up there with that ·303 rifle in those flats who got you!'

Harold Rhodes

The Derbyshire fast bowler played his only two Tests with Ken Barrington in 1959. For most of his career Rhodes played under the threat of being banned as a thrower, and it was only two years before he retired that he was officially cleared.

I think I must be one of the few players who got Kenny for a pair. I looked on it as one of the highlights of my career. It happened at the Oval in 1968, and I got him lbw for 0 first ball in the first innings, and bowled him second ball in the second innings.

I can't remember him saying much. It wasn't something you could have a joke about, because he cared about his batting. I never had a plan of campaign against him although I played against him a lot of times.

I bowled off-stump and was quick, and that's all I did. I didn't have theories about bowling this line or that line to different batsmen. The odd thing about it was that 1968 was my benefit year and the year before I asked Kenny if he could write a piece in my benefit brochure.

He started off his article:

> One of the most satisfying experiences of my 14 years in first-class cricket and playing Tests throughout the world, came one day last season when I stroked Harold Rhodes for 24 runs in one over. That was during Surrey's Gillette Cup match against Derbyshire at the Oval when overs were running out and I chanced my arm. I managed two sixes and three fours against Harold.
>
> This may sound a strange way to start a tribute to a fellow professional cricketer but it is, in fact, a tribute. It gave me great satisfaction because it was one of the few occasions that I have come off best when facing Harold. Usually his speed and accuracy prevent any batsman taking liberties.

It wasn't long before I had a chance to take any revenge! Ken never really scored a lot of runs against Derbyshire. In fact, his batting average against us was his worst against any of the counties.

He had a low average because we had such good bowlers! Seriously, I think he did have great respect for bowlers like Les Jackson and Cliff Gladwin and the players who followed them in the Derbyshire side.

Charles Robins

Chairman of Middlesex, and formerly a player on the Middlesex staff. His father, Walter, was a former England captain, and managed the England tour of the West Indies in 1959–60, when Ken Barrington was a member of the party.

The England players had a pretty rough time in the West Indies, what with the crowds and the fast bowling, and my father told Ken off for the way he was behaving.

Ken used to turn his bat round and 'shoot' at the bowlers when they bowled a bouncer, or at the crowd, and my father said, 'It's hard enough without you inciting them.'

When Ken was manager in Pakistan I shall always remember his kindness to my sister Penny and a friend she was staying with. The two girls watched a Test at Karachi, and couldn't find a single ladies' loo in the ground.

I explained their predicament to Ken, and he said he would clear the area in the England dressing-room and they could use the players' toilets . . . and they did.

They must have been the only women who have used the visiting dressing-room toilets at Karachi!

Gordon Ross

Cricket writer, author of many cricketing books and now consultant to the National Westminster Bank Trophy.

Kenny, Stuart Surridge and I used to attend the annual dinner of the Nidderdale League in Yorkshire, and while staying in the area would go shooting. Stuart is one of the best shots in the country. Kenny was one of the worst.

At one of the dinners I announced that Kenny had at last succeeded in shooting a pheasant. 'But I also have to tell you that the bird is recovering well in Leeds Infirmary,' I said.

Kenny used to supply my wife with a list of horses he thought would do well, and were worth a modest investment. Unfortunately, few of them seemed to win! In his last Christmas card to us he wrote: 'I have a lot of good horses for 1982.'

It was such a tragedy he died so young. He brought joy and happiness to so many people.

Fred Rumsey

The 46-year-old former Worcester, Somerset and England bowler in 1965 took part with Ken Barrington in what was then a record last-wicket stand for England, against New Zealand. That was the Test where Ken was criticized for slow scoring, and was dropped by the selectors as a disciplinary measure. Rumsey – now in the travel business – played in five Tests in 1964–5.

Kenny scored 137 in 7¼ hours, and the selectors left him out of the side to set an example to the others. I thought it was a ridiculous decision. Anyone who scored 137 today would be considered a hero. I think the selectors – Doug Insole, Alec Bedser, Peter May and Don Kenyon – did it to appease public opinion.

The weather during that Edgbaston Test was the worst I ever

encountered in a Test Match. It was so cold they brought out hot coffee for drinks. Charlie Elliott, one of the umpires, wore two pairs of trousers on top of his pyjamas, and was still complaining about the cold! I wore two shirts and four sweaters when I went out to bat.

England were 394–9 when I joined Kenny. He had completed his century – after remaining scoreless on 85 for 62 minutes – and was striking the ball better than earlier in his innings, but he was still unhappy.

'I'm trying to get on with it but it won't happen,' he said. At the time he was using an exaggerated one-eyed stance to counter the left-arm over-the-wicket bowling of Dick Collinge, the young New Zealand pace bowler. Dick bowled 29.4 overs in that innings and took 3–63, excellent figures considering he was only nineteen and it was his first Test. Playing for England were some fine cricketers – Geoff Boycott, Bob Barber, Ted Dexter, Kenny, Mike Smith, Colin Cowdrey and Jim Parks. Only Dexter, with 57, got past 50.

Kenny and I put on 41. He made 20 and I had 21, and he was the man who was out. In the dressing-room afterwards he was very apologetic. He said he hadn't been able to find his form, and Mike Smith was philosophical. I don't remember that anyone criticized him in any way.

The New Zealanders didn't fare too well in their first innings. They were all out 116. Bert Sutcliffe, their veteran left-handed batsman, one of their best players in his day, ducked into a bouncer from Fred Trueman which didn't get up on the slow pitch, and was hit behind the ear. He batted on for a short time before retiring, and in the second innings, we were told not to bowl bouncers at him.

It was a most extraordinary request. I'd never known anything like it before. Bert had been hit on the head in South Africa, and there was a fear that it could be the end of his career if he was injured again. He made 53 in the second innings.

Fred wasn't too happy, as you'd expect. Bert didn't face him with any confidence. I remember Fred saying to me, 'If he backs away any further, he'll be in the bus queue for Birmingham.'

We won that Test by 9 wickets, but it wasn't a memorable game. Perhaps the trouble was that it was Kenny's thirteenth Test hundred. It certainly didn't bring him any luck. He missed the Second Test and Lord's, but came back at Leeds and scored 163, which included twenty-six fours and a seven.

Willie Rushton

Comedian, writer, TV personality and raconteur.

The Colonel – or Captain Barrington, as we called him – led a Taverners side in a tour of Corfu I went on in 1978. The Greeks addressed him as 'Captain Barrington' and he loved it, notwithstanding the demotion.

Platia Down, the Corfu cricket ground, is half Fuller's Earth dotted with grass-like tuffs and half failed tar macadam. The earthy area is next to the Judas Trees, under which the natives anxiously worry at their beads, sitting at tables served from the cafés behind them. Woe betide the men who field on the boundary!

The ground had apparently been flattened by countless feet of Regiments of Foot in the halcyon days of Empire, and never since. We gathered that the locals took their cricket most seriously, and indeed they did.

Saturday the 10th of June was bright and very hot. The opening ceremony was unashamedly based on that used in the World Cup in Buenos Aires that same summer, and we marched in with bands, Scouts and banners. The crowd seemed enormous, and divided evenly between our own tourists waving Union Jacks and light ales, and the locals thirsting for blood. Ours.

You would have been proud. The Taverners, Cleese, John Price, Jack Robertson, John Alderton, Peter Gordeno, Nick Parsons, Brian Rix, Bill Simpson, Ed Stewart, Roy Kinnear, the captain, Barrington, and myself – marched in to the middle of the ground, chests out, stomachs in, whistling *Colonel Bogey* to a solo kettle-drum. The national anthems were played, and speeches intoned. His Worship the Mayor was seemingly more at home in the open, and gifts were exchanged, beer mugs for tasteful medals. Then battle commenced.

Perhaps because it was a Saturday, it could not be described as a charitable match. We realized at once that the Corfu Select XI was keen to rub our faces in the Fuller's Earth. They batted first in a style of their own. The defensive stroke to them is not so much a dead bat as a dead body. Indeed, the crack as one opener played John Price with his elbow caused several of the local gendarmerie to reach for their Lugers.

Anything hittable was vigorously scooped somewhere in an arc between square leg and square leg. It was all effective stuff, however, and given the Taverner tradition of two overs each, suitably amended to give Big John exercise and keep their score somewhere in bounds, they scored something in the region of 220.

Captain Barrington bowled an over or two, and as I remember, bowled exceedingly well, pitching wide of the stumps on either side and turning the ball yards. His bounce was also memorable, often reaching the wicket-keeper above his head. He was too good for the Greeks, who had seen nothing like it. He was, in short, too good for them. They weren't good enough to get an edge, and bouncing and turning so much as that, the Captain failed to take a wicket.

Getting the runs was a formidable task, but the Captain was determined to win, and the general feeling was that he was right. Queen and country called. Corfu were taking no prisoners. Not for them our idiotic tactic of sharing the bowling round. Their captain and another fast bowler bowled short and brisk throughout. The Captain and Big John became increasingly irate at these tactics. 'Good God, bouncers at non-recognized batsmen!' they exclaimed.

Big John went in and scored a towering 120-odder, and the Captain made a brilliant 50. He was an angry man that day, the Captain, and he made the bounders pay for their impertinence. Together the pros brought a famous British victory.

There was a wild taverna party that night, and Jolly Jack Alderton, in a fit of machismo, karate-chopped a plate and had to retire to a local maternity hospital to have his hand sewn back on. 'We don't do hands,' said an unwilling gynaecologist.

Andrew Sandham

The former Surrey opening batsman was one of Ken's first coaches when he joined the Oval staff. Born on 6 July, 1890, Andrew Sandham played fourteen times for England in the Twenties, and set many batting records with Sir Jack Hobbs. He died in April 1982.

Ken was my best pupil. I wrote that on the wreath I sent for his funeral. He was always willing to learn and take advice. He was very determined to succeed. It was in his make-up.

I didn't think when I first saw him that he would eventually become a great player, but he made himself into a great player by hard work. He was a bit slow in those days, and we used to tell him to open up a bit.

He used to bat with his nose in the air, and I was always telling him to keep his head down. Once when he was playing for the Second XI he scored 179 despite having a boil on the back of his neck.

'Pity you didn't have one there all the time,' I said. 'It would help keep your head down.'

He was very good at correcting his mistakes once you had pointed them out. He used to get caught a lot at point trying to force the ball square off the back foot. I tried to get him to cut later. I was a bit of a cutter myself. I used to score a lot of my runs with the cut. When I see these present-day batsmen let balls go back outside the off-stump I wish I was still playing!

But to be fair, the pitches are not as even as they were in my day. The present batsmen are right when they say the bounce is uneven. That doesn't encourage you to cut.

Ken Barrington used to bowl a lot when I first met him, but I could never see him being successful as a bowler. He wasn't accurate enough.

At one game, a Club and Ground match, he was being hit all over the place, and I had to go off somewhere. When I came back the batting side was all out and I asked who had taken the wickets. 'Ken Barrington got four,' I was told.

'Well, I don't know,' I said. 'There must be some mugs about!'

It was a tragedy when he died so young. He was a very nice man, always smiling. Everyone liked him.

John Savage

The former Leicestershire off-spin bowler who is now Lancashire's coach.

Ken's technique against spin bowling was second to none. If the ball was turning a bit but not bouncing, he was the type of player who would bat all day. You would never get him out.

But when it was lifting as well as turning – well, you were in with a chance. There was one game at Ashby de la Zouch, the only time he played at Ashby I think, when I dismissed him twice, for 5 in the first innings and 1 in the second. That was one of the few occasions I came out on top against him.

It was a rain-affected pitch, and I took 8–78 in the second innings. That was the game when someone drove the ball back and I dived, and it hit the stumps to run Micky Stewart out when he had just hit a few boundaries and was going well.

Brian Scovell

Cricket and soccer reporter on the Daily Mail *and formerly Ken Barrington's 'ghost' when he worked first for the* Daily Sketch *and then for the* Mail *between 1969 and 1975.*

When we travelled around together Kenny delighted in taking part in the impromptu nets and back-garden cricket sessions which I used to arrange. I remember taking him round to tea at a friend's house in Bingley, Yorkshire, and before tea could be served he was out in the garden with the host's seven-year-old son showing him how to bowl leg-breaks.

The coaching session had to be abandoned when the ball went through a neighbour's hedge and couldn't be found. But I found it more difficult to coax him to play for the Press side. 'I know what those games are like,' he said. 'You get some eighteen-year-old fast bowler out to prove himself on a green pitch and the ball's flying round your ears. I can do without that.'

He wasn't afraid of fast bowling on poor pitches. His record proved that. But as a man who had been one of the world's finest technicians, he wasn't going to risk that reputation in a knockabout match. He had his pride, and it wasn't going to desert him.

After a year or two, I persuaded him to play for the *Sketch* editorial team against the print-workers at the Northcliffe Sports Ground in Worcester Park. It was coarse cricket at its worst. We had few good players, and the print-workers had even fewer. The pitch was grassy and hard underneath, but neither side possessed a quick bowler.

The print-workers batted first, and it was a limited-overs game with a limit of six overs per bowler. The print-men were most impressed when Kenny came on to bowl his leg-breaks, googlies and flippers. Their batsmen whirled away vainly, but failed to connect.

Kenny kept beating them, and several times an over the ball would defeat the batsmen and somehow contrive to miss the stumps. By the end of his six overs he had failed to take a wicket, and to console him, I asked the print-workers if they minded him exceeding his quota of overs.

'Let him carry on,' said the opposing captain. 'It's an education to watch him.' By this time one of the batsman had started to connect, and was smashing Kenny's bowling to all parts, mostly off the edge. Kenny was becoming more and more exasperated.

'It's harder work getting a wicket here than in a Test Match,' he said. Eventually, in his tenth over, the batsman mishit and the ball went high into the air in the direction of mid-on.

Kenny could have caught it himself, but he deferred to the fielder who was in the mid-on position, a sub-editor on the *Sketch* named Len Kirtland. Len hadn't played cricket for some years, and wasn't shaping too well as the ball hurtled downwards.

He held his hands high above his head, and I thought there might be a nasty incident if he failed to hold it. The ball crashed through his fingers and struck him a sickening blow on the eyebrow, causing a gusher of blood to shoot out of the point of impact like a miniature oil-well. The ball bounced back into the air, but Kenny and I were so shocked that neither of us moved to catch the rebound.

Poor Len had to be taken off to hospital, and it was the last game of cricket he played. That was the closest Kenny came to taking a wicket that day!

He made up for it, however, with an innings of 64 not out which won us the game. For several overs at the start he played himself in against some wild bowling, and soon started pulling sixes into the trees on the top side of the ground. He played that innings as professionally as any of his Test innings.

I tried to get him to play in more Press matches after that, notably the annual English Press *v.* Overseas Press game at Harrogate but for some reason he always opted to play golf!

Peter Short

President of the Barbados Cricket Association and former secretary of the West Indies Board of Control.

Kenny loved bands, and I remember once when he took the baton from the bandmaster at a concert at the Marine Hotel in Bridgetown. He was in his element, and conducted the band as well as the bandmaster had done. But he was stymied when the band suddenly changed to calypso music!

Peter Smith

Cricket correspondent of the Daily Mail, *and formerly a cricket writer with Hayter's Reporting Agency and the* News of the World. *Author of several books, including the official TCCB book of the 1980–1 England tour of the West Indies.*

One story always springs to mind about Kenny. Early in his career Surrey were playing Lancashire, and Brian Statham was one of the fastest bowlers on the circuit.

Brian bowled a short-pitched delivery, and Kenny made a mess of hooking it. The ball hit the splice of his bat, and he was lucky to survive. Brian told Jim Laker, who was batting at the other end, 'Tell that lad not to hook like that; he doesn't get into position quickly enough, he'll get himself out.'

In Statham's next over Barrington again attempted a hook shot, but failed once more. When Ken got up Brian's end 'George' said to him, 'Leave 'em alone. Look, next over I'll bowl you a couple of short ones to see if you've learned your lesson.'

'George' duly bowled a couple of short ones in his next over . . . and was promptly warned by the umpire for intimidatory bowling!

John Snow

Played many of his 49 Tests for England with Ken Barrington, when Ken was a player or a manager. Now retired, Snow runs a travel agent's business in Crawley.

Kenny always recognized a good thing when he saw one – a horse that he knew he had to back, or a match he felt his side could win. He was the positive influence in the dressing-room at Port of Spain in March 1968, when Colin Cowdrey's side won the only Test in the 1967–8 series in the West Indies.

Gary Sobers had become bored with the way the series had gone – too many drawn games – so he declared on the last day and set us to score 215 in 165 minutes. He couldn't have expected to bowl us out in that time, especially as Charlie Griffith was injured and he only had Lance Gibbs, Willie Rodriguez and himself to bowl.

We started slowly, and at tea were 73–1 and behind the clock. There was a general discussion at tea about whether he ought to go for the runs. Colin wasn't sure. Tom Graveney said, 'I'm not so sure we should.' But Kenny said, 'Come on, we can get these.' He talked the others round, and we won with three minutes to spare.

I remember another occasion on that tour when we were playing Jamaica Colts at Montego Bay. The ground was near the airport, and as Kenny was fascinated by planes, he suggested some of us ought to go down to the airport.

We lounged around watching the planes come and go, when suddenly someone said we were six wickets down and people were panicking about us. We returned just in time for me to go in.

Kenny was in the cricket trouser business as most cricketers know and another story I recall about him concerned Colin Milburn. Kenny's company supplied all Colin's trousers, and after one pair split Colin said, 'Where are those new trousers you promised me?'

'Give us a chance, Ollie,' said Kenny, 'we've got four men working on them. It takes time, you know.'

Micky Stewart

Was on the Surrey staff with Ken Barrington between 1952 and 1972, and was captain from 1963–72. He is now manager of Surrey.

The day we won the championship in 1954, Kenny and I arrived back at Paddington at twelve-thirty at night with the team gear. As the youngest players in the side, it was our job to look after the bags. We got them on to a trolley and took them outside to join the queue for a taxi.

It was a big queue, and a long time went by, and Kenny was getting more and more impatient. 'We're never going to get up in time to get to the Oval tomorrow,' he said.

When it was our turn at the head of the queue we had to wait for a taxi which had a roof-rack in order to get the bags on. An hour must have gone by before one appeared. Sandy Tait, the physio, was with us. We started throwing the bags on, and the taxi-driver said, 'What the hell are those?'

Kenny said, 'They're cricket bags. We're Surrey cricketers. We've just won the championship.'

The taxi-driver must have had a hard day, because he said, 'I couldn't care less what you've won.' Sandy Tait said, 'Hey, what did you say?'

'I said I couldn't care less about what you've won,' said the cabby. Sandy became very angry. 'Get those bags off,' he said. 'We're not going with this fellow.' So Kenny and I had to drag the bags off, and Kenny nearly got knocked over by one which fell on him. It was a long time before another taxi with a roof-rack came along. Kenny never stopped complaining next day when we arrived at the Oval for the first day of a county match! Kenny was the player who made me feel most at home when I joined the staff. In those days he had the reputation of being a bit careful with his possessions, including money, and Geoff Kirby (who travelled up to London every day with him on the train) used to complain that when he bought a packet of sweets Kenny would take most of them.

Kenny used Brylcreem in those days. It was the Denis Compton era, and a lot of players used it at the time. Kenny used to stick his fingers in the Brylcreem jars of some of the other players, and once when we were on a second-eleven tour of Cornwall, Ron Tindall decided to catch him out.

Ron scraped out the Brylcreem from his jar and put tooth-paste in it instead. Kenny used to apply a little water as well as the hair cream, and when he helped himself to Ron's jar and applied it his hair started frothing up and he looked like some kind of monster.

I must say, though, despite that early reputation Kenny was a very kind man who would do anything to help people. He was a humorous man, a kindly man and a good friend.

In his early days he was known as the cherry brandy drinker. He didn't really like light ale, or Guinness, which the other players drank, and one day he tried a cherry brandy and liked it. Whenever he was asked what he was drinking, he said, 'Give me a cherry brandy.' It became a joke in the team.

He was never much of a drinker. If he had one or two a sparkly look would come into his eye. After he stopped playing he had an occasional Scotch, but never more than one or two. He was a man of sound habits. He and I shared a room for several years until I became captain and qualified for a room on my own.

In those days he wasn't the insomniac he began to be later. He didn't use to keep me awake at night. Out in the middle, he was a cavalier of a batsman who could smash the ball all over the place. I remember him once taking 24 off an over from Harold Rhodes in a Gillette Cup match, and in second-eleven games he was murderous.

I was with him the day he changed his approach to batting and began more of a grafter. It happened when we were playing together in 1960. He had just had a very successful tour in the West Indies, and was feeling in great form at the start of the domestic season.

'Right, that's it,' he told me. 'I'm really going to enjoy myself this season.' He started off in magnificent fashion, scoring quickly with shots all round the wicket and not failing in a single innings. Then just before the First Test team was picked he made a pair at Hove, and followed it with a 1 at Trent Bridge. He was lucky not to get another pair, because he was missed by Cyril Poole at leg-slip before he scored.

He hadn't been in long enough to say that he was out of form. After such a good start, he'd lost his wicket four times in about ten deliveries, something that can happen to a batsman when he's going well.

He was chosen for the First Test at Edgbaston, but was made

twelfth man. That night in Nottingham he was in tears in our hotel bedroom. 'They'll never be able to leave me out again,' he said. 'I'm going to see to that.' After that he began an accumulator, concentrating on making big scores.

When I became captain there were occasions when I had to gee him up and tell him to get on with it. One of them was when we were playing Essex on a flat pitch at the Oval and he patted back 18 deliveries in a row off Paddy Phelan, the Essex off-break bowler. Paddy must have been as amazed as I was.

It was a Saturday game with a fair crowd, and I went potty. 'What do you think you're up to?' I said. 'He's bowling so accurately I can't get him away,' he said.

'Not the way you're playing, you won't,' I said. 'You've got to play a few shots and attack him sensibly.'

In the next over he hit three 6s in 4 balls, and that made me even madder. 'I didn't tell you to throw your wicket away,' I said. 'I dunno,' he complained, 'I never seem to please you!'

He provoked so much fun in the dressing-room. He had phobias about the pitch, the grass and everything else, and the others used to take the mick all the time.

There was that occasion when we were playing Derbyshire at Chesterfield, and that season he kept on being bowled through the gate. Jim Laker and Tony Lock were always on at him about it.

It was a rain-affected pitch at Chesterfield, and Edwin Smith, their off-spinner, was bowling when the game resumed after bad light. Kenny played forward and gave an almighty bat-pad catch to short leg. He was smiling when he came into the dressing-room.

'What the hell are you smiling about?' asked Lockie. 'He didn't bowl me through the gate this time,' said Kenny.

Lockie was always giving him rollickings. In one game on a slow turner at Swansea he wanted him to field closer at slip. I was at second slip, and level with Arthur McIntyre, who was keeping wicket and Kenny wasn't far behind.

Peter May was captain, and when Lockie asked for Kenny to move up a yard Peter waved him forward.

'Cor, I don't know, I'll be standing next to him soon,' said Kenny. The batsman was Gilbert Parkhouse, who played 7 times for England in the fifties.

Up came Lockie . . . and bowled the faster one. It hit Parkhouse on the foot and rocketed straight up into Kenny's forehead, laying him out. He had to go off to hospital, and he couldn't win there either.

The doctor told him, 'I can't see you yet, I've got three miners to attend to. You should have done it later in the day!'

At the end of the 1966 season, when he'd had a tough time with the Charlie Griffith business, we were invited to go to Bermuda with Frank Russell's side for three weeks. Kenny didn't want to go. 'Go on,' I said, 'it will do you good. You can take it easy with Ann and get some sunshine. It will do you the world of good.'

He finally decided to come, and we played the first match on a matting wicket on concrete. I was batting with him just before lunch when he spooned one up on the leg side and was caught. 'I shouldn't have come,' he said. 'It's all your fault.'

As he came up the stairs to the pavilion it was rather dark, but I could just make out the figure of a rather large man at the top of the stairs . . . Charlie Griffith! 'Christ,' said Kenny, 'that's all I need.' The two weren't speaking at the time, and they brushed past each other. By coincidence, Charlie was there on holiday at the time.

The pitch had Coca Cola tops covering the pins which held down the mat, and when Kenny came on to bowl a batsman drove the ball and it bounced back off one of the tops and smacked Kenny in the head. Down he went. 'I knew I shouldn't have come,' he said.

Most of us had their favourite 'flipper' story about Kenny, and mine was about the time when he met Richie Benaud in a benefit match on a Sunday at Slough and Richie was bowling it rather well. Next day we were playing in a county match at Lord's and Kenny decided to have a go with it. I was fielding at second slip, looking at the bat, when suddenly I saw the ball hurtling towards me. Too late! It hit me on the knee, and the rest of the side fell about convulsed with laughter.

When I toured India with him in 1964 most of us were ill, but he wasn't as bad as some of us. That was because he wouldn't eat the local food. He would always order what he called 'an egg omelette'. One day we were in our room together in Peshawar when the orderly came in with his omelette, smothered in onions.

'Here, I didn't order that,' he said. 'I ordered a plain egg omelette.' In the excitement the plate crashed to the ground, spewing omelette and onions all over the floor, and he finished up having nothing.

When he was asked how he got on with the food he would reply, 'I stuck to omelette and chips the whole time. They can't muck around with that, can they?'

Every time we arrived at an airport we were given a very enthusiastic reception, with garlands of flowers being put around our necks. Kenny advised us early on not to accept them if we could diplomatically avoid it. 'You'll be covered in ants,' he said.

That was the tour when he broke a finger and went home early – lucky blighter! I went home early too after constant stomach trouble which also affected Brian Close, Barry Knight, Jim Parks, John Mortimore, John Edrich, Fred Titmus and Phil Sharpe. Before the Second Test we were down to ten fit men, and had to borrow a substitute fielder from the Indians.

During the First Test in Madras Nadkarni, the Indian spin bowler, sent down 131 deliveries without a run being scored – some kind of record, I believe. Ken was batting with Brian Bolus, and the reason they blocked it out was that the only other English player in the dressing-room ready to bat was the number eleven, Dave Larter. The rest of us were back at the hotel suffering from the runs! Bolus batted nearly seven hours for his 88, and Ken was in 5¼ hours for 80. Nadkarni's figures at the end of the innings were a bit unusual: 32–27–5–0.

That was one slow innings where no one criticized Ken. It was one of the great holding operations of all time, and enabled us to draw the match. His humour on that tour was a blessing, because there wasn't much to laugh about. He was a man who brought a great deal of pleasure and mirth to many people. There haven't been too many like him in the game.

Stewart Storey

The former Surrey all-rounder is now chief coach to Sussex.

One of the funniest times we had with Kenny when I was at Surrey was the time we sent him to Coventry. It was a county game at Trent Bridge, and Kenny was grinding away all day on a good batting track. Four hours for 90 or something like that. Ron Tindall, the next man in, sat there fuming in the dressing-room, and Micky Stewart, the captain, was livid.

Eventually Kenny reached his hundred, got out and started walking back to the dressing-room. Ron passed him on the pitch, but didn't say a word. Micky got him in the back room at the back of the dressing-room and gave him an almighty rocket for going slow when he wanted to declare.

When we were out in the field in the final half-hour none of us said a word to Kenny. He kept chipping away, but Arnold Long and I didn't reply. This went on for nearly half an hour before he finally said, 'All right, then, what did I do?' That used to be one of the jokes in the side, the day we sent Kenny to Coventry.

Although he used to bat slowly at times, he probably had more shots than almost any batsman in the country. In the nets he was great, smashing it all over the place.

But sometimes the practice pitches at the Oval would be a bit green, and the ball would seam about, and Geoff Arnold and I used to hit him on the legs. He used to grunt away. 'I'd love to get you buggers out to Australia,' he said. 'You wouldn't be able to do that out there.'

I went to the Oval a few years after Kenny started in 1948, and the stories about him were part of the tradition of the place. The players used to tell us of the days when Kenny and a mate of his, George Kirby, a wicket-keeper, used to travel up together from Reading to the Oval, where Kenny was employed on the ground-staff.

They got up at six and travelled up in the train with the City types.

George would sit in the carriage humming away like a bee, and the City types in their pin-stripes would start looking round for the bee. Kenny used to screw up his copy of the *Daily Mirror* and pretend to smash the bee. Then they used to pull out a tennis ball and bounce it around.

Kenny started work as a garage mechanic before he had an offer to join the Surrey staff, and his love of cars never left him. He'd get very upset if you said anything critical about one of his cars.

I remember we were playing at Bradford once, and Kenny had an Austin-Cambridge at the time. He took Dave Sydenham there from London, but didn't arrive until 3 a.m. A hose-pipe went, and it was raining so heavily that water started seeping through the windscreen. Dave sat in the front seat in his mackintosh with his feet in a pool of water.

Next day we were sorting out which players should go to the ground in which car, and 'Ob' Long said, 'All those with a mac had better go with Kenny.' Kenny didn't see the joke!

Stuart Surridge

Captain of Surrey between 1952 and 1956, when they won the championship in five successive seasons. An amateur, he played for Surrey in 1947–56. He is now a member of the committee, and recent President of the Club. He was a close personal friend of Ken Barrington.

My company supplied Ken with his bats, the Ken Barrington autograph bat. He used to come down to our factory at Witham with Micky Stewart and choose his bats every year. He would choose one and Micky would promptly grab it, so he'd have to choose another one.

He preferred a light bat, about 2 lb 3 oz without the grip, 2 lb 4½ oz with the grip. He never worried about whether it was a wide grain or a narrow grain. As long as the pick-up was right and he liked the balance, that was sufficient.

Few players looked after their bats as well as Ken. He used to sandpaper it down after use, and it was as clean at the end of the season as it was at the start.

One year when he brought his bat back we found it was an eighth of an inch narrower. That doesn't sound a lot, but it means a lot to these players. Peter May and Herbert Sutcliffe used to be the same. They were obsessive about their bats.

I can't remember Ken breaking a bat. He used to chip a bit off occasionally and we would have to repair it, but it wasn't unusual for him to use the same bat right through a season.

The bat he was using in the West Indies when he died was a Jumbo, heavier than the bats he used in his playing career, but he liked the balance. The England players signed it, and had a silver-plated inscription put on it which read: 'In memory of the life and dedication of "Our Colonel", friend and counsellor.' I thought that was a nice gesture. It showed what the players thought about him.

I was out having dinner with him when there was a message to ring Lord's after it was announced that Alan Smith was to be manager in the West Indies and Ken wasn't to go as cricket manager. The decision to leave Ken behind upset him terribly. I remember him saying at the time, 'What have I done wrong?'

I told him that wasn't the way to look at it, and perhaps it would be better if he had a winter at home. He was delighted when the Test and County Cricket Board changed their minds and he was invited to accompany the team.

He was a great fighter. No one fought harder than he did when he was batting. The critics used to give him stick, but as I always said, if he didn't get the runs, who would?

He invariably went into bat when there was a crisis and England were two or three wickets down. He didn't go in very often when it was 200–1. If he failed the team often failed, and I don't think the critics took that into account. After he retired, he worked in the Press, and was with some of the people who had criticized him, but he never bore grudges.

He was a terrible worrier, not just about cricket but about everything. If he had your car to service he would worry that it was done just right. I can't speak too highly of him. When he joined the committee at the Oval he was the first to volunteer to do things. He was a very generous man – too generous sometimes.

If he hadn't been a great cricketer he could have become a pro golfer. He started late at golf, but within a short time got down to single figures and frequently played to scratch. He was good at all sports.

I often took him shooting, and he became a good shot. He was a safe shot. I had to talk him into firing many times, because the grouse would fly low and he would say, 'I'll hit the beaters if I'm not careful.' The beaters would be half a mile away!

Like all good players, he was best off the back foot. As Sidney Barnes the Australian said, 'If you want to learn to bat, you have to learn to play back.'

He got more square on as he grew older, but he could still drive. He was a good driver. He could play all the shots. Throughout my time with him when he was a player – and I didn't play with him long – I never had to bully him. Coax him, yes, but not bully.

One of the few times I had to give him a rocket was in a match at the Oval when he threw the ball in slowly from cover. The next time the ball came to him he threw it in like lightning. 'We've got a lethal weapon out there,' said one of the other players.

He was full of fun. He kept players amused round the world, particularly with his imitations. When he was abroad he used to correspond with me and keep me in the picture. He was optimistic about English cricket and his role in it.

When he was a player, I didn't think he had it in his make-up to be a captain, although he had a deep knowledge of the game. He was too much of a worrier. Some great players can lead, but not too many. Ian Botham proved that. Whatever he said about captaincy not affecting his performance, the figures showed that it did. When he lost the job, he was a new man. He won us the Ashes in 1981, almost off his own bat.

David Sydenham

Was on the Surrey staff between 1952 and 1965, and later skippered the second eleven. Now an administrative officer in chiropody for the National Health Service, he is a member of the Surrey committee.

Soon after Kenny went into partnership with some people producing sports clothing he told the Surrey players that he would fit them all up with new trousers, very cheaply! He went round taking the measurements and wrote them all down. Later, during a match at Lord's, he came back with the finished items. Unfortunately, the labels were muddled up, and he wasn't able to tell us whose trousers belonged to whom.

So we had a manikins' parade in the dressing-room. Someone looked like Coco the Clown in a pair of trousers a few sizes too big. Someone else looked like a skinned rabbit. It was hilarious, and we ribbed Kenny unmercifully.

He was a powerful man physically, and used to specialize in putting paralysing grips on people. He did it to me on that occasion, I remember, and when the game resumed I couldn't bowl!

Then there was that time when Kenny was out of form and we arranged a simulated game for him at the Oval to enable him to put things right.

After net practice the whole team went out to a pitch on the edge of the square where the stumps had been set up and had a session with him. I bowled the first over, and the ball was swinging about all over the place.

First ball went through the gate and knocked the off-stump over. Kenny wasn't too pleased about it. Second ball did him as well. Third one missed, but the fourth did him again and he was livid. It didn't do his confidence much good.

There were plenty of laughs when he was around, and he never minded being on the receiving end himself. I remember my last game for Surrey, the Gillette Cup Final against Yorkshire in 1965, the one *Wisden* described as 'a surprisingly one-sided match'. The game should never have been played. The ground was saturated. The water didn't seep over your boots, it ran over them.

It was impossible to run up and bowl properly, and FST (Fred Trueman) was still moaning about it halfway through our innings, so goodness knows what he would have said if he'd had to bowl before lunch as we had to.

Micky Stewart and Arthur McIntyre went out to look at the pitch before the match started, an hour and a half late, and they said they thought it would fly as the sun dried it out. But it was the slowest, deadest pitch I've ever bowled on, and Geoff Boycott got that record 146.

Eventually Micky Stewart gave Kenny a bowl, everything else having failed. Kenny pitched so short that some of his deliveries were almost double-bouncers, and Jackie Hampshire scooped him for several sixes.

At the end of the over Kenny grunted, 'I don't think it's my wicket, captain.' It wasn't anyone's wicket! His five overs cost 54 runs, and his state of mind wasn't made any better when he got a duck.

We had a dressing-room of characters in that side, rather what Essex are today. Even when we were up against it we could still see the funny side of things.

Earlier in my career we were at a early-season drinks party with the committee, and a committee man came up to me, patted me on the back, and said, 'Hello, Barrington; wintered well?'

Kenny had just come back from Australia and was as brown as a berry. I'd been working as a chiropodist in London all winter, and was as white as a sheet. He was stocky and muscular. I was fat and flabby. He had that distinctive profile.

It wouldn't happen today. We have a good committee at Surrey, and we're very much involved with the players. Kenny was a member himself, and I'm only sorry that he's gone because he had so much to offer.

Derek Taylor

The Somerset wicket-keeper who played for Surrey during 1964–9. His twin brother Mike is the Hampshire assistant secretary. They both started their careers with Buckinghamshire, and are both nicknamed 'Tay'.

Ken's career was at its height during my early days at Buckinghamshire. The word 'professional' was still rather taboo among the amateurs I was playing with, but it didn't deter me in my appreciation of Ken Barrington's ability and dedication.

When I had the opportunity to join the staff at the Oval in 1964 I met him, and found him to be a far more sensitive and caring person than the rugged professional image that he portrayed to the public. That was his benefit year, and he and his wife really made it a bumper year on and off the field. I was invited to numerous functions, and played in several of his benefit games, meeting many personalities from the stage and TV. I was an overawed youngster, but Kenny always made time for the young players.

One of my first opportunities to play for Surrey was in the then big match of the season at the Oval against Yorkshire. I found myself batting with Ken. The second new ball had just been taken by Freddie Trueman, and the inexperienced Taylor was getting the full treatment from F.S.

Fortunately, I was able to heed Ken's words of encouragement and wisdom as we managed to put on a century partnership, and I achieved my first first-class 50.

'The Colonel' had quite a game, going on to score an undefeated 158 and then taking 7 wickets with his leg-breaks. Kenny's ups and downs with Charlie Griffith in the late Sixties ended up with several appearances in the Second XI, and instead of putting his own game first, he was always helping and cajoling the boys. That presumably was the start of his enthusiasm, which led him to coaching and managing the future England team of the Seventies. Ken Barrington was certainly one of the major influences of my career, for which I shall remain eternally grateful.

Bernie Thomas

The England physiotherapist and medical man went on five tours with Ken Barrington.

One free day in Australia Kenny was playing golf with Ronnie Corbett and Geoff Boycott, and Geoff got into a bunker. There was a loud cry of anguish as Geoff played his shot, and we thought he had lost one of his contact lenses in the sand. But in fact he'd fallen over because he was trying to play over the steepest part instead of taking an easier way, and as he landed he dislocated a finger.

'It's just like D-Day down there,' said Kenny, 'sand all over the place, flags flying!' You can imagine the mirth, especially with someone like Ronnie Corbett there! Golf was Kenny's only relaxation, but he played it competitively, often for a sidestake. He never minded playing with someone like me, who isn't a good player. He used to take delight in coaching me.

Although he had a strong constitution, Kenny would usually have a tummy upset at some time on a tour, and I used to give him tablets. When we were in India with Tony Greig's side I gave the players a package containing all the things they would need, including Vitamin C tablets which were rather large and effervescent. The first time Kenny took one he said, 'Cor, these tablets don't half make your mouth froth!'

The younger players, particularly Graham Dilley, used to worship him. Graham would come in and say, 'Have you heard the latest from Kenny?' And he would repeat Kenny's newest malapropism or funny remark. Kenny played a big part in the improvement in Graham's batting. He helped him a lot, and thought he could develop into a good all-rounder. As Graham showed a few times, he was capable of making runs.

Although he had been to India several times, Kenny had never been into a bazaar until our last trip there. One day I persuaded him to make the effort because he was meeting Ann when the team went on to Australia and he wanted to buy her a present. We walked down this narrow street which was full of bazaars and they were all there, the writing man who writes letters, the hubbly-bubbly man and so on.

We went into a place selling leather goods and Ken fancied a handbag. The shop-owner was rather unresponsive, and to help things along I said, 'This is Mr Ken Barrington, manager of the England cricket team, and he wants a present for his wife. How much is this bag?'

'Four hundred rupees,' said the man. 'Come off it,' I said. 'You can get a bag like that cheaper in England.' We started bartering, and were enjoying it when a man arrived who owned the shirt-shop opposite.

'How much will you pay?' said the first owner. But the second man was insistent. 'Here, have it and come with me,' he said. He led us across to his shop where a large crowd had gathered. They had all recognized Kenny, and the owner wanted them in his shop. He spent some time talking cricket, and the owner was delighted because it had attracted custom to his shop.

Before we left I said to Kenny he ought to pose for a picture with a donkey that was passing. He took up his position, surrounded by all the locals, and just as I was about to take the picture the donkey shook itself and we were all covered in dust. I couldn't take the picture. The lens was covered in dust!

During that tour Kenny had some trouble with a tooth and was talking about going to a dentist, but changed his mind when we walked past a dentist's premises and saw a patient come out and spit a mouthful of blood into the street. They didn't have running water! And when he saw the dentist wave to us, transferring the drill which he was using on a patient from one hand to another to continue drilling as he looked at us, Kenny decided to grin and bear it until we got to Australia!

When the players were thinking about refusing to play if Pakistan used their Packer players in Karachi on the 1977–8 tour, Kenny was very much the negotiator. He spent hours on the phone to London, and it was a worrying time for him. He was always a worrier, and whereas some people can have exercise and work it off and come back and relax, Kenny would come back after nets some days tired and still uptight.

There wasn't much to laugh about that time in Karachi, but I always remember the comment made by Derek Randall. 'We should go out on the pitch on the first day on time and sit down and tell them we're not going to stand for it,' he said.

On a trip to the north of Pakistan, where it can get very cold at night, Kenny went to bed one night wearing his pyjamas under an MCC sweater, his track suit and socks. Next morning he complained of neck and back ache. 'It's that Portland Cement pillow they gave me,' he said. Except for an isolated occasion like that, he was always very meticulous about dress and standards of behaviour.

He had come up through the ranks himself, and he recognized the importance of putting over the right image. When some people wore risqué T-shirts to events he would remind them that they were representing their country abroad. I don't think the Establishment realized what a great job he did for his country.

He took great pride in everything. His cricket bag would always be the tidiest in the dressing-room, and he would put brown paper, or a plastic sheet, over the contents, so that dust wouldn't get in when the bag was thrown about on coaches and aeroplanes.

Taking so much exercise, as he did when he was abroad on tour, probably prolonged his life. He loved being in the nets with the boys. When there was a function to attend he was usually the first to volunteer to go. He usually wanted a couple of players to go with him, to show the flag. He got on so well with everyone, and seemed to have friends wherever we went.

The players loved the stories he used to tell, and the stories he inspired himself. His favourite story was about a lady in war-time who got into a train carriage with three Polish soldiers. They were chatting, and the lady asked one of the soldiers whether he had any children.

'No,' said the soldier, and searching for the right word, said, 'My wife is impregnable.' The second soldier interrupted. 'No, you mean she is inconceivable.' The third one spoke up. 'No, she is unbearable.'

Fred Trueman

England's highest wicket-taker in Tests (307 wickets at 21·57). One of the game's great story-tellers, he now reports cricket for the Sunday People, *and is one of the BBC's team of sound commentators and experts.*

One of the stories I am supposed to have recounted about Ken was about why it took so long for him to start a family. I was supposed to have said it was because he occupied the crease so long that he never got his box off! I don't remember telling this story, but they said I did.

Bless his heart, he was a lovely lad. I remember on the boat going to Australia for the 1962–3 tour, the Duke of Norfolk's tour, we had Marylebone Calypso Club with all the players dressed up in fancy dress. Ken was done up as a Mexican bandit.

He was a fine batsman, one of the best. Once at the Oval – 1964, I think it was – I beat him four times in an over, and at the end of it he said, 'That's the greatest over I've ever faced.' He was like that, very generous to his opponents. A very fair person on the field.

Frank Tyson

The ex-Northamptonshire and England fast bowler is now director of coaching to the Victorian Cricket Association in Australia. Tyson played seventeen times for England in the fifties, including two Tests with Ken Barrington in 1955.

As my playing experience with Kenny was limited, my impressions of him lack the intimacy and humour of the dressing-room, and are confined to the respect which a commentator pays to a great player. In particular I remember the young Barrington, the splendid and fearless hooker who disciplined himself, as he was to teach other England players to do when he was their touring mentor, until he became the most self-demanding player in the game, and the most feared opponent of thinking Australian bowlers, who rarely relished attempting to shake the unshakeable.

Occasionally he would emerge from his chrysalis of concentration and show us what might have been had he not subordinated his stroke-making talents to the needs of his side.

In Melbourne in February 1966 he took 115 runs off an Australian attack which included Neil Hawke and Graham McKenzie, 102 of those runs coming under two and a half hours off 122 balls.

The innings included two sixes, and one of them was a glorious flat-batted drive over long-off. As was his habit, he appeared to reach a long way from his body for the ball. His two-eyed approach to the drive normally did not speak well for his chances of hitting the ball powerfully, but on this occasion, as on many others, he sent the ball skimming over the far-distant boundary of the huge Melbourne Cricket Ground.

Peter Walker

The Glamorgan and England all-rounder played three times for England against South Africa in 1960. He is now a cricket commentator with the BBC.

Glamorgan were playing Surrey at Neath in the county championship, and Surrey were batting. Don Shepherd, a bowler who was never given the recognition by the public that he had within the game, was bowling on a very helpful pitch, and the ball was lifting and turning in a remarkable manner.

Ken came in number three, and first ball, played forward and missed. He was then at the peak of his powers, perhaps the premier batsman in the country.

Don bowled again, and the ball jumped over Ken's shoulder. Third ball, Ken stretched forward . . . missed . . . and the ball went through to the keeper.

Fourth ball, the same thing. Again he played forward and missed. Before Don could bowl the fifth Ken walked down the pitch towards him with his arms raised.

'All right,' he said. 'I surrender!'

On a personal note, I shall always remember what he said to me on my Test debut as Edgbaston in 1960. England picked thirteen players, and Bob Barber and I were the new boys.

On the morning of the match Ken – who was one of England's finest, if not the finest, batsman of the day – was the one who was left out.

He was the first person who came up to me and shook hands and offered congratulations.

'Butch' White

The former England, Warwickshire and Hampshire pace bowler is now a groundsman in Sussex.

Kenny and I shared a room during the tour to India in 1961–2. We had many a friendly row when he used to come and find me lying on his bed dripping with sweat!

Our main entertainment used to be an arm-wrestling championship which went on for weeks. That was one of the few things you could do. You had to make your own amusements out there.

Kenny was a marvellous bloke to tour with. He was like a god in India. He will never be replaced. They loved his antics on the field, including his imitation of Gary Sobers's duck walk. I found him a great help to me in my career. He was wonderful with younger players.

They haven't found a manager to replace him, but if they want a suggestion, my nomination is Bob Willis. He'd do a great job. He thinks about the game, and cares about it.

Mike Willett

On the Surrey staff at the same time as Ken between 1949 and 1966. He now runs a garage, and still plays club cricket.

Very early in Kenny's career, we were having lunch at a ground when Bernie Constable said, 'Hey, Kenny, you should have your blazer on when you're eating lunch with us. Where is it?'

Kenny had a blazer, but it was still in its wrappings. He was very fussy about his possessions, and didn't want to dirty his brand-new blazer.

Next day at lunch he had it on, and a waitress who was serving his salad tripped and a bowl of salad cascaded down his blazer, with most of it ending up in his pocket.

Kenny was quite upset, and said to Bernie, 'It's all your fault. If you hadn't told me to put it on this wouldn't have happened.'

The rest of us were laughing uproariously as Bernie replied, 'If you'd had it on yesterday at least you would have had one day's wear out of it!'

Then there was the story of his brand-new A55 car. Onc day at the Oval he discovered there was a slight mark on it. No one else noticed it, but he did.

During the lunch interval he went out into the car park and inspected the cars of the other players to see if there was any black paint on them from his car. No one let on, and we were all treating it as a joke. At tea he went out and had a look at the committee men's cars which had arrived for a meeting. He still couldn't find the culprit.

He had a fine sense of humour himself, and one of the funniest things he did was in a match against Derbyshire on a pig of a wicket at the Oval. Harold Rhodes was hitting him on the chest, the arms, the gloves – everywhere – and he was laughing it off, although it was no laughing matter really.

After being struck another painful blow, Kenny threw his bat on to the ground, picked up the three stumps and marched off ten yards towards the middle of the square – we were playing near the edge – where he proceeded to bang the stumps in. 'Let's have another game on this pitch,' he said, and Harold Rhodes joined in the laughter. So did John Langridge, who was umpiring.

I joined the staff after he did, but we played a lot together in the club and ground side and the second eleven. One of the other players at the time was Lord Ebbisham, and Kenny was very impressed at being in the same side as a lord.

We were playing in a match at Kew one day, and I was posted at mid-wicket while Kenny was bowling. In those days Kenny was capable of bowling the most awful junk – double bouncers and long hops – and mid-wicket was the kamikaze position.

Kenny was taking a bit of stick, and I was moved back to the boundary to save my hands further punishment. The batsman kept hoicking him into the churchyard there, and after I'd had to run for the ball five times in succession I shouted out, 'That's enough. You get it yourself. I'm bowling at the other end, and I won't be able to carry on if this keeps up!'

Bob Willis

The England vice-captain and fast bowler was a nineteen-year-old second-eleven player on the Surrey staff when Ken Barrington played his last season. Despite being said to be injury-prone, Willis is England's fifth highest wicket-taker, and could still overhaul Alec Bedser's total of 236.

I always get a bit soppy when I talk about Ken, because he meant so much to my career. It was he and Tony Greig who straightened me out in India in 1976 the year after I was operated on for knee trouble. I was running in at an angle, and Kenny said, 'You've got to come in straight.' I spent a long time working at it, and there's no doubt that was the making of me, and I've got Kenny and Tony Greig to thank.

After that I only missed one Test through injury before I had to fly home from the West Indies in 1980–1.

I remember how much I was impressed by Kenny's attitude when I was a kid at the Oval. On the Saturday of the Fifth Test against the Aussies in 1968 – the match when 'Deadly' Underwood cleaned them up – I was watching along with some other second-eleven players, and Kenny invited me to have lunch and have a chat. For some reason, I think he had a soft spot for me.

When I came back from Australia and decided I wanted to leave Surrey he drove round to my grotty little flat in Streatham and tried to talk me into staying.

He really cared about me! After I came home from the West Indies I rang him up at the Holiday Inn to pull the Battoo Brothers joke on him again.

'Hello, Mr Barrington, Battoo Brothers, overseas division here.' But the call was put through to Ann because he was at a team meeting, and then it was transferred to the room where the meeting was taking place, and A.C. (Alan Smith, the manager) took it, and everyone knew it was me by that time.

Wilf Wooller

The former Glamorgan captain and secretary had the reputation of being one of the most competitive players in the game.

If I had to pick out players who were the most pleasant chaps I'd played against in forty years, Kenny Barrington would be in the top six. He was a man without a scrap of duplicity.

You never had to goad him a bit as I sometimes goaded other batsmen. If he hit it, he walked. He was the perfect gentleman in every sense. He was a very quiet, pleasant opponent who got on with the game. No, I can't remember him giving us a moment's trouble. And he wasn't a moaner, either.

I went up to London for his funeral. I thought I had to pay my respects to a fine cricketer and a fine man.

Bob Woolmer

The Kent and England batsman went on the MCC tour to India, Sri Lanka and Australia in 1976–7 when Ken Barrington was manager.

Kenny was King in India. The people there loved him from when he played out there on previous tours. At most of the functions we attended we would tell a few stories, and one of the best received was his coconut story.

Apparently he had been ill on a previous tour, and someone had prescribed a diet of coconut juice. After eight coconuts the trouble cleared up. One day a bearer came to his room and asked if he wanted a drink, and Kenny replied, 'Yes, please, a coconut.' The bearer came back with a coke and a peanut!

Kenny was a great forecaster of how pitches would play. Most of the pitches out there took turn on the first day, but when we played against Central Zone in Jaipur Kenny went out to inspect the pitch and returned to say that it wouldn't take much spin. 'It will play straight,' he said.

Dennis Amiss and I opened the innings, and Kenny's forecast appeared to be accurate until a slow left-armer came on and his first ball pitched leg-stump and jumped over Dennis's shoulder. We ribbed Kenny about it. 'What about this pitch that is going to play straight?' I said. He vowed he wouldn't prejudge another pitch on the tour.

And a final word from Ian Botham

England's captain when Ken Barrington died in Barbados.

Ken was more than an assistant manager. He was a friend, a pal, a father to us all who understood the individual needs of every player in the party.

Surely no other captain in cricket history has led a side out on the field knowing that eight or nine of the men behind him were openly crying. There were tears in my eyes too, and it was a good ten minutes before most of us could focus properly, eyes drying in the need to perform to the standard Ken would have wanted. You had to be a member of the party to realize what he meant to us all.

The Right Rev David Sheppard, Bishop of Liverpool
Speaking at the Service of Thanksgiving for Ken Barrington at Southwark Cathedral, 28 April, 1981.

There is a great company here today, colleagues and friends, Surrey, England, Lord's Taverners, and from the whole of the cricketing world. Business colleagues and friends – and family.

Very specially, we want to stand with Ken's family, particularly with Ann and Guy, with our thoughts and prayers as they work through their shattering loss. Together we want to give thanks for the life of Ken Barrington.

Ken was a very, very talented cricketer. My first memories were of a bit of a dasher, cutting and hooking. But first time round he didn't make it as a Test cricketer. He had a brief chance with England in 1955. Then no more. He batted number five for Surrey, and with Stuart Surridge as captain and four great bowlers waiting you couldn't hang around and make hundreds and 150s. I think he made up his mind, especially on those tours of India, that he would cut out the risky shots and make so many runs that they couldn't leave him out.

Out of that came an enormously determined player, total concentration, not giving up when he was stuck and the crowd was on his back. Determined is one of the words which comes to the top of my mind as I think about Ken. I also think of him as a sensitive man.

In some ways quite an anxious person. He didn't like conflict. It was quite an ordeal for him as manager when the team was confronted by incidents. There is a lot of real courage in someone who is sensitive, vulnerable, sometimes anxious, yet not giving up. This sensitivity made him understand younger players.

Ken was a very warm person, a very funny person who made people laugh a lot. He told stories well, usually affectionate stories about people. I can remember in the dressing-room, Colonel Barrington as we knew him playing the drums on a tin tray plus vocal effects plus sergeant-major's voice, keenly observed by a soldier's son.

He might have been waiting to go into bat all day, chain-smoking and biting his nails. Then at the end of the day's play he would start playing the drums and make everyone laugh.

To use an overworked word among sportsmen, Ken was a team man, totally committed to the team enterprise. I know Mike Gatting said you felt he was a member of the family. Mike Brearley told me after four tours with Ken as manager, 'You felt he was completely with you. He never harked back to tell you how he and his contemporaries did it. He always said it was more difficult now.'

He gave a lot to the game. He said it was such an honour to be asked to be a manager and a selector. He gave a lot through being enormously willing to play charity games and Lord's Taverners matches and go to cricket dinners, youth clubs and so on.

I doubt if any previous cricketer was better known among his fellow-cricketers. He stood for so much that speaks of a true professional cricketer.

He took that same determination into building with Ann a very thriving motor business. He thought a lot about his team there too. Grace and I had a long talk with him at Old Trafford last year. He found it hard to understand those who had less motivation who were less successful in making their way.

Ken loved his home. He and Ann were very happy. Ann faces a huge sense of loss. I know that the Christian faith is very real to her. Having faith doesn't mean you have no questions, no rebellions.

Many are bound to be asked in this context why should someone's life be cut off when he has so much to give? Coming back to Southwark brings back a vivid memory. When I was at Woolwich, driving home to Peckham from visiting a friend in St Olave's Hospital, Rotherhithe – it was a while before he died, that lively, sensitive man was the victim of a disease which wasted away his body. As I drove, I found myself thinking how angry I felt. I have learned that, if God is my father, I should pour out my heart to him, not just a censored, religious, suitable-for-prayer set of words.

In 1 Cor 13 v. 12 'Now we see only puzzling reflections in a mirror, but then we shall see face to face. There is a great hope and there is a not yet.'

On an occasion like this I feel that many people look at someone like me and want to say 'Come, on, tell us if you really believe all that stuff about Resurrection.' My years in Inner City London and Liverpool have made me much more aware of the bad experiences of life which many people face than I was when I was a cricketer. I feel angry and indifferent sometimes, as I did coming from that hospital.

But my answer is Yes, I do truly believe that on Easter Day God raised Jesus from the dead and that those who trust in him however simply will see him face to face and will enter a further life beyond the world.

There is a great hope and I believe it. And there is a Not Yet. We do not yet see all things in subjection to man. In Jesus, however, who for a short while was made lower than the angels, we do see one crowned now with glory and honour because he suffered death.

In the Not Yet, along with the puzzling reflections in the mirror, we see Jesus Christ. We can know him as our friend and saviour and Lord. He's entered into the worst of our sufferings. Understandably he stands with us, helps us to learn and work out in our lives those things which last – faith, hope and life.

Address at the Service of Thanksgiving for Kenneth Frank Barrington (1930–81) at Southwark Cathedral at 11 a.m., Tuesday, 28 April, 1981. The lessons were read by Peter May and Ian Botham.

PART THREE
FACTS AND FIGURES

Personal File

Born Reading.
Date 24 November, 1930.
Educated Katesgrove School, Reading.
Father Percy, a former PoW in the First World War, served in the Royal Berkshire Regiment. An all-rounder in the regimental side, bowling medium-pace. Gave his son his first cricket lesson when Ken was four.
Brothers and sisters Brothers Roy and Colin and sister Sheila.
Other sporting interests as a boy Soccer. Played as a half-back for Reading Schools with Roy McCrohan (Reading, Norwich and Colchester) and Johnny Brooks (Reading, Chelsea, Brentford and England).
First job Apprentice motor-mechanic at the age of fourteen, earning 17*s*. 6*d*. a week.
Height 5 ft 8½ in. At the age of eighteen was 5 ft 4½ in.
Professional cricketer Joined Surrey staff at the age of seventeen.
Debut 6 May, 1953. Surrey *v*. MCC at Lord's, scoring 8 and 17. Dismissed both times by Alan Oakman (Sussex).
Capped by Surrey 1955.
Benefit 1964 – £10,711.
Career figures 583 matches, 831 innings, 136 not outs, 256 highest score, 31,714 runs, 45·63 average, 76 hundreds, 171 fifties, 515 catches, 17,300 balls bowled, 564 maidens, 8,907 runs, 273 wickets, 32·62 average.
Batting run-rate 51·48 runs per 100 balls.
Wicket-taking 63·36 balls per wicket.
Century in each innings 186 and 118 not out, Surrey *v*. Warwickshire at Edgbaston, 1959.
Double hundred in successive innings 256, England *v*. Australia at Old Trafford and 207, Surrey *v*. Nottinghamshire at the Oval, 1964.
Century before lunch 8 to 111, Players *v*. Gentlemen, at Scarborough, 1960.
Highest score 256, England *v*. Australia, Old Trafford, 1964.
Best bowling 7–40, MCC *v*. Griqualand West (Kimberley), 1964–5.
Best bowling in England 6–70, South *v*. North, Torquay, 1955.

Highest score for Surrey 207, Surrey *v.* Nottinghamshire at the Oval, 1964.
Best bowling for Surrey 5–46, Surrey *v.* MCC, Lord's, 1964.
Fast scoring Won Lawrence Trophy for fastest 100 after scoring 115 in 148 off 122 balls at Melbourne for England *v.* Australia, 1965–6.
Test 100 on every English Test ground Became first player to achieve this feat with innings of 142 *v.* Pakistan at the Oval in 1967.
'Pair' Surrey *v.* Derbyshire, 1968. Each time the bowler was Harold Rhodes.
Last innings 8 in 25 minutes for Surrey *v.* Hampshire at the Oval, September 1968. Dismissed by Danny Livingstone with a ball that bounced twice. Livingstone's first first-class wicket.
1,000 runs in a season 12 times in UK and 3 times overseas.
Other Test batting records Scored centuries against each of England's six opponents, and his total of 20 for England is only exceeded by Walter Hammond (22), Colin Cowdrey (21) and Geoff Boycott (22). His aggregate of 55 scores of 50 and over is bettered only by Cowdrey's record of 58. He scored a century on his first appearance against the West Indies, Pakistan and New Zealand and shared in 35 century stands, the highest being 369 for the second wicket with John Edrich against New Zealand at Headingley in 1965.
Test batting record 82 Tests, 131 innings, 15 not outs, 6,806 runs, 256 highest score, 20 hundreds, 35 fifties, 58·67 average.
Test bowling 2,715 balls, 102 maidens, 1,300 runs, 29 wickets, 44·82 average.
Best Test bowling 3–4 *v.* South Africa at Cape Town, 1964–5.
Test catching 58 catches.

Ken Barrington in Statistics

BATTING

In England

Year	Matches	Inns	Not Out	Runs	HS	100s	50s	Average	Catches
1953	9	14	1	237	85	0	1	18·23	4
1954	19	25	4	845	108*	3	3	40·23	16
1955	35	55	7	1,580	135*	2	9	32·91	21
1956	31	54	10	1,323	109*	2	6	30·06	20
1957	35	53	11	1,642	136	6	7	39·09	64
1958	34	45	9	1,147	101*	1	5	31·86	55
1959	32	52	6	2,499	186	6	13	54·32	45
1960	31	53	9	1,878	126	2	16	42·68	22
1961	24	42	7	2,070	163	4	15	59·14	30
1962	29	46	8	1,865	146	6	9	49·07	24
1963	28	45	7	1,568	110*	2	11	41·26	18
1964	22	35	5	1,872	256	4	9	62·40	20
1965	28	41	4	1,384	163	4	6	37·40	36
1966	20	33	6	987	117*	3	4	36·55	18
1967	28	40	10	2,059	158*	6	10	68·63	24
1968	25	43	5	920	75	0	5	24·21	23
Total	430	676	109	23,876	256	51	129	41·75	440

In Australia

Year	Matches	Inns	Not Out	Runs	HS	100s	50s	Average	Catches
1962–3	17	27	5	1,763	219*	6	6	80·13	17
1965–6	11	17	3	946	158	3	9	67·57	10
Total	28	44	8	2,709	219*	9	15	73·85	27

In South Africa

Year	Matches	Inns	Not Out	Runs	HS	100s	50s	Average	Catches
1959	2	4	0	165	111	1	0	41·25	3
1960	4	7	0	164	66	0	1	23·42	3
1964–5	13	18	5	1,128	169*	4	4	86·76	7
Total	19	29	5	1,457	169*	5	5	50·47	13

In West Indies

Year	Matches	Inns	Not Out	Runs	HS	100s	50s	Average	Catches
1959–60	12	19	1	830	128	3	4	46·11	7
1967–8	11	16	3	591	143	2	3	45·46	6
Total	23	35	4	1,421	143	5	7	45·78	13

In India

Year	Matches	Inns	Not Out	Runs	HS	100s	50s	Average	Catches
1961–2	10	15	5	786	172	3	3	78·60	6
1964	4	4	1	336	108	1	3	112·00	2
Total	14	19	6	1,122	172	4	6	95·30	8

In Pakistan

Year	Matches	Inns	Not Out	Runs	HS	100s	50s	Average	Catches
1955–6	12	17	2	586	87	0	5	39·06	6
1961–2	6	9	1	448	149*	2	2	56·00	5
Total	18	26	3	1,034	149*	2	7	47·53	11

In Ceylon

Year	Matches	Inns	Not Out	Runs	HS	100s	50s	Average	Catches
1961–2	1	2	1	95	93	0	1	95·00	1

All First-class

	Matches	Inns	Not Out	Runs	HS	100s	50s	Average	Catches
	533	831	136	31,714	256	76	170	45·63	513

How he was dismissed

Bowled	163
Caught	402
Lbw	89
Stumped	20
Run out	21
Total	695

County Championship Matches

Year	Matches	Inns	Not Out	Runs	HS	100s	50s	Average	Catches
1953	7	10	1	198	81	0	1	22·00	3
1954	16	23	4	715	108*	2	3	37·63	12
1955	25	38	6	1,262	135*	2	7	39·43	10
1956	23	41	6	1,051	109*	2	4	30·02	17
1957	28	41	9	1,129	129*	3	6	35·28	52
1958	26	33	7	656	101*	1	2	25·23	45
1959	18	32	4	1,498	186	5	6	53·50	25
1960	19	32	5	1,004	126	1	9	37·18	15
1961	14	24	5	1,348	163	4	7	70·94	24
1962	20	34	7	1,310	130*	3	7	48·51	14
1963	19	29	6	1,090	100*	1	9	47·39	15
1964	16	25	4	1,263	207	3	6	60·14	17
1965	18	28	1	608	109	1	3	22·51	21
1966	17	29	6	928	117*	3	3	40·34	18
1967	17	22	6	1,058	158*	3	5	66·12	16
1968	20	36	4	671	71	0	4	20·96	19
Totals	303	477	81	15,789	207	34	82	39·87	323

For Surrey Against Other Counties

Counties	Matches	Inns	Not Out	Runs	HS	100s	50s	Average	Catches
Derbyshire	12	20	2	362	50	0	1	20·11	19
Essex	19	32	9	1,186	130*	2	8	51·56	18
Glamorgan	14	18	0	403	59	0	4	22·38	15
Gloucestershire	21	35	8	1,254	124*	3	9	46·44	18
Hampshire	16	27	3	1,052	151*	4	3	43·83	15
Kent	21	32	8	1,120	150*	3	3	46·65	25
Lancashire	16	24	7	1,277	135*	4	7	75·11	16
Leicestershire	17	25	5	592	101*	1	2	29·60	21
Middlesex	26	42	2	1,273	166	3	7	31·82	28
Northamptonshire	19	27	4	905	109*	2	6	39·34	24
Nottinghamshire	27	43	10	1,856	207	6	7	56·24	28
Somerset	12	19	2	480	73	0	2	28·23	17
Sussex	21	36	6	923	96*	0	7	30·76	23
Warwickshire	16	24	5	992	186	3	4	52·21	11
Worcestershire	19	29	5	910	142*	2	2	37·91	13
Yorkshire	27	44	5	1,204	158*	1	10	30·87	32
Totals	303	477	81	15,789	207	34	82	39·87	323

Other Matches for Surrey

Counties	Matches	Inns	Not Out	Runs	HS	100s	50s	Average	Catches
Cambridge U.	13	14	4	731	149	1	5	73·10	15
Oxford U.	9	10	4	509	146	1	3	84·83	9
Combined Services	1	2	1	117	110*	1	0	117·00	1
MCC	13	21	2	506	82	0	4	26·63	9
Rest of England	3	6	0	178	136	1	0	29·66	5
Australians	5	8	1	160	68*	0	1	22·85	1
South Africans	1	2	0	39	34	0	0	19·50	0
New Zealanders	3	4	1	228	129*	1	1	76·00	7
West Indies	4	7	2	330	110*	2	0	66·00	3
Indians	3	6	3	327	85	0	3	109·00	3
Pakistanis	2	3	0	118	102	1	0	39·33	1
Totals	57	83	18	3,243	149	8	17	49·89	54

Other Matches

	Matches	Inns	Not Out	Runs	HS	100s	50s	Average	Catches
Players *v.* Gents.	7	11	0	484	111	2	3	44·00	14
Others	17	32	3	1,013	107	1	6	34·93	15
Totals	24	43	3	1,497	111	3	9	37·42	29

Batting on English Grounds

Ground	Matches	Inns	Not Out	Runs	HS	100s	50s	Average	Catches
Ashby-de-la-Zouch	1	2	0	6	5	0	0	3·00	0
Basingstoke	1	2	0	30	22	0	0	15·00	1
Blackheath	9	13	2	419	121	1	2	38·09	13
Bournemouth	1	2	0	31	19	0	0	15·50	0
Bradford	5	8	0	197	76	0	2	24·62	9
Bristol	4	6	0	86	56	0	1	14·33	4
Cambridge	8	8	1	415	97	0	4	59·28	8
Cardiff	3	5	0	91	59	0	1	18·20	4
Cheltenham	4	8	1	236	103	1	1	33·71	2
Chesterfield	2	1	0	3	3	0	0	3·00	2
Clacton	3	5	1	169	129*	1	0	42·25	4
Colchester	1	2	1	34	32*	0	0	34·00	1
Coventry	1	2	0	83	49	0	0	41·50	0
Derby	2	4	2	38	27*	0	0	19·00	4
Eastbourne	1	2	0	77	50	0	1	38·50	1
Edgbaston	13	21	3	917	186	4	2	50·94	10
Gloucester	3	5	1	219	89	0	2	54·75	3
Gravesend	1	1	1	150	150*	1	0	—	0
Guildford	15	22	7	1,040	149	3	5	69·33	18
Hastings	1	2	0	113	95	0	1	56·50	1
Headingley	10	16	2	726	163	1	3	51·85	11
Hove	7	13	4	318	96*	0	3	35·33	9
Hull	1	2	0	19	10	0	0	9·50	1
Ilford	1	2	0	62	39	0	0	31·00	0
Kettering	1	2	0	39	22	0	0	19·50	1
Leicester	5	7	1	183	101*	1	0	30·50	3
Leyton	2	4	1	112	62*	0	1	37·33	2
Lord's	47	76	4	2,259	166	2	18	31·37	44
Neath	1	2	0	41	24	0	0	20·50	0
Northampton	8	10	2	471	109*	1	4	58·87	7
Nuneaton	1	—	—	—	—	—	—	—	—
Old Trafford	15	25	6	1,475	256	4	7	77·63	14
Oxford	3	2	0	56	30	0	0	28·00	2
Portsmouth	3	5	0	218	100	1	1	43·60	5
Romford	1	2	1	47	41	0	0	47·00	1
Scarborough	12	21	2	804	111	3	2	42·31	12
Sheffield	5	10	2	291	79*	0	2	36·37	2
Southampton	3	5	1	293	100*	1	1	73·25	0
Southport	1	2	0	80	68	0	1	40·00	1
Stroud	1	2	1	112	61*	0	2	112·00	0
Swansea	2	2	0	69	59	0	1	34·50	0
Taunton	2	3	0	15	8	0	0	5·00	4
The Oval	186	287	51	9,977	207	21	53	42·27	206
Torquay	3	6	0	298	75	0	3	49·66	4
Trent Bridge	18	29	9	1,132	113*	5	4	56·60	19
Weston-super-Mare	3	5	1	101	40*	0	0	25·25	4
Worcester	9	15	1	324	99	0	1	23·14	3
Total	430	676	109	23,876	256	51	129	42·10	440

Batting on Australian Grounds

Grounds	Matches	Inns	Not Out	Runs	HS	100s	50s	Average	Catches
Adelaide	6	10	2	748	132*	3	7	93·50	7
Brisbane	4	7	3	464	183*	1	3	116·00	4
Hobart	1	1	0	37	37	0	0	37·00	2
Launceston	1	1	0	73	73	0	1	73·00	1
Melbourne	6	11	3	752	219*	3	2	94·00	6
Perth	3	4	0	71	44	0	0	17·75	1
Sydney	3	5	0	252	101	1	1	50·40	1
Total	24	39	8	2,397	219*	8	14	77·32	22

Batting on New Zealand Grounds

Grounds	Matches	Inns	Not Out	Runs	HS	100s	50s	Average	Catches
Auckland	1	1	0	126	126	1	0	126·00	1
Christchurch	1	2	0	92	47	0	0	46·00	1
Dunedin	1	1	0	18	18	0	0	18·00	0
Wellington	1	1	0	76	76	0	1	76·00	3
Total	4	5	0	312	126	1	1	62·40	5

Batting on South African Grounds

Grounds	Matches	Inns	Not Out	Runs	HS	100s	50s	Average	Catches
Bloemfontein	1	2	1	37	34*	0	0	37·00	2
Bulawayo	1	2	0	24	20	0	0	12·00	3
Cape Town	2	4	2	314	169*	1	1	157·00	0
Durban	2	3	1	159	148*	1	0	79·50	2
Johannesburg	5	7	0	450	169	2	1	64·28	0
Kimberley	1	1	0	10	10	0	0	10·00	0
Pietermaritzburg	1	1	0	6	6	0	0	6·00	0
Port Elizabeth	2	2	0	74	72	0	1	37·00	2
Pretoria	1	1	0	45	45	0	0	45·00	2
Salisbury	3	6	1	338	111	1	2	67·00	2
Total	19	29	5	1,457	169*	5	5	60·70	13

Batting on West Indian Grounds

Grounds	Matches	Inns	Not Out	Runs	HS	100s	50s	Average	Catches
Antigua	2	2	1	183	100*	1	1	183·00	0
Berbice	1	1	0	103	103	1	0	103·00	0
Bridgetown	5	7	2	426	128	1	4	85·20	3
Georgetown	2	4	0	31	27	0	0	7·75	0
Grenada	1	1	0	9	9	0	0	9·00	1
Jamaica									
(Melbourne Park)	1	1	0	30	30	0	0	30·00	1
(Sabina Park)	3	6	0	134	63	0	1	22·33	0
Pointe-à-Pierre	1	2	1	10	8	0	0	10·00	1
Port of Spain	6	10	0	471	143	2	1	47·10	7
St Lucia	1	1	0	24	24	0	0	24·00	0
Total	23	35	4	1,421	143	5	7	45·83	13

Batting on Indian and Sri Lankan Grounds

Grounds	Matches	Inns	Not Out	Runs	HS	100s	50s	Average	Catches
Ahmedabad	1	1	0	72	72	0	1	72·00	1
Bangalore	2	2	1	79	76	0	1	79·00	0
Bombay	1	2	2	203	151	1	1	—	1
Calcutta	1	2	0	17	14	0	0	8·50	1
Colombo	1	2	1	95	93	0	1	95·00	1
Cuttack	1	2	2	84	80*	0	1	—	0
Delhi	1	1	1	113	113*	1	0	—	0
Hyderabad	2	3	0	122	108	1	0	40·66	4
Jaipur	1	1	0	91	91	0	1	91·00	1
Jullundur	1	—	—	—	—	—	—	—	—
Kanpur	1	2	0	193	172	1	0	96·50	0
Madras	2	3	0	148	80	0	1	49·33	0
Total	15	21	7	1,217	172	4	7	86·92	9

Batting on Pakistan Grounds

Grounds	Matches	Inns	Not Out	Runs	HS	100s	50s	Average	Catches
Bahawalpur	2	2	0	18	18	0	0	9·00	0
Chittagong	1	1	0	65	65	0	1	65·00	1
Dacca	2	3	0	138	84	0	1	46·00	1
Hyderabad	1	1	0	66	66	0	1	66·00	0
Karachi	2	4	2	112	70*	0	1	56·00	1
Lahore	3	5	0	221	139	1	1	44·20	1
Lyallpur	2	3	0	142	87	0	2	47·33	1
Multan	1	1	0	41	41	0	0	41·00	2
Peshawar	1	2	0	32	32	0	0	16·00	0
Poona	1	1	1	149	149*	1	0	—	1
Rawalpindi	1	2	0	15	11	0	0	7·50	2
Sargodha	1	1	0	35	35	0	0	35·00	1
Total	18	26	3	1,034	149*	2	7	44·95	11

TEST MATCHES IN ENGLAND

	Matches	Inns	Not Out	Runs	HS	100s	50s	Average	Catches
v. Australia	13	21	3	1,065	256	1	7	59·16	10
v. South Africa	9	16	1	481	91	0	4	32·06	5
v. West Indies	7	14	0	334	80	0	2	23·85	3
v. New Zealand	2	2	0	300	163	2	0	150·00	3
v. India	8	11	0	681	97	0	7	61·90	7
v. Pakistan	7	9	3	486	148	3	1	81·00	6
Total	46	73	7	3,347	256	6	21	50·71	34

TEST MATCHES ABROAD

	Matches	Inns	Not Out	Runs	HS	100s	50s	Average	Catches
In Australia	10	18	3	1,046	132*	4	6	69·73	9
In South Africa	5	7	2	508	148*	2	2	101·60	3
In West Indies	10	16	0	708	143	3	2	44·25	4
In New Zealand	3	4	0	294	126	1	1	73·50	5
In India	6	10	3	674	172	3	2	96·28	2
In Pakistan	2	3	0	229	139	1	1	76·33	1
Total	36	58	8	3,459	172	14	14	69·18	24

CENTURIES IN TEST CRICKET

Edgbaston 137 (1965), Headingley 163 (1965), Lord's 148 (1967), The Oval 142 (1967), Trent Bridge 109* (1967), Old Trafford 256 (1964).
Melbourne 115 (1965–6), Adelaide 132* (1962–3), 102 (1965–6), Sydney 101 (1962–3).
Durban 148* (1964–5), Johannesburg 121 (1964–5), Auckland 126 (1962–3).
Bombay 151* (1961–2), Kanpur 172 (1961–2), New Delhi 113 (1961–2), Lahore 139 (1961–2).
Bridgetown 128 (1959–60), Port of Spain 121 (1959–60), 143 (1967–8).

HOW HE WAS DISMISSED IN TEST MATCHES

Bowled	21
Caught	68
Lbw	23
Run out	4
Total	116

Innings by Innings in Test Cricket

	Tests	Inns	Not Out	Runs	HS	100s	50s	Average	Catches
v. Australia	23	39	6	2,111	256	5	13	63·96	19
v. South Africa	14	23	3	989	148*	2	6	49·45	8
v. West Indies	17	30	0	1,042	143	3	4	34·73	7
v. New Zealand	5	6	0	594	163	3	1	99·00	8
v. India	14	21	3	1,355	172	3	9	75·27	9
v. Pakistan	9	12	3	715	148	4	2	79·44	7
Total	82	131	15	6,806	256	20	35	58·67	58

AGGREGATES

	Matches	Inns	Not Out	Runs	HS	100s	50s	Average	Catches
In England	430	676	109	23,876	256	51	129	42·10	440
In Australia	24	39	8	2,397	219*	8	14	77·32	22
In West Indies	23	35	4	1,421	143	5	7	45·83	13
In South Africa	19	29	5	1,457	169*	5	5	60·70	13
In New Zealand	4	5	0	312	126	1	1	62·40	5
In India	15	21	7	1,217	203	4	7	86·92	9
In Pakistan	18	26	3	1,034	149*	2	7	44·95	11
Total	533	831	136	31,714	256	76	170	45·63	513

TEST INNINGS

			Runs	Average
1955	SA	0, 34, 18	52	17·33
1959	I	56, 80, 80, 87, 46, 8	357	59·50
1959–60	WI	128, 121, 49, 16, 4, 27, 0, 69, 6	420	46·66
1960	SA	24, 80, 1*, 76, 35, 1, 10	227	37·83
1961	A	21, 48*, 4, 66, 6, 78, 5, 53, 83	364	45·50
1961–2	P	139, 6, 84	229	76·33
1961–2	I	151*, 52*, 21, 172, 113*, 14, 3, 20, 48	594	99·00
1962	P	9, 0, 1, 50*	60	20·00
1962–3	A	78, 23, 35, 0*, 35, 21, 63, 132*, 101, 94	582	72·75
1962–3	NZ	126, 76, 47, 45	294	73·50
1963	WI	16, 8, 80, 60, 9, 1, 25, 32, 16, 28	275	27·50
1963–4	I	80	80	80·00
1964	A	22, 33, 5, 29, 85, 256, 47, 54*	531	75·85
1964–5	SA	148*, 121, 49, 14*, 93, 11, 72	508	101·60
1965	NZ	137, 163	300	150·00
1965	SA	91, 18, 1, 1, 18, 73	202	33·66
1965–6	A	53, 38, 63, 1, 60, 102, 115, 32*	464	66·28
1966	WI	5, 30, 19, 5	59	14·75
1967	P	148, 14, 109*, 142, 13*	426	142·00
1967	I	93, 46, 97, 75, 13	324	64·80
1967–8	WI	143, 63, 13, 17, 48, 4, 0	288	41·14
1968	A	75, 0, 49, 46*	170	56·66

KEN BARRINGTON AS A BOWLER

All first-class matches

		Balls	Overs	Mdns	Runs	Wkts	Average
1953		—	—	—	—	—	—
1954		78	13	2	63	1	63·00
1955		207	34.3	0	185	7	26·42
1955–6	(Pakistan)	169	28.1	9	69	2	34·50
1956		177	29.3	3	111	2	55·50
1957		216	36	6	127	4	31·75
1958		930	155	34	444	15	29·60
1959		1,362	227	34	691	20	34·55
1959–60	(Rhodesia)	276	46	8	131	5	26·20
	(West Indies)	1,426	237.4	64	619	17	36·41
1960		1,144	190.4	30	710	7	101·42
1960–1	(South Africa)	348	58	6	200	7	28·57
1961		966	161	28	556	9	61·77
1961–2	(India & Pakistan)	672	112	27	323	9	35·88
1962		477	79.3	11	348	6	58·00
1962–3	(Australia & New Zealand)	1,212	161.4	27	653	17	38·41
1963		462	77	26	167	9	18·55
1963–4	(India)	239	39.5	9	131	7	18·71
1964		838	139.4	34	369	12	30·75
1964–5	(South Africa)	439	73.1	23	174	24	7·25
1965		756	126	26	353	16	22·06
1965–6	(Australia)	260	32.4	1	149	6	24·83
1966		552	92	18	282	10	28·20
1967		1,328	221.2	40	683	23	29·69
1967–8	(West Indies)	1,158	193	33	636	13	48·92
1968		1,608	268	65	733	25	29·32
		17,300	2,883.2	564	8,907	273	32·62

63·36 balls per wicket
Best bowling: 7–40 MCC *v*. Griqualand West (Kimberley) 1964–5
Best bowling (UK): 6–70 South *v*. North (Torquay) 1955

CENTURIES (76)

For Surrey 43

v. Nottinghamshire (6): 207, 163, 126, 113*, 106, 102*.
v. Hampshire (4): 151*, 103, 100, 100*.
v. Lancashire (4): 135*, 125*, 117*, 101.
v. Gloucestershire (3): 124*, 108*, 103.
v. Kent (3): 150*, 126, 121.
v. Middlesex (3): 166, 113, 109.
v. Warwickshire (3): 186, 118*, 101.
v. Essex (2): 130*, 129*.
v. Northamptonshire (2): 103*, 109*.
v. Worcestershire (2): 142*, 136*.
v. West Indies (2): 110*, 103*.
v. Cambridge University (1): 149.
v. Combined Services (1): 110*.
v. Leicestershire (1): 101*.
v. New Zealand (1): 129*.
v. Oxford University (1): 146.
v. Pakistan (1): 102.
v. Rest of England (1): 136.
v. Rhodesia (1): 111.
v. Yorkshire (1): 158*.

Other Matches 33

England *v*. Australia (5): 256, 132*, 115, 102, 101.
England *v*. South Africa (2): 148*, 121.
England *v*. West Indies (3): 143, 128, 121.
England *v*. New Zealand (3): 163, 137, 126.
England *v*. India (3): 172, 151*, 113*.
England *v*. Pakistan (4): 148, 142, 139, 109*.

Players *v*. Gentlemen (2): 111, 100.
MCC *v*. Yorkshire (1): 107.
MCC *v*. Combined Universities (1): 149*.
MCC *v*. South Zone (1): 108.
MCC *v*. Berbice (1): 103.
MCC *v*. Windward Islands (1): 100*.
MCC *v*. Australian XI (1): 219*.
MCC *v*. Queensland (1): 183*.
MCC *v*. South Australia (1): 104.
MCC *v*. Victoria (1): 158.
MCC *v*. Transvaal (1): 169.
MCC *v*. Western Province (1): 169*.

KEN BARRINGTON'S CAREER

Innings by innings plus bowling spells and catches

For	Against	Venue	Score		Bowler	Catches	Bowling O	M	R
1953									
Surrey	MCC	Lord's	8	st	Oakman				
			17	c	Oakman				
"	Australians	Oval	10	c	Archer	1			
			4	c	Archer				
"	Sussex	Guildford	4	lbw	Wood				
			12	c	James				
"	Yorkshire	Oval	24	b	Trueman				
"	Warwickshire	Edgbaston	41	b	Bannister				
			8	c	Grove				
"	Kent	Blackheath	15*						
"	Worcestershire	Oval	81	c	Devereux				
"	Leicestershire	Oval	9	b	Walsh	1			
"	Gloucestershire	Bristol	0	b	Scott	1			
			4	b	Allen	1			
	14 innings; 1 not out; highest score 81; total runs 237					4			
1954									
Surrey	Leicestershire	Oval	24	b	Jackson	1			
"	Sussex	Hove	4	lbw	Marlar				
			54	b	Oakman		7	1	45
"	Somerset	Taunton	4	c	Tremlett	1			
"	Cambridge University	Oval				3	6	1	18
"	Oxford University	Guildford	28	c	Jowett	1			
"	Gloucestershire	Oval	108*						
			68	c	McHugh	1			
"	Pakistan	Oval	102	c	Ghazali				
"	Essex	Colchester	2	b	Bailey	1			
			32*						
"	Kent	Blackheath	1	b	Wright	2			
"	Essex	Oval	89*						
"	Nottinghamshire	Oval	32	b	Goonesena	1			
"	Northamptonshire	Kettering	17	lbw	Broderick	1			
			22	st	Broderick				
"	Middlesex	Oval	31	c	Titmus				
"	Leicestershire	Leicester	24	b	Savage				
			0	c	Savage				
"	Gloucestershire	Cheltenham	3	lbw	McHugh				
			103	b	McHugh				
"	Worcestershire	Worcester	22	b	Ashman				
"	Middlesex	Lord's	9	ro		2			
"	Worcestershire	Oval	10*			2			
"	Lancashire	Oval	43	c	Statham				
			13	c	Hilton				
	25 innings; 4 not outs; highest score 108*; total runs 845					16	13	2	63

or	Against	Venue	Score		Bowler	Catches	Bowling O	M	R	W
955										
irrey	Cambridge University	Cambridge	66	c	Singh		7	0	31	0
,,	MCC	Lord's	14	b	Bannister	1				
			15*							
CC	South Africa	Lord's	3	lbw	Goddard					
			27	lbw	Goddard					
igland	South Africa	Trent Bridge	0	c	Fuller					
igland	South Africa	Lord's	34	b	Heine					
			18	c	Tayfield					
rrey	South Africa	Oval	5	lbw	Tayfield					
			34	c	Tayfield					
ayers	Gentlemen	Lord's	3	c	Warr	1				
			0	st	Goonesena	2				
uth	North	Torquay	25	c	Tattersall	2	5	0	42	1
			52	st	Walsh	1	15.4	0	70	6
rrey	Cambridge University	Oval	9	b	Smith, D.	1				
						1				
,	The Rest	Oval	13	c	Bailey	1				
			0	b	Trueman	1				
,	Essex	Ilford	39	b	Insole					
			23	lbw	Greensmith					
,	Glamorgan	Swansea	59	b	Watkins					
,	Gloucestershire	Cheltenham	12	c	Lambert	1				
			11	c	Mortimore					
,	Hampshire	Bournemouth	19	b	Shackleton					
			12	c	Gray					
,	Kent	Blackheath	5*							
,	Lancashire	Old Trafford	54	c	Tattersall	2				
			38*							
,	Middlesex	Lord's	51	b	Moss	1				
						1				
,	Northamptonshire	Northampton	1	c	Tribe					
			15	b	Broderick		2.5	0	20	0
	Nottinghamshire	Trent Bridge	126	c	Harvey					
							4	0	22	0
	Somerset	Weston-super-Mare	1	c	McMahon					
	Gloucestershire	Oval	46	c	Mortimore					
	Somerset	Oval	64	b	McMahon					
						1				
	Lancashire	Oval	135*							
	Glamorgan	Oval	31	b	Wooller					
	Yorkshire	Oval	1	c	Appleyard					
			11	b	Wardle	2				
	Worcestershire	Oval	32	c	Perks					
	Leicestershire	Oval	27*							
			28*			1				
	Kent	Oval	27	c	Allan					
			72	lbw	Allan					
	Nottinghamshire	Oval	43	b	Stocks					
	Middlesex	Oval	73	c	Titmus					
			2	c	Young					
	Sussex	Oval	39	c	Parks					
	Derbyshire	Oval	1	c	Gladwin					
			50	c	Hall	1				
	Warwickshire	Coventry	49	ro						
			34	b	Bannister					
	Worcestershire	Worcester	18	lbw	Horton					
			8*							
	Yorkshire	Headingley	5	c	Appleyard					
			0	b	Trueman					
	33 innings; 7 not outs; highest score 135*; total runs 1,580					21	34.3	0	185	7
55–6										
C	Karachi	Karachi	70*				4	1	15	0
			4*				6	0	23	0
	Sind	Hyderabad	66	b	Munhf					
	Amir XI	Bahawalpur	18	ro			1	0	3	1
	Combined Universities	Lahore	14	b	Aziz	1	6.1	3	8	1
							10	4	20	0
	Pakistan	Lahore	10	c	Fazal					
			55	st	Alim					
	East Pakistan	Chittagong	65	lbw	Saeed	1				
	Pakistan	Dacca	43	c	Khan					
			11	lbw	Fazal					
	Punjab	Lyallpur	87	lbw	Saeed					
	Pakistan	Peshawar	32	lbw	Kardar					
			0	b	Kardar					
	Pakistan Services	Sargodha	35	c	Shuja	1	1	1	0	0
	Railway XI	Multan	41	c	Qureshi	2				
	Pakistan	Karachi	10	b	Fazal	1				
			28	c	Hussain					
	17 innings; 2 not outs; highest score 87; total runs 589					6	28.1	9	69	2

KEN BARRINGTON

For	Against	Venue	Score		Bowler	Catches	Bowling O	M	R
1956									
Surrey	Australians	Oval	4	c	Johnson				
			15	lbw	Miller				
”	MCC	Lord’s	17	b	Spencer				
			18	c	Spencer				
MCC	Cambridge University	Lord’s	11	lbw	Smith				
			62*						
Surrey	Rest of England	Oval	4	b	Trueman	2			
			21	c	Hilton				
”	Cambridge University	Cambridge	59	c	Smith, D. J.				
						1			
”	Oxford University	Oval	0	c	Allan				
			23*				11	1	38
”	Cambridge University	Guildford	13*						
			25*				1	0	1
”	Derbyshire	Derby	0	lbw	Hall				
			10*						
”	Essex	Clacton	11	c	Bailey				
			4	lbw	Smith, R.				
”	Glamorgan	Cardiff	20	st	Jones				
			59	c	Shepherd	1			
”	Hampshire	Portsmouth	1	c	Burden				
			21	b	Marshall				
”	Kent	Blackheath	32	c	Wright	1			
						1			
”	Leicestershire	Leicester	24	c	Palmer				
”	Middlesex	Lord’s	15	c	Young	2			
			1	c	Young				
”	Northamptonshire	Northampton	109*						
			40	b	Manning		3	0	5
”	Nottinghamshire	Trent Bridge	0	c	Smales				
			8	b	Smales	1			
”	Derbyshire	Oval	13	c	Gladwin				
			41	b	Gladwin	1			
”	Northamptonshire	Oval	15	c	Broderick	1			
			3	b	Tribe				
”	Hampshire	Guildford	7	c	Shackleton	1			
			103	c	Cannings	1	5	0	22
”	Kent	Oval	2	c	Page	1			
			6*			1			
”	Gloucestershire	Oval	7	c	Mortimore		12	2	45
			21*						
”	Essex	Oval	0	b	Bailey	2			
			58	c	Greensmith				
”	Nottinghamshire	Oval	0	c	Jepson				
			63*						
”	Middlesex	Oval	47	c	Warr	1			
			17	b	Edrich				
”	Sussex	Oval	19	lbw	Suttle	1			
			2	c	Marlar	1			
”	Lancashire	Oval	26	c	Hilton				
”	Sussex	Hastings	95	b	Thomson				
			18	lbw	Marlar	1			
”	Warwickshire	Edgbaston	22*						
”	Worcestershire	Worcester	42	c	Berry				
”	Yorkshire	Sheffield	34	b	Broughton				
			35	c	Wardle				
	54 innings; 10 not outs; highest score 109*; total runs 1,323					21	29.3	3	111

or	Against	Venue	Score		Bowler	Catches	Bowling O	M	R	W
957										
urrey	West Indies	Oval	26	c	Ramadhin		4	1	20	0
			2	ro		1				
,,	West Indies	Oval	24	c	Ramadhin	1				
			103*			1	3	0	11	0
,,	MCC	Lord's	5	c	Bennett	1				
			4	c	Marlar	2				
,,	Combined Services	Oval	7	c	Pearson	1				
			110*				3	1	12	1
,,	Oxford University	Guildford	76	b	Jowett					
						1	3	0	14	0
,,	Cambridge University	Cambridge	16	b	Smith, C.	1				
						2				
,,	The Rest	Scarborough	136	c	Bailey	1				
			4	b	Trueman					
,,	Derbyshire	Derby	1	c	Jackson	2				
			27*			2				
,,	Essex	Clacton	129*			2				
			16	c	Preston	1				
,,	Gloucestershire	Bristol	1	c	Smith					
			56	c	Cook					
,,	Hampshire	Portsmouth	52	b	Sainsbury	2				
						1				
,,	Kent	Blackheath	18	c	Brown, A.	1				
			4	b	Brown	1				
,,	Lancashire	Old Trafford	51*							
						1				
,,	Leicestershire	Leicester	26	c	Savage					
			6	c	Munden	2				
,,	Middlesex	Lord's	0	b	Hurst	1				
			6	b	Warr	1				
,,	Northamptonshire	Northampton	10	b	Kelleher					
						1				
,	Nottinghamshire	Trent Bridge	10*							
						1				
,	Somerset	Weston-super-Mare	6	c	Langford					
			32	c	McCool					
,	Glamorgan	Oval	52	c	McConnon	2				
						1				
,	Worcestershire	Oval	36	c	Berry	2				
			30*			2				
,	Sussex	Oval	11	b	Marlar					
			5	b	Thomson					
,	Northamptonshire	Oval	4	b	Tyson	3				
			5	c	Tribe	2	11	1	34	2
,	Essex	Oval	44	c	King					
							8	2	18	1
,	Gloucestershire	Oval	124*							
,	Hampshire	Oval	40*							
						1				
,	Yorkshire	Oval	53	c	Trueman					
,	Kent	Oval	43	c	Pretlove	2				
						2				
,	Derbyshire	Oval	4	b	Morgan	3				
			0	c	Jackson	2				
,	Leicestershire	Oval	59*			2				
						2				
,	Nottinghamshire	Oval	19	c	Goonesena					
			8	st	Morgan	1				
,	Middlesex	Oval	1	b	Warr	1				
,	Warwickshire	Oval	0	lbw	Carter					
,	Sussex	Hove	10	c	Bell	1				
			27*							
,	Warwickshire	Edgbaston	101	b	Townsend	1				
						1	4	1	18	0
,	Yorkshire	Bradford	2	c	Illingworth					
						2				
	53 innings; 11 not outs; highest score 136; total runs 1,642					64	36	6	127	4

For	Against	Venue	Score		Bowler	Catches	Bowling O	M	R
1958									
Surrey	Cambridge University	Cambridge	34	c	Hurd	3	8.2	3	20
							7	2	31
,,	MCC	Lord's	2	c	Moss				
			10	c	Tyson				
,,	New Zealand	Oval	18	c	Moir				
						1			
,,	Gloucestershire	Oval	0	c	Smith	1			
			8*			2	9	2	20
,,	Warwickshire	Oval	1	c	Ibadulla				
						1			
,,	Leicestershire	Oval	33	b	Spencer	1			
						2	6	1	9
,,	Nottinghamshire	Trent Bridge	7*						
,,	Lancashire	Old Trafford	74	st	Hilton	1			
			14	c	Higgs	1			
,,	Essex	Oval	29	c	Preston	2	4	1	9
,,	Northamptonshire	Oval	62*			3	22	6	63
,,	Somerset	Taunton	8	c	Langford	1	15	2	49
			3	c	Langford	2			
,,	Yorkshire	Sheffield	0	ro		1			
			34	lbw	Wardle	1	5	0	16
,,	Derbyshire	Chesterfield	3	c	Gladwin	2			
,,	Cambridge University	Guildford	80	lbw	James				
			40*						
,,	Hampshire	Guildford	9	b	Shackleton	1			
,,	Oxford University	Oval	75*			1			
							15	5	28
,,	Kent	Oval	37	b	Brown				
							5	1	28
,,	Glamorgan	Swansea	10	c	Shepherd				
,,	Glamorgan	Oval	17	c	Shepherd	2			
						1	26	5	64
,,	Yorkshire	Oval	4	c	Illingworth	1			
						1			
,,	Gloucestershire	Bristol	18	c	Smith	2			
							4	0	25
,,	Essex	Leyton	10	b	Preston	1			
			13	c	Ralph				
,,	New Zealand	Oval	11	b	Alabaster	3			
						1	14.4	3	27
Surrey	Nottinghamshire	Oval	17	c	Cotton	1			
						1			
,,	Leicestershire	Leicester	101*						
							2	0	5
,,	Middlesex	Oval	14	lbw	Moss	1			
						1			
,,	Middlesex	Lord's	37	c	Moss				
			9*			2			
,,	Northamptonshire	Northampton				2			
,,	Worcestershire	Worcester	28	c	Pearson	1			
							1	0	1
,,	Somerset	Oval	13	c	Langford	2			
,,	Sussex	Hove	4	c	Bates	2			
			30*						
,,	Worcestershire	Oval	0*			1			
			9	c	Flavell	1			
South	North	Torquay	46	c	Jackson		11	3	49
			44	c	Gladwin				
England XI	Commonwealth XI	Torquay	75	c	Alley				
			56	c	Wight	1			
	45 innings; 9 not outs; highest score 101*; total runs 1,147					55	155	34	444

59

›r	Against	Venue	Score		Bowler	Catches	O	M	R	W
ırrey	Cambridge University	Cambridge	97	c	Kirby					
,,	MCC	Lord's	25	c	Langford	1				
			8	lbw	Moss	1	3	0	13	0
,,	Warwickshire	Edgbaston	186	c	Ibadulla		9	2	21	0
			118*							
,,	Indians	Oval	85	ro			2	1	2	0
			59*				4	0	22	1
,,	Nottinghamshire	Trent Bridge	4	c	Springall		11	1	36	0
			113*				13	1	33	1
,,	Glamorgan	Oval	21	c	Clarke	2				
,,	Somerset	Oval	73	c	Palmer	1	7	0	22	0
			13*							
,,	Kent	Oval	35	c	Page					
			40	lbw	Page		19	3	58	1
ıgland	India	Trent Bridge	56	b	Nadkarni	1				
ırrey	Yorkshire	Oval	81	b	Platt	4				
			3	lbw	Platt					
ıgland	India	Lord's	80	c	Desai					
ırrey	Cambridge University	Guildford	149	c	Hurd	1				
						1	10	3	26	0
,,	Sussex	Guildford	25	c	James	2				
			6*			1				
ıgland	India	Headingley	80	c	Nadkarni					
						1				
ırrey	Glamorgan	Cardiff	5	c	Ward	2				
,,	Kent	Blackheath	16	c	Brown	1				
						3	6	2	16	0
ayers	Gentlemen	Lord's	4	c	Sayer	1				
						3	9	2	25	1
ırrey	Yorkshire	Bradford	3	c	Platt	2				
			3	c	Trueman					
ıgland	India	Old Trafford	87	lbw	Surendranath	1	14	3	36	3
			46	lbw	Nadkarni	1	27	4	75	2
ırrey	India	Oval	47	b	Gupte					
			25*			1	3	2	1	0
,,	Nottinghamshire	Oval	4	b	Springall					
			51	c	Morgan	1	5	0	12	0
,,	Worcestershire	Worcester	99	c	Flavell	1	9	0	36	0
			11	c	Pratt					
,,	Middlesex	Lord's	166	lbw	Titmus					
,,	Lancashire	Oval	64	c	Hilton, C.	1	9	1	22	0
			19	b	Hilton, C.					
,,	Hampshire	Portsmouth	44	c	Cannings	2				
			100	b	Cannings					
ıgland	India	Oval	8	c	Gupte	1	6	0	24	0
ırrey	Gloucestershire	Gloucester	12	c	Smith	1				
			49	c	Cook					
,,	Middlesex	Oval	40	lbw	Titmus		9	1	37	1
			7	ro		1				
,,	Northamptonshire	Oval	0	lbw	Tyson	1				
			87	b	Manning					
ayers	Gentlemen	Scarborough	32	b	Bailey	1	15	2	59	4
							6	2	10	1
N. Pearce's XI	India	Scarborough	48	b	Surendranath	2				
			32	st	Nadkarni	2	4	0	15	0
ıe Rest	Yorkshire	Oval	15	st	Illingworth		5	0	18	3
			18	c	Illingworth		22	4	72	2
	52 innings; 6 not outs; highest score 186; total runs 2,499					45	227	34	691	20

959–60

›r	Against	Venue	Score		Bowler	Catches	O	M	R	W
ırrey	Rhodesia	Salisbury	111	c						
			30	c			23	5	48	3
,,	Rhodesia	Bulawayo	4	c		1	23	3	83	2
			20	c		2				
	4 innings; highest score 111; total runs 165					3	46	8	131	5
CC	Windward Islands	Grenada	9	b	Redhead	1	5.2	3	6	2
CC	Barbados	Bridgetown	79	lbw	Griffith		17	2	58	1
			79	b	Weekes					
gland	West Indies	Bridgetown	128	c	Ramadhin		18	3	60	1
CC	Trinidad	Port of Spain	1	c	Corbie	2	7	1	17	0
			16	st	Singh		10.1	3	23	2
CC	Trinidad	Pointe-à-Pierre	8	c	Aleong	1	15	1	63	1
			2*				14.5	4	42	3
gland	West Indies	Port of Spain	121	c	Hall	1	16	10	15	0
			49	c	Hall	1	25.5	13	34	2
CC	Jamaica	Kingston	30	c	Valentine	1	9.5	0	44	2
							14	4	48	0
gland	West Indies	Kingston	16	c	Watson		21	7	38	1
			4	lbw	Solomon		4	4	0	0
CC	Leeward Islands	Antigua	83	lbw	Matthew		24.4	4	56	0
							8	1	27	0
gland	West Indies	Georgetown	27	c	Sobers		6	2	22	0
			0	c	Worrell					
CC	Berbice	Berbice	103	b	Benjamin		5	0	18	0
gland	West Indies	Port of Spain	69	c	Ramadhin		8	0	21	0
			6	c	Sobers		8	2	27	1
	19 innings; 1 not out; highest score 128; total runs 830					7	237	64	619	17

1960

For	Against	Venue	Score		Bowler	Catches	Bowling		
							O	M	R
Surrey	Cambridge University	Cambridge	67	lbw	Hurd				
,,	MCC	Lord's	82	c	Allen		4	0	33
			65*						
,,	Northamptonshire	Oval	10	c	Watts	1	3	0	9
			8	lbw	Watts		2	1	1
,,	Worcestershire	Oval	38	c	Slade	1			
,,	Lancashire	Old Trafford	93	c	Higgs	2			
			44*						
,,	Sussex	Oval							
,,	Gloucestershire	Stroud	51	b	Mortimore		5	2	8
			61*						
,,	Somerset	Oval	34	b	Wight	2	21	4	52
			0	c	Alley		2	0	6
,,	Sussex	Hove	0	c	Mordaunt		15	0	60
			0	b	Thomson				
,,	Nottinghamshire	Trent Bridge	1	c	Wells	2	7	1	40
			13*			1			
,,	Kent	Oval	126	c	Dixon				
						1			
,,	Warwickshire	Edgbaston	21	c	Cartwright				
			63	lbw	Ibadulla		5	2	9
,,	Yorkshire	Oval	4	c	Close		18	3	53
			62	b	Trueman				
England	South Africa	Lord's	24	lbw	Goddard				
Surrey	Oxford University	Guildford	44*				23.2	7	47
			61*			2	10	1	43
,,	Kent	Blackheath	72	c	Halfyard	1	7	0	32
			3	lbw	Ridgway				
England	South Africa	Trent Bridge	80	c	Goddard				
			1*				3	1	5
Players	Gentlemen	Lord's	32	b	Sayer	2	11	0	81
Surrey	Yorkshire	Sheffield	65	c	Wilson				
			1*						
England	South Africa	Old Trafford	76	b	Goddard				
			35	c	Goddard				
Surrey	Nottinghamshire	Oval	11	b	Cotton	2			
			12*				4	1	6
,,	Glamorgan	Cardiff	2	c	Shepherd	1			
			5	b	Evans, J.				
,,	Middlesex	Oval	0	c	Warr				
			26	c	Drybrough				
,,	Hampshire	Southampton	46	c	Piachaud				
,,	Middlesex	Lord's	67	c	Titmus		10	2	32
			13	lbw	Moss		0.2	0	5
England	South Africa	Oval	1	lbw	Pothecary				
			10	c	McKinnon				
Surrey	Glamorgan	Oval	52	b	Evans, J.	1			
							1	0	4
T. N. Pearce's XI	South Africa	Scarborough	19	b	Adcock		14	1	67
			27	lbw	Wesley	1	15	0	94
Players	Gentlemen	Scarborough	71	b	Hurd		2	1	4
			111	st	Hurd		1	0	4
Rest	Yorkshire	Oval	19	c	Trueman				
			11	c	Cowan		5	1	15
MCC	Yorkshire	Scarborough	16	b	Cowan	2	2	2	0
			22	b	Illingworth				
	53 innings; 9 not outs; highest score 126; total runs 1,878					22	190.4	30	710

1960–1

For	Against	Venue	Score		Bowler	Catches	O	M	R
Commonwealth XI	Rhodesia	Salisbury	31	c		1	12	1	37
			66	b		1			
,,	Transvaal	Johannesburg	7	c					
							13	1	44
,,	Natal	Durban	4	c					
			7	b			10	1	32
,,	Combined XI	Johannesburg	41	c			10	1	45
			8	c		1	13	2	42
	7 innings; highest score 66; total runs 164					3	58	6	200

For	Against	Venue	Score		Bowler	Catches	Bowling O	M	R	W
1961										
Surrey	Cambridge University	Cambridge	35	c	Willard					
,,	Hampshire	Oval	151*			2	15	2	36	0
						1	6	0	32	1
,,	Australians	Oval	4	c	McKenzie		6	1	31	0
			43	ro			2	0	8	0
,,	Nottinghamshire	Trent Bridge	75	c	Davison	2				
			47	c	Forbes	2	6	1	31	0
,,	Warwickshire	Oval	10	c	Bannister	1	3	0	8	0
			37*			1	8	3	17	0
MCC	Australians	Lord's	55	c	Davidson	1	7	1	28	1
			35	lbw	McKenzie		3	0	21	0
Surrey	Gloucestershire	Oval	93	c	Mortimore	1				
						1	26	5	67	1
,,	Northamptonshire	Northampton	57	b	Ashenden					
England	Australia	Edgbaston	21	c	Mackay	1				
			48*							
Surrey	Sussex	Hove	8	c	Thomson	2	5	1	18	1
			96*				7	0	24	0
,,	Yorkshire	Oval	17	c	Gillhouley					
						1	20	2	69	0
England	Australia	Lord's	4	c	Davidson	2				
			66	lbw	Davidson					
Surrey	Kent	Blackheath	121	c	Baker	1	6	1	27	0
			38	lbw	Halfyard	1	5	0	36	0
England	Australia	Headingley	6	c	Davidson					
Surrey	Leicestershire	Oval	6	c	Boshier	2				
			7	c	Spencer	1				
,,	Middlesex	Oval	0	lbw	Titmus					
			1	b	Bennett	1				
Players	Gentlemen	Lord's	53	b	Drybrough					
			53	c	Wheatley	1	1	0	5	0
Surrey	Yorkshire	Headingley	1	c	Illingworth		12	6	32	2
			65*			1	8	0	33	1
England	Australia	Old Trafford	78	c	Simpson	1				
			5	lbw	Mackay					
Surrey	Australians	Oval	12	c	Misson					
			68*							
,,	Nottinghamshire	Oval	163	c	Corran	1				
			95	c	Forbes	1	6	1	15	1
,,	Lancashire	Old Trafford	125*			2	9	4	18	1
			40	c	Green					
,,	Middlesex	Lord's	17	c	Hooker					
			78	b	Drybrough					
England	Australia	Oval	53	c	Gaunt					
			83	c	Benaud					
	42 innings; 7 not outs; highest score 163; total runs 2,070					31	161	28	556	9

For	Against	Venue	Score		Bowler	Catches	Bowling O	M	R	W

1961–2

For	Against	Venue	Score		Bowler	Catches	O	M	R	W
MCC	President's XI	Rawalpindi	11	b	Akhtar	1				
			4	c	Akhtar	1				
,,	Governor's XI	Lyallpur	55	c	Afaq	1				
			0	b	D'Souza		9	2	24	0
,,	Pakistan	Lahore	139	ro			6	0	25	0
			6	lbw	Mahmoud					
,,	Combined Services	Poona	149*			1	6	2	11	0
							3	0	3	2
,,	India	Bombay	151*			1				
			52*				3	0	18	0
,,	President's XI	Hyderabad	6	c	Prasanna	2				
			8	b	Surti	1	13	1	53	2
,,	Rajasthan	Jaipur	91	c	Raj					
						1				
,,	India	Kanpur	21	b	Gupte					
			172	ro						
,,	North Zone	Jullundur					7	0	18	2
							3	1	13	1
,,	India	Delhi	113*				9	1	39	0
,,	East Zone	Cuttack	80*				21	6	63	2
			4*							
,,	India	Calcutta	14	b	Durani					
			3	c	Desai	1				
,,	South Zone	Bangalore	3	b	Kasturirangan					
,,	India	Madras	20	c	Durani					
			48	lbw	Nadkarni					
,,	Pakistan	Dacca	84	b	D'Souza	1	11	1	39	0
							21	13	17	0
,,	Combined XI	Bahawalpur	0	b	Fazal					
,,	Ceylon	Colombo	93	b	Fuard					
			2*			1				
	26 innings; 7 not outs; highest score 172; total runs 1,329					12	112	27	323	9

For	Against	Venue	Score		Bowler	Catches	Bowling O	M	R	W
1962										
Surrey	Glamorgan	Oval	3	c	Walker					
						1				
,,	Lancashire	Oval	56	lbw	Greenhough	1				
,,	Northamptonshire	Oval	27	c	Watts, P. D.					
						1				
England	Pakistan	Edgbaston	9	lbw	Mahmood	1	2	2	0	0
Surrey	Pakistan	Oval	3	c	Nasim		7	0	36	0
			13	c	Munir	1				
,,	Nottinghamshire	Trent Bridge	26*							
			102*			1	1	0	7	0
,,	Lancashire	Old Trafford	29	c	Greenhough	2				
			101	c	Barber		2.1	1	7	0
,,	Essex	Oval	130*							
			21*			1	11	2	43	1
England	Pakistan	Lord's	0	c	Farooq					
							1	0	8	0
Surrey	Oxford University	Guildford	146	c	Majendie	1	3	0	14	1
						1	5	1	23	0
,,	Yorkshire	Sheffield	18	st	Taylor					
			23	c	Wilson					
England	Pakistan	Headingley	1	c	Farooq	1				
						1	1	0	4	0
Surrey	Sussex	Oval	5	c	Thomson	1				
			89	ro						
,,	Gloucestershire	Gloucester	57	c	Mortimore					
			12*							
,,	Somerset	Oval	48	lbw	Alley					
			34	b	Alley					
,,	Kent	Blackheath	76	c	Halfyard					
			18	c	Baker					
,,	Worcestershire	Oval	19	c	Standen					
,,	Middlesex	Oval	63	c	Moss	1				
			91*			2	6	2	25	0
,,	Worcestershire	Worcester	8	b	Coldwell					
			27	st	Slade					
,,	Nottinghamshire	Oval	1	lbw	Cotton					
,,	Derbyshire	Oval	31	c	Morgan	1				
			9	b	Smith					
,,	Middlesex	Lord's	16	lbw	Titmus	1				
England	Pakistan	Oval	50*							
							2	0	10	0
Surrey	Essex	Leyton	27	lbw	Bailey					
			62*			1				
,,	Yorkshire	Oval	2	b	Trueman		4.2	0	25	2
			8	c	Ryan					
,,	Hampshire	Southampton	26	c	Sainsbury		6	0	27	0
			45	c	Burden		6	2	21	0
MCC	Yorkshire	Scarborough	55	c						
			107	c			5	0	11	1
T. N. Pearce's XI	Pakistan	Scarborough	46	lbw	Nasim					
						1				
Players	Gentlemen	Scarborough	100	b	Drybrough	1	17	1	87	1
			25	b	Drybrough	2				
	46 innings; 8 not outs; highest score 146; total runs 1,865					24	79.3	11	348	6

For	Against	Venue	Score		Bowler	Catches	Bowling O	M	R	W
1962–3										
MCC	Western Australia	Perth	24	c	Hoare					
							10	1	47	0
,,	Combined XI	Perth	0	c	McKenzie	1	2	0	8	0
			44	c	Hoare		4	0	35	0
,,	South Australia	Adelaide	104	c			4	0	27	0
,,	Australian XI	Melbourne	219*							
			19	c	Veivers	1				
,,	Queensland	Brisbane	183*				8	1	71	1
							12	3	28	0
England	Australia	Brisbane	78	c	Benaud	1	12	3	44	1
			23	c	Davidson					
MCC	South Australia	Adelaide	52	ro		2	18	2	55	3
			52*							
England	Australia	Melbourne	35	lbw	McKenzie	2	6	0	23	0
			0*				5	0	22	0
MCC	Combined XI	Launceston	73	c	Patterson	1	2.4	1	16	0
							2	0	8	1
England	Australia	Sydney	35	lbw	Davidson	1	8	0	43	0
			21	b	McKenzie					
MCC	Victoria	Melbourne	33	c	Guest		2	0	14	1
			66	c	Meckiff	1	17	3	60	2
England	Australia	Adelaide	63	b	Simpson					
			132*			2				
England	Australia	Sydney	101	c	Benaud					
			94	c	McKenzie		8	3	22	0
	22 innings; 5 not outs; highest score 219*; total runs 1,451					12	121.2	17	523	10
England	New Zealand	Auckland	126	c	Cameron		12	4	38	0
,,	New Zealand	Wellington	76	c	Reid	1	2.3	1	1	1
						3	11	3	32	3
,,	New Zealand	Christchurch	47	lbw	Motz	1	5	0	18	0
			45	c	Blair					
MCC	Otago	Dunedin	18	lbw	Cameron					
							9.5	2	41	3
	5 innings; highest score 126; total runs 312					5	40.2	10	130	7

or	Against	Venue	Score		Bowler	Catches	Bowling O	M	R	W
963										
urrey	MCC	Lord's	4	b	Bailey					
,,	Kent	Oval	30	c	Sayer	1	7	2	13	1
			39*			2				
,,	Derbyshire	Oval	48	b	Buxton					
							6	1	16	1
,,	Leicestershire	Oval	94*			1				
,,	Worcestershire	Worcester	8	ro						
			38	c	Horton	1	9	6	11	0
,,	Essex	Oval	95	lbw	Preston	1				
			7	c	Phelan	1	6	2	12	2
,,	West Indies	Oval	110*				7	2	20	0
,,	Nottinghamshire	Trent Bridge	2	c	Forbes		8	1	24	0
			25	st	Wells					
ngland	West Indies	Old Trafford	16	c	Hall					
			8	b	Gibbs					
ırrey	Hampshire	Oval	20	c	Shackleton					
			17	c	Wassell					
ıgland	West Indies	Lord's	80	c	Worrell	1				
			60	c	Griffith					
ırrey	Sussex	Guildford	77	st	Bell	1				
						1				
,,	Leicestershire	Ashby	5	c	Savage					
			1	c	Savage					
ıgland	West Indies	Edgbaston	9	b	Sobers					
			1	b	Sobers	1				
ırrey	Yorkshire	Oval	84*							
						1				
CC Touring XI	The Rest	Lord's	23	b	Shackleton					
			1	c	Palmer		1	0	4	1
rrey	Yorkshire	Sheffield	2	c	Nicholson		1	0	16	0
			79*							
gland	West Indies	Headingley	25	c	Gibbs	1				
			32	lbw	Sobers					
rrey	West Indies	Oval	43	c	King					
			22	ro						
,,	Nottinghamshire	Oval	53	c	Wells		25	8	40	4
,,	Hampshire	Southampton	76	lbw	Shackleton					
			100*							
,,	Middlesex	Oval	75	c	Hooker					
							5	3	4	0
,,	Lancashire	Oval	8	b	Statham	2	2	1	7	0
,,	Essex	Clacton	9	b	Edmeades					
						1				
gland	West Indies	Oval	16	c	Gibbs					
			28	b	Griffith					
rrey	Somerset	Oval	15	c	Hall	1				
			26	c	Rumsey	1				
,	Middlesex	Lord's	6	b	Titmus					
			0	b	Titmus					
,	Warwickshire	Oval	51*							
	45 innings; 7 not outs; highest score 110*; total runs 1,568					18	77	26	167	9
963–4										
CC	President's XI	Bangalore	76*				8	2	16	0
CC	South Zone	Hyderabad	108	c	Kumar	1	5.2	2	11	3
							14	4	45	2
gland	India	Madras	80	c	Borde		4	0	23	0
							2	0	6	0
CC	West Zone	Ahmedabad	72	lbw	Surti	1	1.3	1	1	1
							5	0	29	1
	4 innings; 1 not out; highest score 108; total runs 336					2	39.5	9	131	7

For	Against	Venue	Score		Bowler	Catches	Bowling O	M	R	
1964										
Surrey	MCC	Lord's	55	lbw	Knight		14	3	46	
			23	c	Hobbs		7	1	35	
,,	Northamptonshire	Oval	43	c	Larter		6	0	27	
			14	c	Larter					
,,	Leicestershire	Oval	24	c	Boshier		3	0	10	
			19	c	Smith	1	4	1	12	
,,	Kent	Gravesend	150*							
England	Australia	Trent Bridge	22	c	Veivers	2				
			33	lbw	Corling					
Surrey	Worcestershire	Oval	0	lbw	Coldwell					
			136*			1				
,,	Essex	Oval	70	c	Phelan					
			50*				24	8	50	
England	Australia	Lord's	5	lbw	McKenzie					
Surrey	Yorkshire	Bradford	76	c	Illingworth	1				
						1	8.4	0	26	
England	Australia	Headingley	29	b	McKenzie					
			85	lbw	Veivers	1				
Surrey	Derbyshire	Oval	31	c	Smith		25	7	59	
			45	c	Jackson	1	8	3	20	
,,	Gloucestershire	Gloucester	89	c	Mortimore	1				
						1				
,,	Lancashire	Southport	12	b	Higgs	1				
			68	c	Pullar					
,,	Sussex	Hove	76*			1				
						2				
England	Australia	Old Trafford	256	lbw	McKenzie		1	0	4	
Surrey	Nottinghamshire	Oval	207	c	Forbes		7	1	16	
							20	6	43	
,,	Sussex	Oval	22	c	Snow					
			13	c	Buss, M.					
,,	Middlesex	Lord's	2	lbw	Price	1				
			37	b	Titmus	1	7	2	14	
England	Australia	Oval	47	c	Hawke					
			54*							
Surrey	Warwickshire	Edgbaston	34	b	Edmonds	1				
			1	b	Webster					
,,	Yorkshire	Oval (benefit match)	8	c	Illingworth					
,,	Warwickshire	Oval	36	b	Hitchcock	2				
						1	5	2	7	
	35 innings; not outs 5; highest score 256; total runs 1,872					20	139.4	34	369	1

For	Against	Venue	Score		Bowler	Catches	Bowling O	M	R
1964–5									
MCC	Rhodesia	Salisbury	74	c	Bennett				
			26*						
,,	Transvaal	Johannesburg	169	c	Thorp				
,,	Eastern Province	Port Elizabeth	2	c	Barlow				
							4.1	1	17
,,	Western Province	Cape Town	169*						
			82	ro					
England	South Africa	Durban	148*			1			
MCC	S. African Universities	Pietermaritzburg	6	c	Hall		10	2	29
							20	9	25
,,	North East Transvaal	Pretoria	45	c	Hall	2	1	0	1
,,	South Africa	Johannesburg	121	c	Pollock, P. M.		4	0	29
England	South Africa	Cape Town	49	c	Pollock, P. M.				
			14*				3.1	1	4
MCC	Orange Free State	Bloemfontein	3	c	Macaulay	1			
			34*			1			
England	South Africa	Johannesburg	93	c	Barlow				
			11	c	McKinnon				
MCC	Griqualand West	Kimberley	10	c	Burrow		18	5	29
							12.5	5	40
England	South Africa	Port Elizabeth	72	c	Goddard	2			
	18 innings; 5 not outs; highest score 169; total runs 1,128					7	73.1	23	174

r	Against	Venue	Score		Bowler	Catches	Bowling O	M	R	W
'65										
rrey	Cambridge University	Cambridge				1				
			41*							
,,	MCC	Lord's	23	c	Underwood	2				
,,	Hampshire	Oval	21	c	Wassell					
			3	b	Sainsbury					
,,	Warwickshire	Oval	7	b	Edmonds	1	1.2	0	9	2
			5	b	Cartwright		6	2	18	0
,,	Sussex	Hove	6	lbw	Buss	1				
			3	c	Thomson					
,,	Leicestershire	Oval	0	c	Cotton					
			15	lbw	Spencer	2				
,,	Worcestershire	Oval	18	c	Coldwell					
			35	b	Gifford					
gland	New Zealand	Edgbaston	137	c	Collinge	1	5	0	25	0
rrey	Nottinghamshire	Nottingham	23	c	Johnson	1				
,	New Zealand	Oval	70	c	Pollard	2	29	2	88	5
			129*							
,	Oxford University	Oxford				1	11	2	27	2
							9	5	13	0
,	Gloucestershire	Bristol	7	c	Windows					
,	Kent	Oval	5	c	Dye					
,	Essex	Oval	60	c	Knight					
							23	9	50	1
,	Northamptonshire	Northampton	32	ro		2				
,	Yorkshire	Bradford	0	c	Hutton	2				
			76	b	Hutton					
gland	New Zealand	Headingley	163	c	Motz					
						2				
rrey	Middlesex	Oval	109	c	Titmus		6	0	21	0
						1				
gland	South Africa	Lord's	91	ro		2				
			18	lbw	Dumbrill	1				
rrey	Lancashire	Old Trafford								
,	Nottinghamshire	Oval	10	c	Forbes		3	0	5	0
			36	st	Gillhouley	1				
gland	South Africa	Trent Bridge	1	b	Pollock, P. M.					
			1	c	Pollock, P. M.					
rrey	Somerset	Weston-super-Mare	22	c	Alley	3				
			40*			1	2	0	2	1
,	Yorkshire	Oval	54	c	Hutton	1	11	2	30	2
			4	c	Hutton	2	11	3	28	2
,	Worcestershire	Worcester	9	c	Coldwell		6	1	23	0
			3	c	Gifford					
gland	South Africa	Oval	18	b	Botten	1				
			73	lbw	Pollock, P. M.	1				
rey	Sussex	Oval	5	lbw	Thomson	3				
			0	lbw	Snow					
gland XI	Rest of World	Scarborough	11*			1	2.4	0	14	1
	41 innings; 4 not outs; highest score 163; total runs 1,384					36	126	26	353	16
65–6										
CC	Combined XI	Perth	3	c	Mayne					
,	South Australia	Adelaide	69	c	Hawke	1				
			51	c	Sincock	2	3	0	22	0
,	Victoria	Melbourne	12	c	Stackpole		4	0	9	0
			158	c	Connolly		7	1	24	4
,	Queensland	Brisbane	80*			2				
			9*							
gland	Australia	Brisbane	53	b	Hawke	1				
			38	c	Cowper					
CC	South Australia	Adelaide	63	st	Sincock		1	0	5	0
gland	Australia	Melbourne	63	c	Veivers	2	7.4	0	47	2
,	Australia	Sydney	1	c	Hawke					
						2				
CC	Combined XI	Hobart	37	c	Hooper					
							10	0	42	0
gland	Australia	Adelaide	60	lbw	Walters					
			102	c	Hawke					
,	Australia	Melbourne	115	c	Walters					
			32*							
	17 innings; 1 not out; highest score 158; total runs 946					10	32.4	1	149	6

For	Against	Venue	Score		Bowler	Catches	Bowling O	M	R	W
1966										
Surrey	MCC	Lord's								
,,	Derbyshire	Oval	0	b	Smith	2	8	0	21	
			48	c	Smith	1				
,,	Sussex	Oval	41	c	Bates					
,,	Glamorgan	Oval	2	ro		1				
			10	c	Davis		9	3	6	
,,	Hampshire	Basingstoke	8	lbw	Shackleton	1				
			22	c	Sainsbury		5	1	18	
,,	Northamptonshire	Oval	103*							
			1	c	Crump					
,,	Nottinghamshire	Nottingham	49*							
			106	c	White	3	22	7	45	
England	West Indies	Old Trafford	5	c & b	Griffith					
			30	c	Holford					
Surrey	Kent	Oval	7	c	Underwood					
			68	c	Brown		1	0	1	
England	West Indies	Lord's	19	b	Sobers					
			5	b	Griffith					
Surrey	Leicestershire	Leicester	2	c	Marner					
,,	Essex	Oval	19	b	Knight					
			13*							
,,	Nottinghamshire	Oval	36	c	Taylor	1				
						1	7	2	27	
,,	Middlesex	Lord's	0	c	Stewart					
			20	c	Hooker					
,,	Yorkshire	Bradford	33	b	Close	1				
			4	b	Illingworth					
,,	Gloucestershire	Cheltenham	76	c	Smith					
			9*				2	1	4	
,,	Sussex	Eastbourne	27	c	Bates		15	4	34	
			50	b	Buss, A.	1	10	0	39	
,,	Gloucestershire	Oval	0	lbw	Smith	2				
			57*			1	13	0	87	
,,	Yorkshire	Oval	0	c	Close	2				
						1				
,,	Lancashire	Old Trafford	117*							
	33 innings; 6 not outs; highest score 117*; total runs 987					18	92	18	282	1

For	Against	Venue	Score		Bowler	Catches	Bowling O	M	R	W
1967										
Surrey	Oxford University	Oxford	26	c	Barker	1	10	3	27	3
							13	2	30	0
,,	MCC	Lord's	62	st	Hobbs					
,,	Warwickshire	Oval	63*							
			95	c	Edmonds					
,,	Hampshire	Oval	41	b	Cottam	1	3	0	20	0
			60	c	Cottam					
,,	Northamptonshire	Northampton	82	c	Kettle					
,,	Derbyshire	Chesterfield								
,,	Warwickshire	Nuneaton								
,,	Essex	Oval	14	c	Hobbs	1	8	1	48	2
,,	Indians	Oval	84	b	Guha					
			27*			2	6	0	27	0
,,	Leicestershire	Guildford	32	c	Lock					
						1	5	1	11	0
England	India	Headingley	93	ro		1				
			46	c	Chandra		9	1	38	0
Surrey	Worcestershire	Oval	142*							
England	India	Lord's	97	b	Chandra					
Surrey	Kent	Oval	0	c	Graham	1				
			5	lbw	Underwood					
,,	Glamorgan	Oval	14	c	Davis		10	2	31	1
							10	1	39	3
,,	Lancashire	Old Trafford	20	c	Higgs					
			33*				5	0	14	0
,,	Middlesex	Oval	113	c	Parfitt		6	2	19	1
			10	lbw	Titmus	2	10	1	15	0
England	India	Edgbaston	75	c	Prasanna					
			13	c	Chandra	1				
Surrey	Northamptonshire	Oval	13	b	Sully	2				
						2	7	2	18	2
,,	Yorkshire	Oval	158*			2	20.2	5	51	5
						1	25	7	54	2
England	Pakistan	Lord's	148	c	Asif	1	11	1	29	1
			14	b	Intikhab	1	13	2	23	2
Surrey	Gloucestershire	Oval	20	c	Bissex		10	1	23	0
			36	c	Mortimore		6	2	16	0
England	Pakistan	Trent Bridge	109*							
						1				
Surrey	Middlesex	Lord's	0	c	Herman	2				
England	Pakistan	Oval	142	c	Salim					
			13*				8	2	29	0
Surrey	Nottinghamshire	Oval	59*			1	11	4	28	0
			48*							
T. N. Pearce's XI	Pakistan	Scarborough	29*				8	0	41	0
			2	c	Arif					
England XI	Rest of World	Scarborough	8	b	Gibbs		5	0	31	1
			13	c	Gibbs		2	0	21	0
	40 innings; 10 not outs; highest score 158*; total runs 2,059					24	221.2	40	683	23

1967–8

For	Against	Venue	Score		Bowler	Catches	Bowling			
							O	M	R	W
MCC	President's XI	Bridgetown	1	ro		2	27	4	99	5
			53*				4	0	30	0
,,	Trinidad	Port of Spain	1	c	Rodriguez	1	21.1	2	52	1
			17	c	Hall	1	7	0	27	0
England	West Indies	Port of Spain	143	c	Gibbs		18	6	44	1
							15	0	69	1
MCC	Jamaica	Kingston	6	c	Wellington		1	0	6	0
			32	lbw	King		11	4	34	2
England	West Indies	Kingston	63	c	Holford					
			13	lbw	Griffith		6	1	14	0
MCC	Leeward Islands	Antigua	100*				12.5	4	35	0
							10	1	40	0
,,	Barbados	Bridgetown	69*				6	1	23	0
							12	3	27	0
England	West Indies	Bridgetown	17	c		1	8	1	29	1
							4	0	17	0
MCC	Windward Islands	St Lucia	24	c	Laurent		2	0	6	0
England	West Indies	Port of Spain	48	lbw	Gibbs	1	10	2	41	1
,,	West Indies	Georgetown	4	c	Sobers		18	4	43	1
			0	c	Gibbs					
	16 innings; 3 not outs; highest score 143; total runs 591					6	193	33	636	13

For	Against	Venue	Score		Bowler	Catches	Bowling O	M	R	W
1968										
Surrey	MCC	Lord's	24	c	Shuttleworth	1				
			25	st	Allen		1	0	8	0
,,	Northamptonshire	Oval								
,,	Derbyshire	Oval	0	lbw	Rhodes					
			0	b	Rhodes	1				
,,	Oxford University	Oxford	30	lbw	Khan					
,,	Essex	Romford	41	c	Hobbs	1				
			6*				5.4	3	6	1
,,	Warwickshire	Edgbaston	4	b	Bannister	1	26	7	57	4
			5	c	Gibbs		4	0	23	0
,,	Leicestershire	Oval	1	c	Birkenshaw	2	12	2	51	1
			25	c	Birkenshaw					
,,	Essex	Guildford	11	b	Turner	1	8	0	58	0
			52	b	Turner	1	7	2	23	0
England	Australia	Lord's	75	c	Connolly					
							2	1	12	1
Surrey	Somerset	Oval	44	b	Chappell	1				
,,	Middlesex	Lord's	3	c	Parfitt		3.3	1	5	2
			0	c	Titmus	1	18.5	5	42	0
,,	Sussex	Oval	29*			2	18	8	26	1
			11	c	Lewis		29	5	64	2
England	Australia	Edgbaston	0	lbw	Freeman	1				
Surrey	Nottinghamshire	Oval	16	c	White					
			43	b	Taylor		10	2	24	3
,,	Yorkshire	Oval	37	b	Illingworth		13	2	35	1
			11	c	Wilson					
England	Australia	Headingley	49	b	Connolly	1				
			46*			1	6	1	14	0
Surrey	Gloucestershire	Oval	13	b	Green					
							26	9	42	1
,,	Nottinghamshire	Trent Bridge	29	c	Sobers	1	11	1	49	0
			63	lbw	Forbes	1				
,,	Kent	Oval	4	lbw	Shepherd	1				
			5*							
,,	Gloucestershire	Cheltenham	21	c	Allen	1	17.2	4	47	5
			1	c	Bissex					
,,	Glamorgan	Neath	17	b	Shepherd		4.4	1	20	2
			24	b	Lewis, B.		6	1	15	0
,,	Northamptonshire	Northampton	71	b	Sully	2	13	5	28	1
			54*				5	0	31	0
,,	Yorkshire	Hull	10	c	Illingworth	1				
			9	c	Wilson					
,,	Worcestershire	Worcester	2	b	Coldwell					
			1	c	Gifford		21	6	53	0
,,	Hampshire	Oval	0	ro		1				
			8	c	Livingstone					
	43 innings; 5 not outs; highest score 75; total runs 920;						**Total**			
						23	268	65	733	25

INDEX OF NAMES

N.B. All the contributors to Part Two appear in this Index. In the case of peripheral references to personages in Parts One and Two, the more important are also to be found here.